Classroom Decision-Making
Negotiation and process syllabuses in practice

CAMBRIDGE LANGUAGE TEACHING LIBRARY

A series covering central issues in language teaching and learning, by authors who have expert knowledge in their field.

In this series:

Affect in Language Learning *edited by Jane Arnold*

Approaches and Methods in Language Teaching *by Jack C. Richards and Theodore S. Rodgers*

Appropriate Methodology and Social Context *by Adrian Holliday*

Beyond Training *by Jack C. Richards*

Classroom Decision-Making *edited by Michael P. Breen and Andrew Littlejohn*

Collaborative Action Research for English Language Teachers *by Anne Burns*

Collaborative Language Learning and Teaching *edited by David Nunan*

Communicative Language Teaching *by William Littlewood*

Designing Tasks for the Communicative Classroom *by David Nunan*

Developing Reading Skills *by Françoise Grellet*

Developments in English for Specific Purposes *by Tony Dudley-Evans and Maggie Jo St John*

Discourse Analysis for Language Teachers *by Michael McCarthy*

Discourse and Language Education *by Evelyn Hatch*

English for Academic Purposes *by R. R. Jordan*

English for Specific Purposes *by Tom Hutchinson and Alan Waters*

Establishing Self-Access *by David Gardner and Lindsay Miller*

Foreign and Second Language Learning *by William Littlewood*

Language Learning in Intercultural Perspective *edited by Michael Byram and Michael Fleming*

The Language Teaching Matrix *by Jack C. Richards*

Language Test Construction and Evaluation *by J. Charles Alderson, Caroline Clapham, and Dianne Wall*

Learner-centredness as Language Education *by Ian Tudor*

Managing Curricular Innovation *by Numa Markee*

Materials Development in Language Teaching *edited by Brian Tomlinson*

Psychology for Language Teachers *by Marion Williams and Robert L. Burden*

Research Methods in Language Learning *by David Nunan*

Second Language Teacher Education *edited by Jack C. Richards and David Nunan*

Society and the Language Classroom *edited by Hywel Coleman*

Teacher Learning in Language Teaching *edited by Donald Freeman and Jack C. Richards*

Teaching the Spoken Language *by Gillian Brown and George Yule*

Understanding Research in Second Language Learning *by James Dean Brown*

Vocabulary: Description, Acquisition and Pedagogy *edited by Norbert Schmitt and Michael McCarthy*

Vocabulary, Semantics, and Language Education *by Evelyn Hatch and Cheryl Brown*

Voices from the Language Classroom *edited by Kathleen M. Bailey and David Nunan*

Classroom Decision-Making

Negotiation and process syllabuses in practice

Edited by

*Michael P. Breen and
Andrew Littlejohn*

CAMBRIDGE
UNIVERSITY PRESS

PUBLISHED BY THE PRESS SYNDICATE OF THE UNIVERSITY OF CAMBRIDGE
The Pitt Building, Trumpington Street, Cambridge, United Kingdom

CAMBRIDGE UNIVERSITY PRESS
The Edinburgh Building, Cambridge CB2 2RU, UK   http://www.cup.cam.ac.uk
40 West 20th Street, New York, NY 10011–4211, USA   http://www.cup.org
10 Stamford Road, Oakleigh, Melbourne 3166, Australia
Ruiz de Alarcón 13, 28014 Madrid, Spain

First published 2000

Printed in the United Kingdom at the University Press, Cambridge

Typeface Sabon 10.5/12pt. *System* 3B2 [CE]

A catalogue record for this book is available from the British Library

Library of Congress Cataloguing in Publication data applied for

ISBN 0 521 66192 7 hardback
ISBN 0 521 66614 7 paperback

Contents

Contributors   *page* vii

Acknowledgements   x

Introduction and overview   1

1   The significance of negotiation   5
      Michael P. Breen and Andrew Littlejohn

Part 1   **Accounts of practice in primary and secondary schools**   39

      Overview   39

2   Negotiated evaluation in a primary ESL context   44
      Anne MacKay, Kaye Oates and Yvonne Haig

3   Negotiating assessment with secondary-school pupils   55
      Kari Smith

4   Introducing negotiation processes: an experiment with   63
      creative project work
      Ramon Ribé

5   'We do what we like': negotiated classroom work with   83
      Hungarian children
      Marianne Nikolov

6   Is a negotiated syllabus feasible within a national   94
      curriculum?
      Pnina Linder

7   Refining negotiated classroom work in a Spanish   108
      secondary school
      Isabel Serrano-Sampedro

Contents

Part 2   **Accounts of practice in tertiary institutions**   133

Overview   133

8   Negotiation in tertiary education: clashes with the   138
dominant educational culture
Stefaan Slembrouck

9   Syllabus negotiation in a school of nursing   150
Elaine Martyn

10   Negotiating the syllabus: learning needs analysis through   163
pictures
Eddie Edmundson and Steve Fitzpatrick

11   Reality therapy: using negotiated work in a technical-   176
writing class
Wendy Newstetter

12   Negotiation of outcome: evaluation and revision decisions   185
in the writing curriculum
Margaret Sokolik

13   Learners, practitioners, teachers: diamond spotting and   195
negotiating role boundaries
Lucy Norris and Susan Spencer

Part 3   **Accounts of practice in teacher education**   205

Overview   205

14   A process syllabus in a methodology course: experiences,   209
beliefs, challenges
Suzanne Irujo

15   Discourse, process and reflection in teacher education   223
Michael McCarthy and Michael Makosch

16   Negotiation, process, content and participants' experience   233
in a process syllabus for ELT professionals
Roz Ivanič

17   Negotiation as a participatory dialogue   248
Kate Wolfe-Quintero   272

Conclusions   272

18   The practicalities of negotiation   272
Michael P. Breen and Andrew Littlejohn

References   296
Index   305

Contributors

Michael P. Breen is Professor of Language Education and Director of the Centre for English Language Teaching at the University of Stirling, Scotland. He has taught in primary and secondary schools and five universities and has been directly involved in teacher education for 27 years. He became interested in the practicalities of teacher–student negotiation in the late 1970s from which he deduced the potential of process syllabuses for language classrooms.

Eddie Edmundson is the British Council Director for North East Brazil. He has 31 years' experience in ELT as a teacher, teacher trainer and manager in Latin America. His interest in negotiation stems from work on student self-evaluation in 1986.

Steve Fitzpatrick works as teacher, teacher trainer, and manager in the British Council Teaching centre in Recife, Brazil. He started negotiating syllabuses in the Centre 10 years ago. This has developed his interest in attempting to humanise assessment in language learning.

Yvonne Haig has been involved in ESL/EFL education for 23 years, both in Australia and Western Samoa. She has worked as a teacher, advisory teacher, administrator, consultant and sessional teacher educator. She is presently undertaking a PhD at Edith Cowan University, Western Australia. She believes negotiation is the 'way to go' even though her natural inclinations are towards a benevolent dictatorship.

Suzanne Irujo is Professor Emerita of Education at Boston University, USA. After 10 years in a bilingual/ESL classroom, she worked as a teacher educator for 15 years. As an education consultant, she continues to negotiate the content of courses and workshops.

Roz Ivanič is a Senior Lecturer in the Department of Linguistics and Modern English Language at Lancaster University, UK. She taught in secondary and adult education for 15 years, and has been involved in post-experience MA courses for ELT professionals for 12 years. Her interests include issues of access to higher education and alternative forms of knowledge and learning.

Contributors

Pnina Linder has been an EFL teacher in Israel at all levels since 1960 and a teacher educator at Oranim School of Education of the Kibbutz Movement, University of Haifa, Israel for the past 27 years. She also teaches at the Haf Hacarmel Regional Secondary School. Her interests in student choice and education for democracy led to her working with staff and students at the secondary level on aspects of curriculum planning.

Andrew Littlejohn teaches for the Institute of Education, University of London and is the author of a number of textbooks. His first experience of negotiated classroom work was in the Middle East in the early 1980s since when he has been refining the process involved and supporting teachers in attempting negotiation, particularly through the design of classroom materials.

Michael McCarthy is Professor of Applied Linguistics at the University of Nottingham, UK. He has 32 years' experience as a language teacher and teacher trainer. He is joint Director (with Ronald Carter) of the Cambridge and Nottingham (CANCODE) five-million-word conversational corpus project.

Anne MacKay has been involved in ESL/EFL education in Australia and Papua New Guinea as a teacher and teacher educator for many years. Her present work as a teacher at Graylands Intensive Language Centre, Western Australia has involved developing the concept of negotiated evaluation for use with primary ESL learners.

Michael Makosch is Head of Languages for Switzerland's largest adult education institute, the Club Schools. He has represented Switzerland on the Council of Europe Modern Languages Project and is chairman of the International Certificate Conference.

Elaine Martyn has been a Language Instructor in the English Centre at The University of Hong Kong for seven years. She has also taught EFL in Nigeria, China and Pakistan. Her interest in syllabus negotiation, self-access and self-directed learning derives from her belief that negotiation empowers students as they build communication skills in meaningful interactions.

Wendy Newstetter is a Research Scientist with the EduTech Institute in the College of Computing at the Georgia Institute of Technology, USA. At present, she teaches courses in human–computer interaction, computerisation and society and ethnographic and qualitative methods in systems design. Her belief in negotiated work has been heightened since working with engineering students who must embrace life-long learning as a fact of the profession.

Marianne Nikolov is a Senior Lecturer/Associate Professor at the Department of English Applied Linguistics of Janus Pannonius University, Pécs, Hungary. She taught children in a primary school for 18 years and has been working as a teacher educator for over two decades. She has used negotiation not only with children of 6 to 14 years but also with pre- and in-service students.

Lucy Norris is Director of Studies at the Cairns Language Centre, Australia and a tutor for the Cambridge/RSA CELTA scheme. Fourteen years in ELT embraces European and Asian teaching contexts, and her interest in negotiation arises from learning and teaching exchanges in cross-cultural settings. She has initiated negotiation into the Cairns Language Centre's curriculum to good student and teacher response.

Kaye Oates, as the administrator of Graylands Intensive Language Centre, Western Australia, has been responsible for co-ordinating the implementation of negotiated evaluation as a tool for assessment. She has been involved in ESL/EFL as a teacher, teacher educator and administrator in Australia and Papua New Guinea.

Ramon Ribé is an Associate Professor at the University of Barcelona, Spain where he co-ordinates postgraduate programmes in Applied Linguistics. A former high-school teacher and trainer, he has experimented and published in the area of negotiated task-based learning, language creativity and project work.

Isabel Serrano-Sampedro is the Head of English at the Instituto de Educacíon Secundaria Avempace (the Avempace Secondary School), Zaragoza, Spain. An EFL teacher for twenty-four years, she has worked in teacher education since 1982. She has practised negotiation work with students of secondary, university and teacher education since 1986 and is the author of teacher resource books for implementing negotiated programmes in the new curriculum for Spanish schools.

Stefaan Slembrouck is Professor of English Language and Linguistics at the University of Gent, Belgium. Although a discourse analyst by vocation, the nature of modern-languages degrees in Belgian universities has granted him some 8 years of intensive teaching experience in TEFL.

Kari Smith has the Chair of the Education Department, Oranim School of Education of the Kibbutz Movement, Haifa University, Israel. She has 21 years' experience in teaching and 11 years' in teacher education working with teachers of all subjects in the secondary school. Her main interest is alternative approaches to assessment which would involve learners in the process.

Margaret Sokolik is a lecturer at the University of California, Berkeley's College Writing Programs, USA. She has been in the ESL/EFL field since 1984. She both practises negotiation with university students of writing and trains graduate students in this approach in writing-pedagogy seminars.

Susan Spencer now works as a Language and Curriculum Development teacher for the Cambridgeshire Multicultural Service at Chesterton Community College in Cambridge, UK. She has worked as a project co-ordinator, consultant, manager and teacher in Britain, Indonesia, Bangladesh and Tanzania.

Kate Wolfe-Quintero is an Associate Professor of ESL and Director of two ESL programmes at the University of Hawaii at Manoa, USA. For the past several years, she has explored issues surrounding negotiation in her own graduate courses as well as with graduate students who teach in the Department of ESL.

Acknowledgements

We would like to give our thanks to the many, many teachers and students who, over the years, have offered their insights, uncertainties and experiences of negotiated classroom work and who have been the inspiration for developing this collection. We would also like to thank the contributors for their patience in awaiting the publication of the book. At Cambridge University Press, we would like to thank Alison Sharpe and Mickey Bonin who made the collection possible; thanks also to Martin Mellor for his careful editorial support. We also received many useful, constructive comments from four anonymous readers. Thanks go to them and also to Alison Hill and Emma McEvoy for their detailed work on parts of the text.

Introduction and overview

The focus of the collection

Over recent years, interest in the concepts of 'negotiation' and 'process' in language teaching have come from two main areas of professional debate. On the one hand, research has looked closely at the process of second language acquisition and how interaction may contribute. Studies have examined, for example, how in native/non-native interaction speakers may modify their language in response to requests for clarification to bring about a message comprehensible to the listener. At the same time, a different, though related use of the concept of 'process' and 'negotiation' has emerged in the realm of classroom pedagogy. In this, 'process' has been defined as taking students through various stages in producing language, most notably in the area of academic writing where students are encouraged to collect ideas, draft, redraft, seek feedback and negotiate with peers and with 'the reader' to accomplish a successful text.

Both these avenues of debate have made important contributions to the development of professional knowledge. It is, however, a third, broader, view of the terms 'process' and 'negotiation' which is the focus of this collection. Developing from moves towards communicative language teaching, recent innovations in classroom practice have emphasised the value of collaborative learning, learner-centredness, autonomy and shared decision-making in the classroom. The motivation for developments in this area have come from many sources but a strong element in this is a desire to create forms of classroom interaction which give voice to students in the management of their learning. Through making explicit the typically 'hidden' views of students, the intention is to arrive at more effective, efficient *and* democratic modes of classroom work. In the context of these accounts presented in this book, therefore, negotiation refers to discussion between all members of the classroom to decide how learning and teaching are to be organised.

Interest in the potential of negotiation in this respect has stimulated work aimed at providing structures which can enable this to happen. Fundamental to the nature of classroom work is the type and content of the syllabus which frames the work teachers and students do together. We have become familiar, for example, with grammatical syllabuses functional syllabuses, lexical syllabuses, and task-based syllabuses. A natural evolution in the desire to establish shared decision-making in the classroom has therefore focused attention on the nature of the syllabus, for it is clear that, in the accomplishment of any educational aim, a structure – however loosely defined – needs to be provided for this to happen. Process syllabuses have therefore evolved as a means of planning, implementing and evaluating negotiation in the classroom, and the decisions to which teachers and students may jointly arrive.

While interest in the concept and potential of negotiation and process syllabuses is high, there is relatively little in the professional literature which documents practical work in this area. Indeed, many commentators have dismissed the concept of a process syllabus as untested and impractical, with scant evidence on which to base such a view. A key aim of this book, then, is to provide a 'landmark' volume which explores the rationale of classroom negotiation and provides accounts of its practicality in diverse contexts.

Organisation

Chapter 1 sets out in detail the meanings and significance of the concept of negotiation, and traces the origins and rationale of the concept into the fields of applied linguistics, educational philosophy and psychology. It also outlines a framework for the application of a process syllabus. Accounts of classroom practice then follow. These are divided in three parts, each of which relates to a different sector of educational practice. Part 1 (Chapters 2 to 7) contains accounts of negotiated work with children in primary and secondary schools, Part 2 (Chapters 8 to 13) provides accounts of work in tertiary education (including universities and language schools), while Part 3 (Chapters 14 to 17) documents work in teacher education. The final chapter in the collection, Chapter 18, draws together some practical implications of classroom negotiation and provides a resource to guide those wishing to introduce negotiation into their own classrooms. Table 0.1 provides an overview of the content of each chapter, indicating in each case the context for negotiated work.

Each of the chapters provides an account in which a teacher has undertaken negotiation with language learners. A distinctive feature of

Table 0.1   *Overview of negotiated work*

1	*Michael P. Breen and Andrew Littlejohn*	Definition, origins and rationale for negotiation; a framework for process syllabuses

Part 1   Accounts of practice in primary and secondary schools

2	*Anne MacKay, Kaye Oates, Yvonne Haig*	Primary-school pupils learning ESL in Australia
3	*Kari Smith*	Secondary-school students in Israel
4	*Ramon Ribé*	Secondary-school students in Spain
5	*Marianne Nikolov*	Primary-school pupils in Hungary
6	*Pnina Linder*	Secondary-school students in Israel
7	*Isabel Serrano-Sampedro*	Secondary-school students in Spain

Part 2   Accounts of practice in tertiary education

8	*Stefaan Slembrouck*	University students in Belgium
9	*Elaine Martyn*	School of nursing students in Pakistan
10	*Eddie Edmundson and Steve Fitzpatrick*	Language-school students in Brazil
11	*Wendy Newstetter*	Institute of higher education in USA; engineering students studying written English
12	*Margaret Sokolik*	University writing class in USA
13	*Lucy Norris and Susan Spencer*	Pre-departure language course in Indonesia for teachers of a wide range of disciplines

Part 3   Accounts of practice in teacher education

14	*Suzanne Irujo*	Teacher education at a university in USA
15	*Michael McCarthy and Michael Makosch*	Teachers participating in a two-week residential seminar in UK
16	*Roz Ivanič*	MA students at a university in UK
17	*Kate Wolfe-Quintero*	Teaching of writing course at a university in USA
18	*Michael P. Breen and Andrew Littlejohn*	Overview of practical aspects of negotiation

the accounts which the collection provides is the broad range of contexts which are reported. These include those as geographically and culturally diverse as Australia, Belgium, Brazil, Britain, Hungary, Indonesia, Israel, Pakistan, Spain and the USA, with examples of work in state and private institutions, with small and large classes, and with learners of diverse age ranges and educational experience. Some of the writers have negotiated with their students about a single aspect of their curriculum or programme, such as end of course assessment, or overall aims and objectives of the course. Other writers report on shared decision-making about much of their work with their students, including purposes, ways of working, contents and evaluation.

Through the collection as a whole, we learn much about the complexities of introducing negotiation, about apparent achievements as well as failures, successes as well as difficulties. Each of the chapters presents direct experience of negotiation and as such reveals factors such as students' affective response, classroom roles, rights and responsibilities, and the influence of educational cultures. These are factors which underpin all classroom work. The collection aims to broaden our understanding of how negotiation may interact with these factors and thereby provide teachers with starting points for their own initiatives in classroom work.

1 The significance of negotiation

Michael P. Breen and Andrew Littlejohn

In this chapter, we explore the origins, rationale and nature of nego-tiated work in a language classroom, setting the scene for the practical accounts which follow. We will principally be concerned therefore with three sets of questions:

1. What is negotiation? Which particular form of negotiation is the focus of this book?
2. What are the justifications for negotiating with students in a language class? What is the rationale for negotiation?
3. Which classroom decisions may be negotiable? How does nego-tiation relate to a process syllabus?

Although these issues are related to one another, we will explore them in turn in the three sections that follow. As we shall see, the broader concept of 'negotiation' is rather like a river, arising from a variety of small streams and gathering its own momentum eventually to pour in quite different directions over a flood plain. Its theoretical sources are diverse. As it has attracted greater interest in terms of its relevance to research and practice, it has become more defined and differentiated so that it no longer has a single meaning. As this book focuses upon only one of these meanings, it is important to clarify from the outset what we intend by the term and how it is implemented in practice by the contributors to this collection. Building on this initial definition, we will then elaborate upon negotiation in the classroom in more detail by tracing some of the influences that have shaped it and by enumerating the main principles underlying its role in language pedagogy in particular. Finally, we will address certain practical implications for classroom decision-making by describing the relationship between negotiation and a process syllabus in the context of a language course or curriculum. In this chapter, therefore, the focus is upon the theory or philosophy of negotiation as a preliminary to teachers' accounts of its practical applica-tion in Chapters 2 to 17. In Chapter 18, we will draw theory and practice together in deducing what may be learned from both.

Forms of negotiation

Negotiation typifies and generates the ways we communicate through written or spoken texts. We can distinguish three kinds of negotiation in terms of the main purposes they serve in particular contexts of communication. We may call these personal, interactive and procedural negotiation. All three involve a struggle for meaning and all three entail the reduction of our uncertainty during learning or communication – both psychological uncertainty and, to differing extents, social or interpersonal uncertainty. All three are related and can co-occur.

Personal negotiation

Personal negotiation is primarily a psychological process because it engages such mental capacities as discriminating, analysing and synthesising, memorising or recalling, and so on. When we interpret meaning from what we read or hear, negotiation occurs between the potential meanings of the written or spoken text and those meanings which we ourselves can attribute to that text from our previous knowledge and experience (Widdowson, 1978). For example, we are all familiar with the experience of 'gaining' more meaning than we had given previously to a novel or a poem when we read it a second time and with our inclination to superimpose our own interpretations upon items in a news broadcast. Such interpretative negotiation is likely to result in different meanings being derived from the same text by different people. Similarly, when we express meaning in what we write or say, we have to negotiate between what we intend to mean and our knowledge of the forms of expression which the rules and conventions of writing and speaking will allow. In certain situations, we are well aware of the frustrations of struggling for the right word or form of expression, whilst we are likely to be most conscious of this mental negotiation when we are trying to write something which we want to make very clear.

Negotiation in this sense therefore refers to the unobservable and complex mental processing that occurs in our search for understanding and our efforts to be understood. This kind of negotiation underlies all the negotiating we do. Meaning is made in our heads, although, of course, the meanings we interpret and express are likely to have been learned in previous social activities and can be regarded as having their roots in the cultural and social worlds which we inhabit. The second two kinds of negotiation are motivated by this mental process and, in turn, serve to influence it in an ongoing way. If we seek meaning through language, personal negotiation is unavoidable whilst interactive and procedural negotiation are always optional and located in overt social activity.

Interactive negotiation

The original use of the term 'negotiation' in the sense we refer to it here derives from researchers investigating the nature of conversational interaction (Garfinkel, 1967). Here the negotiation is overtly social and occurs when people use language either to indicate their understanding or their failure to understand (or, indeed, believe) what another person has said, or in order to modify and restructure their language to make things clearer so that they will be understood. The significance of this for language learning was originally recognised by Evelyn Hatch when she explored how learning might actually *derive* from the kinds of interaction in which learners may be involved (Hatch, 1978). This radical departure from the accepted view that the capacity to communicate was an outcome of the necessary *prior and explicit* learning of the forms of language coincided with Krashen's influential argument that language acquisition primarily depends upon the provision to learners of comprehensible input (Krashen, 1981; 1985).

In representing a synthesis of Hatch's assertion of the importance of conversation and Krashen's assertion of the centrality of appropriate input, M. Long identified the interactive process as pivotal for language acquisition. He elaborated upon the interaction in which a listener requests clarification of someone else's message and the speaker subsequently repeats, simplifies or elaborates upon the original message as the location in which teachers and learners seek and create comprehensible input (M. Long, 1981). He was encouraged in this view by his and others' discovery that this kind of modified interaction occurred more frequently when native speakers communicated with non-native speakers and even more frequently when non-native speakers communicated with each other, particularly in language learning tasks. Debates on the relative contributions of input and interaction have characterised much of second language acquisition (SLA) research since the mid-1970s. Long and other researchers who acknowledged the centrality of conversational interaction in SLA later adopted the term 'negotiation' to describe it and, more recently, specified it as 'negotiation for meaning' (for a review of this work, see Pica, 1994). Interactive negotiation, therefore, occurs in an ongoing and usually spontaneous way within immediate social activity. From the perspective of language acquisition research, however, it also has a psycholinguistic purpose in that it is seen as a facilitative means for generating comprehensible input.

Procedural negotiation

The primary function of personal and interactive negotiation is to uncover and share meaning. Like interactive negotiation, whilst it is also overt and social in nature, the primary focus of procedural negotiation is less upon meaning than upon reaching agreement. Although both understanding and sharing meaning are entailed in the process, these are subordinate to the main aim of procedural negotiation. This kind of negotiation is exemplified by discussions between people who are likely to have different interests or different points of view but who seek to reach agreement on a matter, solve a shared problem or establish ways of working that are acceptable to them. This view of negotiation is probably the interpretation that is used most in everyday usage, and it is regularly used to refer to what diplomats, or trade unions and employers do when differences between various parties arise.

Its relevance to language learning arises because, for many people, such learning occurs in the social context of a classroom. Here, the primary function of procedural negotiation is managing teaching and learning as a group experience. There are certain key decisions which have to be made within this process. These include: who will work with whom, in what ways, with what resources and for how long, upon what subject matter or problem, and for what purposes. In other words, decisions have to be made with regard to the purposes of the work, its particular focus or content, and the ways in which it will be undertaken in the classroom group. In addition, we need to know the extent to which the actual decisions made have been appropriate in enabling the achievement of the chosen objectives. Outcomes from the process have to be evaluated in some way. Conventionally, it is assumed that it is the role of the teacher to make these decisions, both covertly as part of planning and classroom management and through overt instructions to students at key moments in a lesson. As we see in the next part of this chapter, there are several justifications for raising such decisions to the level of overt negotiation *with* students. However, one major justification echoes what we identified as the motivations for both personal and interactive negotiation: reaching and sharing understanding.

We can exemplify this motive in classroom language learning with reference to the common situation of a teacher having to lead students through a pre-designed syllabus which entails specific learning objectives. The teacher has to mediate between the requirements of the syllabus and the different learning agendas of the students in the class. These diverse personal agendas are shaped by the students' prior knowledge and experience, including their earlier experiences of classroom learning. Learning agendas comprise the learners' own learning

8

priorities, their changing learning needs, their different preferred strategies and styles of learning, the different value and functions they give to the language classroom and the people in it, and so on. Such agendas inevitably generate a wide range of interpretations – some of which are unconscious – of the objectives of learning and appropriate content. Similarly, there are a range of preferred ways of learning and differences in how people think they should work in a classroom setting. However, the teacher often has to navigate all the students through a set syllabus towards specific objectives. To achieve this, and responding to emerging learner needs and difficulties, the teacher is the person who most often makes decisions of the kind we identified earlier. The result is the *actual* syllabus of the classroom which is an unfolding compromise between the original pre-designed syllabus and the individual teacher's alertness to those aspects of learner agendas that may be revealed during classroom work.

The teacher's interpretation of a syllabus and reasons for classroom decisions are usually covert. Similarly, learners' own unfolding interpretations of what is done in the classroom and how it relates to their own learning agendas are rarely the focus of overt consideration. Just as the compromise syllabus is essentially the teacher's creation, so it is also differentially interpreted by the students, and it is unlikely to accommodate the more opaque aspects of the diverse language learning agendas of the classroom group. The result is likely to be a lack of harmony between the different versions of syllabuses in the class that, in turn, has the potential to inhibit, disrupt or delay the learning process.

A major purpose of procedural negotiation in the classroom is, therefore, to reach a shared understanding at appropriate moments in classroom work of both the requirements that may be implicit in, for example, an external syllabus or the teacher's experientially informed view of efficient ways of working and the different learning agendas in the class. Through this ongoing process of explicit accommodation, a collective language curriculum of the classroom group can be gradually evolved. Procedural negotiation in the language classroom comprises overt and shared decision-making through which alternative assumptions and interpretations are made clear, the range of achievements and difficulties in the work are identified, and preferences and alternatives in ways of working can be revealed and chosen so that the teaching–learning process within a class can be as effective as possible. *It is this kind of procedural negotiation and the practical experiences of it that is the focus of this book and which defines the nature of a process syllabus.*

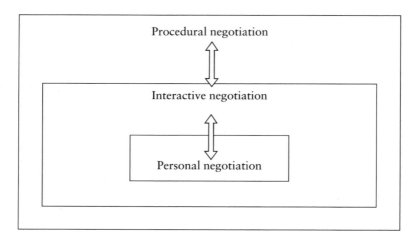

Figure 1.1 Relationship between three kinds of negotiation

Negotiation and language learning

Although we have emphasised the potential contribution of procedural negotiation to the language classroom, all three forms of negotiation which we have identified are highly relevant for language learning. Learners must engage in personal negotiation as a psychological process in order to learn to interpret and express meaning in a new language. If given appropriate scope to occur, interactive negotiation (sharing, checking and clarifying meanings) and procedural negotiation (reaching agreement on decisions) will be part of the communicative and social activity of a language class. Also, and importantly, all three are related. As Figure 1.1 illustrates, the relationship is one of interactivity and entailment. Procedural negotiation entails interactive negotiation for meaning; the search for agreement in decisions requires the resolution of failures to understand or the struggle to be clear. Interactive negotiation is motivated by the wish to interpret personally what is said or express a particular point of view. We can also describe the process in reverse, where the personal struggle to express meaning, for example, is likely to entail noticing when one is not understood and the consequent effort to reformulate or elaborate on one's meaning. Such interactive work will occur in an ongoing and spontaneous way while seeking agreement in relation to a decision about classroom work.

A major significance of procedural negotiation for the language class-room is that it calls upon and activates both personal and interactive negotiation while, in turn, contributing to their scope and quality during learning. All three are mutually supportive processes for developing the capacity to communicate in a new language.

In identifying procedural negotiation of classroom decisions as the particular focus of this book, we have so far emphasised two of its purposes. First, when language learning is undertaken in a classroom group, negotiation is a means for developing a harmonious relationship between three teaching–learning agendas: any external requirements upon the learning in terms of pre-specified knowledge and capabilities, individual learning agendas and the evolving collective curriculum of the group. Second, procedural negotiation entails and engages personal and interactive negotiation as processes for the expression of meanings and the sharing of understandings. All three kinds of negotiation underlie and refine a person's use of language. When we consider the learning of a language, we readily recognise that personal and interactive negotiation are essential. A central argument here is that one of the major purposes of procedural negotiation in a language class is to intensify opportunities for the enactment of personal and interactive negotiation. There are, however, additional and deeper justifications for negotiated decision-making of this kind which we explore in the next section.

The rationale for negotiation

In this section, we present a number of key principles on which negotiation in the language classroom rests. These principles have a long history and express a range of motivations for negotiation with students in classroom settings. We begin, however, with a brief account of influences from theory, research and practice that have shaped them.

The roots of the concept of negotiation in learning

It is not too grandiose a claim to suggest that the direct engagement of students in their learning through democratic decision-making has its roots in the Enlightenment and classical liberalism. The original concept of liberalism, becoming enacted in the gradual spread of democratic forms of government subsequent to the French Revolution, has since been colonised and thereby distorted by state and corporate capitalism – as has the word 'democracy' which, in our own times, is often appealed to on behalf of policies and actions of the powerful that are the least democratic. However, the principles of classical liberalism informed what Bertrand Russell identified as 'the humanist conception' of social development in the first part of the twentieth century. Both Russell in Europe and John Dewey in the USA explored the relationships between an emergent democratic society and an educational enterprise that might give rise to democratic citizenship.

Russell saw education as a means for asserting values over domination and compliance and, crucially, as a means for developing a wise and creative citizenry of a free community to replace the more inegalitarian and dehumanising features of the industrial revolution (B. Russell, 1926). Dewey, writing on education mainly in the years of the Great Depression of the 1930s coincident with the rise of dictatorships in Europe, asserted a humanist conception of education in the context of what he saw as a real struggle for genuine democracy. The expansion of corporate industrial power represented to him, an evolved form of feudal and elitist social structure that classical liberalism had sought to replace. He saw education in the twentieth century as the means towards freedom and independence in thought and action within a co-operative venture towards common goals for the good of the majority rather than a plutocratic minority. And he believed that the educational process should encourage open-mindedness, wholehearted involvement and, significantly, a sense of responsibility to oneself and the wider community (Dewey, 1933; 1938).

The wellspring of these proposals within a humanist conception of education, virtually choked by the horrendous divisions of the Second World War and the subsequent 'Cold War' between western interests and those of state communism, later came to the surface in two distinct streams of theory and research. The first emerged in the work of psychologists who asserted a perspective on human beings as more active agents in their own learning than behaviourism had allowed. The second, coinciding with the significant cultural innovations of the 1960s, emerged in the critical assessments of dominant models of western education by a large number of writers. These streams of influence touched upon or anticipated significant developments in linguistics which were to have a later impact upon both research in second language learning and upon language pedagogy.

The innovations in the psychology of learning were exemplified by the work of George Kelly, Abraham Maslow and Carl Rogers in the 1950s and 1960s. Kelly based his influential notions regarding how we conceptualise our world through personal constructs on the view that all learning is analogous to scientific investigation and the construction of empirically or, more precisely, experientially informed theories (Kelly, 1955). A central idea in his view was that we learn, not by forming habits of behaviour or accumulating wisdom as it is presented to us, but when confronted with discontinuity, puzzles or paradoxes. We best learn at moments when we *must* reduce our own uncertainty. Maslow and Rogers, reflecting a strong focus on the individual that exemplified western psychology, somewhat misleadingly interpreted humanism primarily in terms of a 'person-centred' agenda for 'self-actualisation' through education. In most thoroughly exploring the facilitative role of the teacher within such an agenda, Rogers directly addressed the power and control relations that he saw as existing in 'conventional' education (Rogers, 1969). He envisioned teachers as providing the 'psychological climate' in which learners are able to take responsible control over their own learning. Although identifying power and control as located in interpersonal relations, he did not extend his vision to broader political and social action. This wider perspective would arise later from other sources, mainly European. However, Rogers, like Maslow, argued for a reduction of emphasis upon content-based and fixed-learning outcomes in favour of opening up a space for learners' diversity in learning needs and objectives through a focus upon the process or experience of learning which could be seen as generative and of life-long value. These 'humanistic' perspectives were carried through in certain new directions in language teaching in the 1970s, particularly in the USA exemplified by Moskovitz (1978) and the innovations described by Stevick (1976; 1990). However, as we shall see, another critic of the behaviourist constructs of human learning was to have a significant, though perhaps indirect, impact upon second language teaching.

Meantime, of even more long-term significance for the roots of procedural negotiation in the classroom, and coincident with the growing civil-rights movement, more overtly critical perspectives on the inequalities and divisiveness of contemporary American education were being identified in the work of Holt (1964), Kohl (1968) and Kozol (1967), among others. Their demands for school reform were expressed in terms of the urgent need for more socially inclusive and explicitly democratic forms of pedagogy and curricula (Postman and Weingartner, 1969). Dewey's original agenda was being rewritten at a time when his predictions about the underlying inequalities of American society were being more widely acknowledged.

Educators outside the USA were, meantime, widening this debate. Ivan Illich (1971) asserted that conventional schooling had gone beyond redemption not least because it served the interests of power and wealth in its construction of compliant consuming citizens. Like Russell before him, Illich asserted the need for a return to 'vernacular values' and he identified these as being rooted in community endeavour that was typified by authentic democracy. Paulo Freire's work, primarily in adult literacy in Latin America, similarly located emancipatory education within local cultural action and proposed worthwhile learning as essentially an outcome of social collaboration (Freire, 1970; 1972). Recently, Freire's ideas in particular have been taken up most directly in relation to language teaching through Auerbach's proposals concerning a participatory pedagogy (Auerbach, 1990; 1995; see also Wolfe-Quintero, Chapter 17 of this volume).

In Britain, echoing Russell's and Dewey's liberal democratic agenda for the schooling of young people with an emphasis upon collaborative responsibility rather than competition, and choice rather than coercion, the 1960s and 1970s witnessed a range of practical initiatives within mainstream, state schooling. These included the Plowden Committee's learning-centred agenda for primary education (Plowden, 1967) and the establishment of the first comprehensive high schools intended to replace the binary division between grammar schools (which selected their intake on the basis of seeming academic potential) and secondary schools (for all other students). Both these initiatives attracted strong resistance at the time and ever since from more conservative circles. Coincident with such innovation was a growing interest in less conservative circles in alternative forms of schooling, perhaps most notably in A. S. Neill's Summerhill in which he had transformed liberal views of education into practice thirty years previously, at a time when Russell's and Dewey's ideas were still relatively new (Neill, 1937; 1962; Hennings, 1972).

More liberal directions in practice coincided with critical explorations in theory. Detailed analyses of the transmission of knowledge in schooling in terms of an asymmetry of power and its implications for control in the teaching–learning process were undertaken by a number of British sociologists of education (for example, Bernstein, 1967; Young, 1971). In terms of curriculum innovation, the tenor of this debate in Britain was, perhaps, most accessibly articulated in Lawrence Stenhouse's work (Stenhouse, 1975). In the same climate of critical evaluation, and echoing Bernstein's ideas regarding access to, and control of, knowledge, Douglas Barnes and his co-writers challenged prevailing transmission modes of education with specific reference to the language used in schools and classrooms (Barnes *et al.*, 1969). This remarkable critique initiated a focus among educators upon language across the whole curriculum and anticipated Britten's assertion of the need to see students as active communicating participants rather than quiet spectators in schooling, and Barnes' exploration of small group processes as a means for genuinely interpretative learning. Later advocates of direct student participation through their negotiation of aspects of curriculum, particularly aspects relating to language and literacy, have often cited the work of these authors as highly influential (see, for example, Boomer *et al.*, 1992).

This remarkable upsurge of ideas and action of the 1960s and 1970s flows more recently into the assertively critical work on education in feminist writing and within what we may identify with a post-modern perspective. It is within these that European tributaries of theory and research on emancipatory forms of education begin to dominate the landscape, although the writings of Giroux (1981) and Apple (1986), both North American, perhaps most directly explore implications for teaching and learning in the coming time. Such writers, echoing some of the critics of the limitations of education in the 1960s and 1970s, share the view that pedagogy based upon genuine dialogue both between teachers and taught and also between students is a crucial process characterising emancipatory educational practices. This concern with the contrast between emancipatory and oppressive pedagogies exemplifies European post-modern critiques of contemporary society which derive much of their evidence from theory and research on discourse (amongst others, see Fairclough, 1989). A particular critical stance in our own language teaching profession which identifies coercion and colonisation through certain language education practices has been taken up by a number of writers (see, for example, contributors to Tollefson, 1995). Of course, the post-modern critique of what is seen as the oppressive role of conventional education in our present society goes much further than a humanist or liberal stance, actually questioning the Enlightenment reliance upon 'rationality' and the plausibility of a classical liberalism agenda. What, though, of the more direct impact of this evolution of thinking upon the teaching of language? The twin influences of the 'humanistic conception' of Russell and Dewey and a recognition of the essentially social nature of the learning process – expressed through the critique of its failure to be genuinely democratic in meeting the needs of different groups of learners – can also be traced in certain key developments in views of language learning and teaching since the 1970s.

Chomsky shared with 'humanistic' psychologists a critical disdain for the limitations of behaviourist views of learning but from the perspective of Cartesian and, thereby, Enlightenment thinking, whilst also signalling radical directions for linguistics (Chomsky, 1968). He asserted that he had little to say about language teaching, but his views on the untutored nature of language acquisition and our underlying competence of language knowledge have had lasting effects upon theory and research in our field. Debates about what is innate and what is or is not teachable have dominated second language acquisition (SLA) theory and research to the present time, while the notion of competence, coinciding with the remarkable emergence of sociolinguistic research in the early 1970s, indirectly shaped possibly the most significant shift in our views about language pedagogy in recent years. In what follows, we briefly trace each of these two developments.

Chomsky's assertion, supported by child language research in the 1970s, that a child acquires his or her first language largely without overt teaching by caretakers was extrapolated as part of the first substantial theory of SLA in terms of Krashen's distinction between acquisition and learning and, especially, the primacy of the former. For Krashen, the crucial condition for acquisition to take place was the provision to the learner of comprehensible input (Krashen, 1981; 1985). To date, the significance he attributed to the primacy of the meaning of a new language as the crucible for acquisition remains largely unquestioned in mainstream SLA research except in the matter of how learners might best develop it. Building upon the growth of later studies in first language acquisition which identified interaction between caretakers and young children as the arena for language development, Long launched a research agenda for SLA – currently identified as a 'social interactionist' perspective – which sees interactive negotiation as the means for the creation and uptake of comprehensible input (M. Long, 1981). From such a perspective, the process of language acquisition is extended beyond the mere interaction between input data and the learner's mind to overt negotiation for meaning within social relationships.

The presently influential social interactionist research in SLA also identifies the seminal work of Evelyn Hatch as a formative influence. Through her analysis of the discourse of caretakers and language learners, Hatch revealed that the kinds of conversation in which they participated provided highly appropriate scaffolding for the learning of new linguistic forms (Hatch, 1978; 1992). This concept of scaffolding derives, of course, from the work of Vygotsky who explicitly located learning both *within* social activity and *as* social activity (Vygotsky, 1962). A central process in Vygotsky's account of learning is the scaffolding during a shared activity provided by social interaction between a learner who is not yet capable of independently achieving something and a person who is already knowledgeable and capable. As Hatch revealed when examining caretaker interaction with young learners, caretaker contributions to the flow of conversation, elaboration or reformulation of learner utterances, and input of appropriate vocabulary at certain moments all enabled young learners to contribute to the conversation and to express and understand new meanings. For Vygotsky, the potential for development through social interaction with someone more capable is greater than that which a learner can achieve independently; the difference being referred to as the 'zone of proximal development' (Vygotsky, 1962).

In terms of current directions in the psychology of education, it is significant that the work of Vygotsky is seemingly being rediscovered, not least in the language-teaching profession. His ideas are currently seen to inform a 'sociocultural' perspective on language teaching which partly echoes humanist psychological views of the learner as an *active agent* in the process (Lantolf, 1994; Lantolf and Appel, 1994). However, following the ideas of Leont'ev, one of Vygotsky's successors, sociocultural theory identifies agency as social action and places it within particular contexts or 'activity'. 'Activity' is used in a special sense by sociocultural theorists to refer to the inter-personal nature or inter-subjectivity of collaborative action, the specific settings of colla- borative action, and how actions are actually carried out in those settings (Leont'ev, 1981; Donato and McCormick, 1994).

Turning from views on how language is acquired to Chomsky's concept of underlying competence, the almost simultaneous emergence and expansion of sociolinguistic research enabled Dell Hymes to challenge the apparent narrow mentalism of Chomsky's formulation of underlying linguistic knowledge and to extend it in terms of our knowl- edge of appropriate *use* of language in social situations (Hymes, 1971). It is fair to suggest that Hymes' notion of communicative competence provided one of the key theoretical reference points for the most significant development in language teaching from the late 1970s onwards. Communicative Language Teaching (CLT) reflected a sea change which initially extended our view of the aims and content of language courses. The focus shifted to language use and specifically in terms of notions or frameworks of meaning and, in particular, commu- nicative functions within discourse (Widdowson, 1978). Language learning therefore came to be seen as the development of a range of competencies for use in addition to linguistic knowledge (Canale and Swain, 1980).

Largely because of the significant impetus provided by functionally based pedagogic frameworks of language developed at that time by the Council of Europe, debates about the distinctiveness of CLT centred upon what should be the aims and subject matter of language teaching. Innovations in the design of content syllabuses therefore tended to dominate early formulations; defining language use upstaged discus- sions of how teaching might contribute to its actual development. Perhaps inevitably, this initial narrow focus prefaced the subsequent fragmentation of what the profession intended by the term 'commu- nicative language teaching' so that there are now different lines of development emerging from it. For some proponents of CLT, a primary concern with communicative objectives and content persists, as in certain special-purpose course designs or in a concern with authenticity of classroom texts. For others, *how* the capacity to use language is acquired is the more significant issue. Informed by developments in second language acquisition research, various 'task-based' approaches to language teaching may be seen to exemplify this concern (Long and Crookes, 1992). Similarly, 'learner-centred' syllabus design, minimally in terms of the analysis of learner needs or more overtly involving degrees of negotiation with learners, appears to reflect a stronger focus on learning than upon the content to be learned (Nunan, 1988b; Tudor, 1996).

Just prior to these two developments and in direct response to the initial preoccupation within the CLT movement with appropriately communicative syllabuses, Breen and Candlin proposed a broader *curriculum* framework for CLT. This articulation of a broader view of the possibilities of CLT was influenced by developments in how socio-linguists were investigating and describing language use, by the critiques of prevailing transmission modes of education, and by emerging strands within second language acquisition research at that time (Breen and Candlin, 1980). Defining CLT in curriculum terms enabled language content and classroom methodology to be seen as inextricably related and a specifically communicative perspective on the teaching–learning *process* in the classroom could therefore be explored. A central tenet derived from this perspective was that teachers and students should have the opportunity to undertake procedural negotiation in relation to the curriculum on which they are working as a facilitative and authentic environment for the personal and interactive negotiation processes which current research was identifying as underlying the use and learning of language. Given the preoccupation in the early 1980s with what should serve as appropriate communicative syllabuses (Brumfit, 1984), both writers further explored the implications of negotiation for syllabus design in particular.

Candlin argued that any pre-designed syllabus was rendered redundant from the moment teacher and students began working and that the only genuine syllabus would be a retrospective account of what the work had covered and what had been achieved from it (Candlin, 1984). Breen formulated the concept of a process syllabus in order to locate the conventional content syllabus more explicitly *within* and as *mediated by* the teaching–learning process. In addition, a process syllabus was proposed as a reference point for teachers who wished to engage students explicitly in evolving the actual curriculum of the classroom. The place of such procedural negotiation within the framework of a process syllabus is the focus of the third section of this chapter (see pp. 29ff.). First we need to summarise the theoretical and research motivations for negotiation in the language classroom to which we have so far referred.

The principles underlying negotiation in the language classroom

This necessarily brief historical account of some of the main theoretical and empirical roots of procedural negotiation in language teaching has identified four major perspectives. First, a view of learning contextualised in a wider society in which student responsibility and co-operation during learning can be seen as expressing and enabling participation as a citizen in democratic processes. Second, a view of learning as emancipatory, in contrast to 'conventional' education which may be socially divisive and requiring compliance to the hegemony of a dominating minority. Third, a view of learning as located in social and cultural action wherein what is learned and how it is learned are collaboratively shaped. Finally, a view of the learner as an active agent of his or her learning in which the interpretation and control of knowledge is an attribute of the learner rather than as someone positioned as a mere recipient of selected and transmitted knowledge previously determined as appropriate by others.

In addition to these four perspectives on learning and the learner, our historical overview also identified certain key developments in language pedagogy. Second language research identifies interactive negotiation for meaning within discourse as the crucible for acquisition. A basic tenet of communicative language teaching is that the student is learning to become a member of a new speech community through the development of communicative competence. Personal and interactive negotiation for meaning underlie such competence. Given that many learners learn a language in a classroom group, it has been argued from the perspective of communicative language teaching that opportunities for overt negotiation about the classroom curriculum provide a springboard for the other forms of negotiation and for authentic language use about matters that are of immediate significance to learners.

The principles underlying the use of negotiation in the language classroom can therefore be derived from these four perspectives on learning and the learner and from these more specific proposals within second language research and pedagogy. Given that such perspectives and proposals often flow into one another, even from diverse tributaries of thinking and research, the principles we deduce inevitably overlap. However, six key principles can be identified as follows:

- Negotiation is a means for responsible membership of the classroom community.
- Negotiation can construct and reflect learning as an emancipatory process.

The significance of negotiation

- Negotiation can activate the social and cultural resources of the classroom group.
- Negotiation enables learners to exercise their active agency in learning.
- Negotiation can enrich classroom discourse as a resource for language learning.
- Negotiation can inform and extend a teacher's pedagogic strategies.

In the following sections, we briefly elaborate upon each of these principles in turn.

Negotiation is a means for responsible membership of the classroom community

If we are to learn anything from the history of the twentieth century, it seems clear that mere compliance and consumption in line with the hegemony of the powerful and wealthy actually undermine the rights and security of many people. The coming time appears to need, perhaps more than ever before, people who are self reliant and flexible in their working lives, socially responsible rather than merely self-seeking and collaborative rather than competitive in their dealings with other people. Genuine liberty as exercised through democratic processes depends on informed, questioning citizens who are capable of choosing and discarding and who can think issues through and take responsibility for their decisions and, crucially, be responsible for the impact of such decisions on others.

Any classroom, in its social composition, is a microcosm of the wider society in which it is located. For it to function, a classroom community realises its own values and priorities through either implicitly or explicitly accepted procedures and routines. In this way, a classroom culture can be more or less democratic in the original meaning of this term. The more explicitly ways of working are agreed, the more likely a collaborative approach to achieving shared goals can be fostered. Inevitable tensions between the priorities of the individual in relation to the group are more likely to be worked through and resolved. Additionally, the class of learners is more likely to see itself as a learning community with mutual responsibilities. This may perhaps be seen as a large agenda for the language classroom. However, if we accept that learning a language in a group is inherently a social process with the likely purpose of becoming a member of another community of speakers, we may see that the concept of community endeavour may not be inappropriate.

As a number of feminist and post-modern thinkers in education have argued, our present social and political conditions signal an urgent need for classroom pedagogies that enable learners to uncover the relationship of knowledge to power and vested interests. In this sense, learning a language might be seen as either the taking on of a potentially oppressed identity (see, amongst others, Tollefson, 1995) or as a means of access to greater personal adaptability and influence. It has the potential to provide the student with cultural and intellectual resources and, thereby, the practical means and strategies to seek further knowledge and to challenge structures in society that operate in an oppressive way. Learning a language can also facilitate understanding of cultural diversity and provide access to such diversity as a resource. The recognition and maintenance of cultural diversity is both a means towards and an attribute of genuine democracy. As Nancy Lester put it, negotiation in the classroom, in its microcosmic way, can serve as 'a process through which our beliefs about and our enactments in the social, political, and cultural spheres might be transformed' (Lester, 1992: 214). Perhaps the most obvious enactment of these spheres in the classroom – though not the only one – can be seen in the conventional institutional roles of the teacher and the learners. Negotiation between teacher and learners and among learners necessarily entails different ways of enacting these roles. In this way, it may support learners' capabilities to participate in a responsible and self-empowering manner in the world beyond the classroom and, crucially, as a member of a new speech community and culture.

Negotiation can construct and reflect learning as an emancipatory process

A pedagogy that does not directly call upon students' capacities to make decisions conveys to them that either they are not allowed to or that they are incapable of doing so; or it may convey that the more overt struggle to interpret and plan is not part of 'proper' learning. In classrooms that require conformity to externally determined decisions mediated through the teacher and/or to those of the teacher, students have to try to make sense of the curriculum covertly as best they can or withdraw into surviving as an individual not wishing to appear out of place. Learning becomes, at best, a lonely guessing game or, at worst, simply oppressive.

The potential for emancipation can be identified in a learner's stance as a citizen in the wider society and as a seeker of new knowledge and capabilities in *any* context. Additionally, as we have argued, entering a language community as a new member has emancipatory potential. When a person enters a classroom he or she may or may not be enabled to exercise autonomy, the active expression of emancipation.

Autonomous action is typified by thinking and acting according to one's own principles rather than habitually conforming to someone else's. It can, thereby, express the relationship to oneself as a learner. In the context of a transmissive classroom, the learner is most often obliged to 'exercise' this autonomy by conforming to the ways knowledge, teaching and learning have been defined previously by others. Autonomy becomes enacted as overtly passive and individualist. A classroom based upon negotiated knowledge and procedures allows the learner to exercise autonomy on an equal footing with others in the group and as a contribution to the good of the learning community.

Negotiation within the classroom therefore promotes a learner's power of learning and interdependency in learning when appropriate. However, negotiation entails freedom with discipline. It does *not* mean 'anything goes'. Collaborative decision-making requires the constant balancing of an individual agenda with everyone else's. It also requires the constant balancing of particular goals, be they negotiable or not, with personal purposes and preferences for learning. In the classroom group, genuine autonomy has to be exercised in an interdependent way. Autonomous learning within a group also requires opportunities for critical self-reflection in relation to the learning and ongoing group reflection at appropriate moments so that outcomes from shared decisions can be traced. Classroom negotiation entails evaluation of outcomes from activities and how they were undertaken as a pivotal moment for such reflection. The exercise of emancipatory learning in a classroom can therefore be identified as the shared task of evolving and adapting the curriculum according to emerging needs, difficulties and achievements. Through this, learners construct and reconstruct their own learning both as individuals and as a group, and this kind of social action can also contribute to a learner's self-directed learning beyond the classroom and into the wider community.

Negotiation can activate the social and cultural resources of the classroom group

The knowledge constructed in a classroom, because it evolves through a collective process – through the texts, the classroom discourse and the social practices of the group – is greater than any single individual could create, including the teacher. If the social process is *explicitly* directed at the negotiation of alternative understandings and proposals rather than subjected to 'approved' understandings or the understanding of a single person, the learning can entail a sense of ownership rather than mere reproduction. As a group, teacher and learners work towards new understandings; what is learned, being investigated and shaped through a shared process becomes knowledge that is diverse, dynamic and open to new possibilities.

In the classroom, language input through different media and student output are, most often, channelled through social interaction. In this way, the language made available to be learned is constructed within classroom discourse. In addition to shaping what can be learned, the interpersonal processes of the class also shape how the teaching and learning is actually undertaken. Explicit negotiation about such issues enables exploration and trying out of alternative interpretations as well as uses of the new language and alternative ways of working. The latter can provide opportunities for the individual to extend a repertoire of learning strategies in addition to discovering and refining ways of learning in a group that may have life-long relevance. In this way, participating in negotiation in the language class can contribute towards the disembedding of language learning from the more commonly constrained and relatively predictable discourse of the classroom. It can anticipate and provide the foundations for the student's participation through the new language in *other* discourse contexts beyond the classroom.

Learning a language can be seen as a personal means towards broader cultural engagement and identity. It can entail the taking on of cross-cultural membership and, through negotiation, the classroom culture can be seen as a crucible for this. Just as it is a microcosm of the wider society, a classroom is multicultural in terms of the different voices and perspectives on the new language, on learning and on most things in the world! Language pedagogy that explicitly calls upon these can be a means for the inclusion of, and access to, diverse ways of seeing and meaning. David Stern was one of the few language-teaching theorists and researchers to recognise the importance and potential of what he termed the 'cultural syllabus' for language learning (Stern, 1992), whilst Kramsch has taken this idea further to assert the value of cultural investigation as being an integral part of language learning (Kramsch, 1993). Negotiation can facilitate such endeavours by giving space to the multicultural resources that any classroom group inherently contributes, most obviously in a class of students from different cultural backgrounds. However, if we can also regard the different experiences, knowledges and capabilities of the members of *any* class of students as resources on which to draw explicitly, then this valuing of diversity and alternatives in thinking and ways of working can encourage an openness and flexibility in students' approaches to the learning. And negotiation can contribute to such perceptions and approaches to language learning in particular by repositioning the 'curriculum as cultural conversation' (Onore and Lubetsky, 1992: 259).

Negotiation enables learners to exercise their active agency in learning

Much of the research on language classrooms reveals that many learners are placed in a responsive and seemingly passive role (Chaudron, 1988; van Lier, 1988, Breen, 1998). In such circumstances, learners are positioned like children who may seek to conform to a teacher's expectations and may even underachieve in order to do this. This passive conformity can be misinterpreted by the teacher as a lack of sufficient background knowledge, an unformed learning agenda or a lack of the capacity to participate in decision-making. However, all learners bring prior knowledge and capability to learning and further understanding is sought on the basis of what is already known and not merely given. Negotiation provides a context in which opportunities exist for learners to articulate and, thereby, refine their prior understandings, purposes and intentions as reference points for new learning. All learning also requires intention and decision and, as the humanist psychologists discovered, learners work harder if they can explore and articulate their own ideas, ask their own questions and seek their own answers. Psychologists such as Kelly, Maslow and Vygotsky (see previous section) all identified deeper learning as a gradual quest. Learners need time and space to think things through and to talk, read, write and act themselves into new understandings. They need to confront willingly the risk of the problematic and to identify uncertainties. They also need a sense of continuity and progress and this requires ongoing reflection at appropriate moments. None of these requirements are likely to be attained by a learner without support and feedback from others and negotiating new understandings, uncertainties and evaluative reflections with a group of other people who are sharing the learning experience can clearly provide such support.

Being an active agent of one's own learning in a classroom entails optimising the collective resources of a gathering of people, including a teacher who probably has greater experience of helping people to learn than others in the room. Agency in learning in such circumstances also involves contributing as much as one gains so that a group of learners engaged in shared decision-making can also entail mutual support. From this perspective, negotiation is not strictly a characteristic of what is commonly referred to as 'learner-centred' language pedagogy. Negotiation is *classroom-group* centred, serving a collective teaching–learning process and, thereby, individuals located as members of a group.

In addition to being a stimulus for personal and interactive negotiation for meaning, negotiation is also a means for individual agency in the shaping of the classroom curriculum. It is a process during which the individual and the group *together* map out the routes for learning and the alternative ways in which the journey can be undertaken. Comparing his perceptions of conventional educational processes with those in which negotiation occurred, Garth Boomer adopted a similar metaphor for how we might regard the individual's experience of learning:

> Compare the knowledge of certain terrain in the case of a tourist who has been driven through in a tourist bus with traditional blurbs as opposed to that of an adventurer (under guidance) who has, with map and compass, travelled the same territory and had the opportunity to talk it over with fellow travellers ...   (Boomer, 1992: 286)

Negotiation can enrich classroom discourse as a resource for language learning.

As we have seen, current second language acquisition research appears to provide a number of motivations for procedural negotiation in the classroom. Research on the discourse of language classrooms suggests that opportunities for direct learner participation in it are significantly constrained (Chaudron, 1988; van Lier, 1988). The research suggests that the mainly silent, individual struggle to make sense predominates because most interaction appears to be channelled through the teacher. Greatest emphasis appears to be placed upon personal negotiation by the individual whilst opportunities for interactive negotiation during certain learning tasks may be relatively rare. In these circumstances, learners are most often obliged to navigate language lessons as best they can in order to relate their learning agendas to the overt classroom routines and procedures (Breen, 1998). Such pragmatic compliance is more likely to hide rather than reveal to other learners and to the teacher what is being achieved or what is being misunderstood by any individual. In any learning context, teachers' theories, aims and intentions need to be made clear to learners. However, a key function of procedural negotiation is for learners to reveal *their* theories, aims and intentions as resources for the teacher and each other and, thereby, contribute to the inclusiveness and accessibility of the classroom discourse itself.

Interactive negotiation for meaning is regarded by second language researchers as the catalyst for language acquisition. Procedural negotiation provides an authentic arena for it. In addition, overt negotiation that potentially calls upon the contributions of everyone in the group

25

diversifies the input, extends opportunities for learner output, and allows the exercise of judgements of appropriacy and accuracy in relation to the language made available for learning. Being able to make such judgements is not only facilitative of further learning but is also a crucial component of communicative competence in any language.

Perhaps one of the issues which led to the fragmentation of Communicative Language Teaching in recent years has been disagreement among practitioners about the explicit teaching of formal aspects of the language as exemplified by conventional structural syllabuses. Such a focus on the forms of language is argued to be inappropriate in CLT because it entails teacher and learner work upon language as a decontextualised object rather than as the means for sharing meaning within genuine communication. More recently, such a focus on forms has been distinguished from the appropriate focus on *form* at moments when there is an incidental shift of attention to specific aspects of the language which are causing problems in understanding or expressing meaning (Doughty and Williams, 1998). However, if one of the purposes of negotiation is to accommodate the diverse learning agendas within a class, there is likely to be a need to focus on the workings of language which may be occasionally an agreed focus on forms and, at other times, a spontaneous focus on form. The crucial issue here is that *learners'* overtly expressed need for different kinds of metalinguistic work or spontaneous discovery of problems in relation to specific features of the language – *plus* the teacher's recognition of these – determine timing and focus of metalinguistic work and not, as in a structural approach, a pre-determined syllabus of grammar, pronunciation or lexis assumed in advance to be useful for learners.

Negotiation about the conventions of language and its use locates the study of grammar, for example, within the learning purpose of anticipating and solving often unpredictable problems in understanding and expressing meaning through speech or writing. Clearly, a major advantage of negotiation is that it enables the revealing and more precise specification of such problems. Explicit metalinguistic information – such as rules and conventions governing language use or frameworks for structuring different genres – is most useful at moments:

- when it is most needed *by the learner* or when confronting a problem in communication which requires such knowledge;
- when 'noticing the gap' between target forms in written or spoken input and their own output;
- when seeing it as a short cut in making aspects of the language more manageable for them; or
- when the learner simply has a particular interest in such information.

Negotiation allows for the identification of such needs and for a selection process of the most apposite metalinguistic content and how it may be worked upon.

Negotiation can inform and extend a teacher's pedagogic strategies

Clearly, the teacher is at the centre of the negotiation process. Many teachers are obliged to mediate for their students a language syllabus or curriculum over the design of which they had little or no control. However, whether more or less autonomous in the range of decisions they can make, classroom regimes to which teachers significantly contribute are a microcosm of the kind of society which they value. How learners are expected to work in the classroom is more profound in what this conveys to them about learning a language than the syllabus or curriculum the teacher is mediating. Seeing learner diversity in knowledge, and ways of working as resources to be explicitly called upon during the classroom process, may appear to take more time and may release to the surface unexpected learner difficulties. Through this, however, learners' different contributions to their own learning are foregrounded as valid and shareable resources while difficulties can be worked upon in a more direct and collective way rather than being smoothed over to become a source of continued learner confusion or dissatisfaction. In essence, negotiated decision-making can more overtly locate responsibility for learning in a classroom with the class as a working group including the teacher rather than with the teacher alone.

In the context of negotiation – even negotiation about one or two aspects of the classroom curriculum – the teacher has the opportunity to act as a role model for active learning. The teacher can welcome learners' alternative interpretations and proposals as equal but also identify them as open to the group's judgements, selection and agreement. The teacher can encourage learners' own gradual explicitness and greater precision in the identification of preferred learning purposes, content, ways of working and ways of evaluating outcomes so that such preferences become available for everyone as reference points and alternatives for action.

Procedural negotiation entails that the teacher also has the right to negotiate, and how she or he exercises this right also serves as a model for learner engagement in it. The teacher knows the potential and limits of negotiation in the particular classroom setting and the wider educational and cultural context in which it is located. She or he has to be explicit about what seems non-negotiable whilst seeking feasible opportunities for sharing decisions. In this way, negotiation becomes a solution to the puzzles and difficulties grounded in the daily work of the particular class. It is not an approach, method or technique, but a way of taking decisions and acting in a classroom seen as a dynamic communal resource. It is an alternative open to teachers who believe that there is a need for a decision-making process in the classroom that can engage the responsibilities of the learners for their own learning through the exercise of interdependency in a genuine cultural investigation.

Negotiation is emancipatory for the teacher also. It is sharing the weighty burden of managing other people's discovery of a language directly with the people concerned. It enables opportunities for teacher reflection on the more transparent learning process in the class and upon one's own practice in contributing to the management of learning. Negotiated decision-making does not imply abdication but a shift in self-definition as a language teacher which, in turn, can release adaptability in role. Particularly in its early stages, the teacher is pivotal in the negotiation process. The teacher does not give up his or her status as highly experienced and authoritative in the matter of the language and how learners can work upon it (Underhill, 1989). Nor does it imply power-sharing of the kind in which everyone is reduced to the same levels of opportunity or grey conformity to a group norm. The expressions of individuality and difference are crucial contributions to collectively formed and agreed plans, not least because they generate worthwhile alternatives for consideration. Negotiation entails a dialectic between the various 'power-holders' and 'power-subjects' in any gathering of people. And the teacher or the more confident or proficient learners are never, in fact, the only bearers of power in terms of potentially contributory knowledge, experiences and levels of awareness that are involved in learning a language. This dialectic or 'curriculum as conversation' has the potential to free up the teacher to rely on the learning group to help in a methodical way in creating a specific and ongoing language curriculum as an enriching teaching–learning experience.

Just as shared decision-making requires more classroom time initially, which is likely to be made up later on in terms of the scope and quality of the learning, experience at enabling this kind of conversation also grows over time. The teacher has to define with learners moments of closure and agreement whilst recognising that any one step opens up other possibilities. The teacher has to remind learners, quite often in the early stages, what has previously been agreed and to exploit the key phase of evaluation as the opportunity to enable greater precision in future decision-making against realistic objectives. History is often against the innovative educator, and a teacher who begins to share decisions about some or many aspects of the teaching–learning process in a language class also has to be a pragmatist. However, she or he may discover that the time and energy devoted to procedural negotiation generates levels of interactive and personal negotiation that have deeper and longer term effects upon the learning of the language, not least the greater capacity of learners to negotiate through the new language in other situations long after the course has been completed. If we accept that learners discover a great deal about language learning in a classroom from the stance of the teacher, if the teacher launches an exploration of different ideas and perspectives on the what and how of language learning in the class, this can model to learners the inherent potentials of language knowledge and, crucially, adaptability in its acquisition and use.

Classroom decision-making and negotiation: conceptualising a process syllabus

So far we have identified procedural negotiation as a means for a teacher and students to share decision-making in relation to the unfolding language curriculum of the group. On the basis of a tradition of theory and research, we have also described principles that motivate such negotiation. The final question that we address in this chapter refers to the potential focus of negotiation: Which classroom decisions are open to negotiation?

Just as a conventional syllabus provides a framework for the potential content for teaching, the concept of a process syllabus was originally proposed in order to provide a framework for decision-making during teaching and learning in a classroom setting. It distinguishes itself from conventional, content syllabuses by identifying classroom decisions as potentials for negotiation whereby teacher and students together can evolve and work through the *actual* curriculum of the classroom group. As a framework, a process syllabus identifies:

1. the range of decisions that can be open to negotiation;
2. the steps in a negotiation cycle; and
3. the elements or levels in the classroom curriculum to which the negotiation cycle can be applied.

We explore each of these components of a process syllabus in turn and describe two concepts – the negotiation cycle and the curriculum pyramid – which may help to map out and guide the nature and extent of negotiation undertaken by a classroom group.

The range of decisions open to negotiation

Negotiation can potentially occur in relation to any and all decisions that need to be made in the ongoing creation of the language curriculum of a particular class or group of learners. As we suggested in the first section of this chapter, procedural negotiation can be the means for teacher and students to reach agreement in four key decision-making areas that, in turn, generate such a curriculum. Decisions have to be made in relation to:

- the purposes of their work together;
- the content or subject matter of their work;
- their various ways of working together;
- their preferred means of evaluation of the efficiency and quality of the work and its outcomes so that new directions in the work can be identified.

These four areas of decision-making can be expressed in terms of questions the answers to which may be negotiated by teacher and students together. These questions are illustrated in Table 1.1. Two important characteristics of decision-making become clearer when we consider them as questions. First, as Table 1.1 indicates, each major question is generic in the sense that it can be further specified in terms of contributory questions that may need to be addressed through negotiation. Second, any single decision reached can affect and influence other decisions that have to be made.

As we shall see in the chapters that follow, negotiation between a teacher and students and between the students themselves can be devoted to *any one* of these or similar questions. Not only may negotiation be selective among the range of decisions, it may occur only at certain points depending on the circumstances of each classroom group. Indeed, it would be highly unusual and inefficient for a classroom group to seek negotiated agreement on all of the major questions in every lesson, even if this was feasible. A language lesson is rarely a discrete event although it may follow its own micro-sequence focusing upon a single topic or aspect of language, punctuated by class, group or individual work, involving a particular way of working, and concluding, perhaps, with some form of evaluation and feedback. However, classroom work is most often based on a macro-sequence of related lessons. Content in terms of a topic or specific uses of language may take up a series of lessons and may be recycled. Participation may shift appropriately from whole group, to small group and individual work and back again on a particular set of tasks or larger activity over time. Additionally, assessment of achievements or evaluation of the whole

Table 1.1   *The range of decisions open to negotiation*

Purposes: Why are we learning the language?
What immediate and long term learning need(s) should be focused upon?
What should we aim to know and be able to do? What very specific aims
might we have? etc.

Content: What should be the focus of our work?
What aspects of the language? What topics, themes, or specific uses of the
language? What skills, strategies or competencies when using or learning
the language? What puzzle(s), problem(s) or focus for investigation should
be addressed? etc.

Ways of working: How should the learning work be carried out?
With what resources? What types of texts or materials would be most
appropriate? How long should it take? How will the time available be
organised? What working procedure or set of instructions should be
followed? Who will work with whom? (the teacher with the class, a group
or an individual?; the students in groups, in pairs or alone?). What can best
be done in class and what best outside class? What support or guidance
may be needed, what form should it take, and who should provide it?

Evaluation: How well has the learning proceeded?
What should be the outcomes from the work? Have the purposes been
achieved? Of the intended outcomes, what has not been learned and what
has been learned in addition to these? How should outcomes be assessed
and against which criteria? What will happen with the assessment? etc.

---

process may come only at the end of a number of lessons when the
sequence is completed. Lessons form a kind of narrative, and negotiation seen as part of a cycle is the means for teacher and students to
initiate such a narrative together and for revealing their interpretations
of it as it unfolds as the basis for future decisions.

The negotiation cycle

Figure 1.2 illustrates the negotiation cycle within a process syllabus
indicating three important steps in the cycle. At Step 1, teacher and
students identify and address those decisions from the full range which
may appear to be most appropriate and feasible for them to negotiate in
the context in which they work, or the most urgent, or even ones that
both teacher and students find problematic in some way and about
which negotiation seems to them necessary. As the chapters in this book

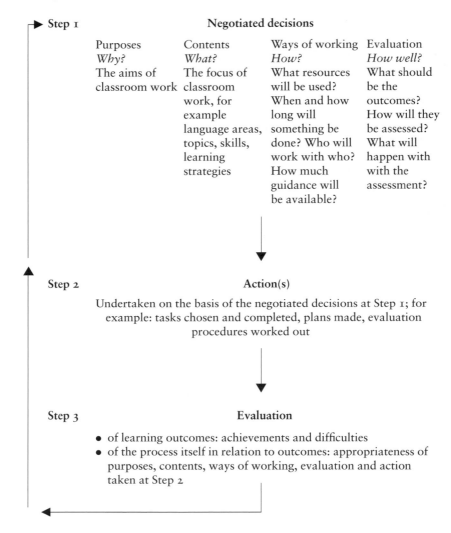

Figure 1.2   The negotiation cycle

illustrate, teachers and students have different reasons for the particular decisions which they choose to negotiate.

Step 2 in the cycle is the resulting action or actions in terms of what is done on the basis of decisions made. We can briefly illustrate such 'actions' by giving examples of what might occur as a result of a negotiated decision within each of the four areas of decision-making.

Implementing decisions made in relation to their Purposes, students might collect and display the short-term and long-term language-learning aims of all class members, or analyse a test or exam that has to be taken at the end of the course in order to plan and map out future work upon unfamiliar aspects, etc. In relation to the Contents of the work, the group may choose to work on a common topic or different topics, undertake tasks that focus on form or use of the language, or they may work on specific problems they have identified, or find out about specific learning strategies that members of the group have found helpful. Implementing decisions made concerning their Ways of Working, students may investigate specific resources beyond the class-room, or agree a particular schedule for an activity and who would be responsible for which parts of it, or specify that a particular task will be a whole class undertaking with the teacher, or something completed in sub-groups, or even partly undertaken by individual students but with a view to sharing outcomes. Concerning Evaluation, students may identify particular criteria for success, choose or design an appropriate test or diagnostic task, or create portfolios of their work and write an evaluative report identifying their strengths and weaknesses, etc., etc.

These few examples of actions resulting from negotiated decisions at Step 1 are merely illustrative and it may be that a classroom group will either implement a decision within only one of the decision-making areas or act upon a set of decisions initially negotiated across all four areas.

Perhaps the most important characteristic of a process syllabus is that it pivots upon the evaluation of an agreed action or set of actions. Identifying learner reflection as a key contributory factor in learning, Step 3 of the cycle involves the classroom group in evaluation of:

1. outcomes in terms of both what is learned and what has proved problematic; and
2. the appropriateness or otherwise of the actual process which they have followed in terms of initial decisions made and subsequent actions undertaken.

A key criterion of appropriateness here is the extent to which initially planned or agreed learning purposes have been achieved. This reflective phase is, of course, unlikely to occur in every lesson or session but more likely at the completion of a large activity made up of a sequence of tasks or after a related sequence of lessons. However, the phase is critical in the whole process because it generates essential information for teacher and students for the next cycle of decision-making.

The significance of negotiation

The curriculum pyramid: levels of application of the negotiation cycle

Negotiation is never undertaken in a vacuum; it is *about* something. As we have seen, it addresses particular decisions at Step 1 in the cycle. However, even these decisions must refer to things that already exist and to the experiences both teacher and students already have concerning language learning in the classroom. The most likely situation is when a teacher and students may be obliged to follow a particular curriculum, or a pre-designed syllabus, or prescribed materials, or an external test that every student must take at the end of the course. Similarly, teacher and students are likely to be familiar with particular ways of working in the classroom; particular methodologies, roles and responsibilities. In such circumstances, any of these things may act as reference points for the negotiation cycle so that what they appear to imply for classroom work can be made explicit and open to adaptation in ways that the teacher and students regard as directly beneficial. Here the cycle itself serves to evolve the actual curriculum which would include the group's aims, content, ways of working or evaluation procedures which are amalgams of what they see as prescribed or required and what they regard as their own priorities and preferences.

In some situations, a particular curriculum, syllabus, materials or test may not be prescribed or the teacher and the learners may feel less constrained by previous ways of working in the classroom. In these circumstances, the negotiation cycle more directly *generates* the classroom curriculum as the work unfolds. However, such circumstances may be unusual and the identification of different levels of focus for the negotiation cycle within a process syllabus assumes that teacher and students very often negotiate between what may be pre-existing or prescribed and their more immediate priorities and preferences. As part of its framework, therefore, a process syllabus identifies different reference points for the negotiation cycle in terms of levels in a curriculum pyramid. Figure 1.3 illustrates these levels on which the cycle may focus at appropriate times.

A feature of each level in the curriculum pyramid is that the higher ones are contained within the levels below and, therefore, negotiation about an appropriate sequence of tasks, for instance, might either follow from or lead to negotiation, perhaps at another time, about an appropriate single task within the sequence. Alternatively teacher and student may choose to focus their negotiation only on one particular level. A second feature of each level in the pyramid is that it may entail *its own* Purposes, Contents, Ways of Working and Evaluation; these are

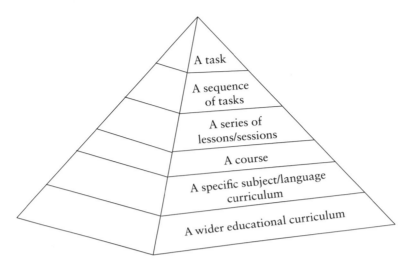

Figure 1.3   The curriculum pyramid: levels of focus for the negotiation cycle

elements that we have identified as open to negotiated decisions at Step 1. A pre-designed task or a course in pre-designed materials, for example, entail the designer's decisions in each of these areas and these would serve as the reference points for negotiated decisions in the classroom.

As Figure 1.3 indicates, the smallest unit on which the cycle focuses is at the level of Task. A task can be seen as the most immediate location of learning work and as a specific social event in the classroom. Of the levels below Task, and therefore entailing it, a Sequence of Tasks, a Series of Lessons/Classroom Sessions and a full Course can be seen also as simultaneous learning and social events but requiring increasing periods of time. The broadest levels of focus for the negotiation cycle are a specific language or subject curriculum – the latter in an immersion programme or in teacher education, for instance – and an all embracing educational curriculum at the institution or state level. Table 1.2 offers brief definitions and examples of each level in the pyramid. As the definitions and examples suggest, the levels of the pyramid cannot be absolutely distinct; each level overlaps to some extent with those above or below it.

Table 1.2 *Levels of the curriculum pyramid*

Level	Definition	Example
A task	Any single structured/planned classroom undertaking which directly *serves* (is directly related to) the teaching–learning of the foreign language. It has its own objective(s), content, working procedure, and implicit or explicit criteria for success in its accomplishment.	A listening comprehension task, an information gap task or a brainstorming task.
A sequence of tasks	A number of tasks which together form a coherent whole or are related parts within a single larger activity.	A 'unit' on a particular topic or language area, which contains a number of different tasks (for example, listening, reading, discussing, practising, etc.).
A series of lessons/ sessions	Several sequences of tasks which form a clear 'series' (related one to the other in some way), and which are undertaken over a number of lessons/sessions.	Work covered during 'this month', progressively covering a series of topics/language areas/ skills, etc. in an organised way so that there is continuity.
A course	One or more coherent series of lessons/sessions plus other work/sessions included within a specified period of time.	Several series of lessons/sessions, each covering a number of topics as the 'core' of the course, plus other work/sessions such as guest talks, visits, games, drama, which may be optional or additional to the envisaged 'core', but which together form the work done carried out during the course.
A specific language/ subject curriculum	A specified set of aims and content (language or other), working procedures, evaluation procedures and criteria which the course is intended to address.	Specifications concerning the aims of a course, what it covers (for example, topics, skill areas, grammar, vocabulary, cognitive development, learning strategies or other subject matter, etc.), how the teacher and students will work (task types, grouping, etc.) and evaluation (what will be evaluated, how and by whom).

A wider educational curriculum	The institutional and social context in which the course is placed: the relationship of the specific language/subject curriculum to the curriculum of other courses (weighting, links, common principles of approach, cross-curricular links, etc.).	Relationship between the teaching–learning of a foreign language and the teaching–learning of other subjects in a school curriculum or professional development programme and other college studies.

Note: Potentially, the levels 'task', 'sequence of tasks', 'series of lessons' and 'course' can overlap. A 'course', for example, may consist of only one 'series of lessons'. Similarly, a 'series of lessons' may have only one sequence of tasks or major activity (such as a simulation, run over several sessions).

A process syllabus in practice

To summarise so far, we have stated that a process syllabus provides a particular answer to the question: Which classroom decisions are open to negotiation? It offers a framework for decision-making for evolving the curriculum of a particular classroom group by proposing the range of decisions open to negotiation, the steps in a negotiation cycle and the levels in a curriculum to which the cycle can be applied. Figure 1.4 summarises the framework we have described.

As the chapters that follow reveal, when a process syllabus is applied in practice in a particular teaching situation, there is not one process syllabus or even a typical process syllabus, but a range of different teacher–student applications of the framework. At Step 1 in the cycle, teacher and students may select one or other of the four main areas of decision-making for negotiation and may focus on only one decision within any of the four. At Step 2, the action chosen through negotiation may be singular and completed relatively quickly within a single lesson or short period of time. At Step 3, joint evaluation may focus either on learning outcomes or on the appropriateness of earlier decisions and actions rather than both subsequent to a chosen action. Minimally, the three steps of the cycle might be applied to only one of the levels of the curriculum pyramid. On the other hand, a fully implemented process syllabus would involve negotiation on all four areas of decision-making at Step 1, appropriate chosen actions at Step 2, and evaluation of both outcomes and the process at Step 3. It would also entail applying this cycle to all levels of the curriculum pyramid. Whilst such a process syllabus could possibly emerge within a classroom group working together over a good period of time, such a maximum implementation

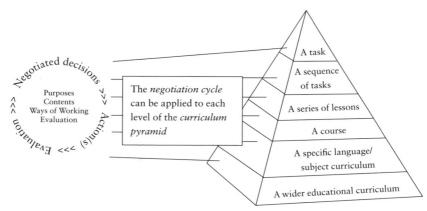

Figure 1.4   A process syllabus

may be unusual. In practice, it may be more a matter of negotiation *within* the full range of decisions to be made, different degrees of explicitness or distinctiveness in the steps taken in the cycle, and specific selections of the levels addressed in the curriculum pyramid. Although even the minimal implementation of a process syllabus entails the practices that we have identified, as a framework offered for negotiated decision-making, it is open to diverse practical interpretations by teachers and to the diverse contributions of the students who participate in such decision-making.

In this chapter, we have defined negotiation in relation to classroom decision-making, we have identified the theoretical and research roots that have motivated it, and we have concluded by describing a process syllabus as a framework for use in a language classroom. It is time we explored negotiation and process syllabuses in practice. Each of the teachers' accounts in Chapters 2 to 17 illustrates the practicalities of negotiated decision-making with different types and levels of students in different teaching situations. Each chapter also illustrates the application of a process syllabus with a negotiation cycle applied at different levels of the curriculum pyramid and with respect to different curriculum decisions. In the final chapter, Chapter 18 we relate the process syllabus framework we have here described more closely to each of the teachers' accounts in order to provide an overall picture of the different negotiation practices which were undertaken.

Part 1 Accounts of practice in primary and secondary schools

Overview

The six chapters in Part 1 describe the authors' experiences in negotiating with their students in primary/elementary and secondary or high school classrooms. In five of the schools, English is taught as one of the foreign languages within the overall school curriculum, whilst one school (described in Chapter 2) is an English Language Centre preparing recent migrant pupils for mainstream classes in an English-speaking environment. The young students participating in negotiation with their teachers on aspects of their language learning are aged between five and 18 years. Most of the chapters in Part 1 refer either directly or indirectly to teacher and student negotiation on the assessment of learning whilst Chapters 2 and 3 in particular focus upon assessment procedures involving negotiation. Chapters 4 to 7 describe how the aims and contents of a course were negotiated with secondary students learning English as a foreign language. However, Chapters 5 to 7 – describing classes of secondary students in Hungary, Israel and Spain – reveal how negotiation focused upon virtually all aspects of the course, with Chapter 7 in particular revealing how the actual curriculum of the classroom group was gradually evolved through negotiation.

Assessment of student progress is a critical moment in the teacher's influence upon the classroom language-learning process. Whatever form it takes, the teacher's judgement of student achievement informs subsequent decisions concerning immediate or future planning and practical intervention. The teacher's explicit expression of that judgement to students provides feedback and this is likely to channel the subsequent extent and focus of energy of students, and to shape how they act as learners. However, assessment is also a highly sensitive moment in the pattern of relationships between teachers and learners. Teachers are constantly making judgements about their students' language learning, often in informal and spontaneous ways, and students will respond to these in ways that reflect their personal investment in learning a particular language in a classroom. More formal assessment, in which grades may be given in class tests or through externally set examinations, is likely to attract higher emotional investment on the part of students, not least because their achievements in such things tend to be more public.

Of course, feedback is essential in language learning. However, the way in which it is carried out, regardless of what is being assessed and why, has the potential to inspire or demoralise students. Being assessed is often viewed by them as a threat to the self unless they enjoy a fairly robust self-image or good measures of confidence and determination. Assessment entails a judgement about one's worth as a learner which is difficult to separate from the mere reception of feedback from the teacher on a particular use of the new language or some more extensive classroom task.

The different reactions of students receiving feedback through assessment are most often shaped by four factors:

1. The extent to which they are aware of the criteria being used.
2. The relative emphasis given to what they have achieved as compared with what they have failed to achieve.
3. The coincidence between what the feedback focuses upon and what the students themselves have recognised as particularly difficult for them.
4. Whether or not they believe they can act on the basis of the feedback in a way that solves a recognised problem.

Given the affective significance for students of teacher judgements and given that the teacher will seek to maximise the benefit of feedback to student learning through assessment, these four factors provide a complex challenge to the teacher in both undertaking assessment and preparing students for some external form of assessment. Establishing and clarifying criteria, identifying achievements as well as those difficulties that are intuitively sensed or explicitly recognised by individual students, and finding alternative ways of acting upon problems all appear to be ideal points of focus for negotiation in the classroom.

All of the teachers contributing the chapters in Part 1 recognise this negotiative potential of the assessment process. Two papers in particular provide detailed accounts of how this process was undertaken through negotiation with young students. In chapter 2, Anne MacKay, Kaye Oates and Yvonne Haig make it clear that negotiation can be undertaken with children who are just beginning to learn a new language and are as young as five years old. Basing their own assessment procedure upon Helen Woodward's (1993) concept of 'negotiated evaluation', the writers describe how the children's language-learning achievements and what they should next focus on, are identified in the context of a three-way 'dialogue' between the teacher, the child and the child's parents. This procedure has been developed by the writers for recent migrant children of multilingual identities in ESL classrooms in Western Australia. In Chapter 3, Kari Smith, on the other hand, is working with secondary students in an EFL context in Israel. She describes a negotiated assessment procedure which involves the students in clarifying the criteria, choosing relative weighting of assessment for particular types of learning activities and undertaking self-assessment. Kari Smith presents this experience as enabling students to make realistic judgements about their own language learning and one which informs their broader approach to learning beyond the school.

Involving learners in project work as the framework in which language learning is undertaken has become well established in some European secondary schools. Project work requires students to focus for an extended period of time upon a particular overall topic or theme involving them in an activity or investigation which typically entails a sequence or range of different but contributory tasks. Examples might include: the creation of a video which is designed as a guide for tourists to the students' town or region; the undertaking of interviews outside the classroom with a view to writing a report on local people's familiarity with and attitudes towards the particular language which the students are learning; or, perhaps, a mini-research project on a topic or set of texts – such as advertisements – that particularly interest the whole class or a sub-group of students. In Chapter 4, Ramon Ribé describes how 16-year-old Spanish students in a mixed ability class of 40 undertook what he describes as a 'creative project'. He takes us through the project step by step, suggesting how negotiation informed each step to a different extent and with different effects. In his account, Ribé presents project work as a framework for the organisation of student contributions, and his experiment with the secondary students has enabled him to develop a blueprint for creative projects of other kinds.

Several contributors to this volume discovered for themselves, at a particular moment in their work, the value of negotiating in the classroom. This personal recognition of its appropriateness in informing one's own pedagogic decisions within a specific teaching situation appears to be a common experience. The discovery often occurs at moments of genuine uncertainty on the teacher's part. When the uncertainty is coupled with the confidence to involve one's own students in helping resolve it, negotiation reveals itself as a genuine resource for classroom decision-making. This is what happened to Marianne Nikolov over 20 years ago when beginning teaching EFL to Hungarian children aged 6 to 14 years. In Chapter 5, Nikolov gives an account of a long-term experiment in her own teaching and describes how her students make decisions about ways of participating, choosing content and tasks, assessing their progress, and expressing their views on the course they have been taught. A particularly revealing aspect of Nikolov's chapter is the relationship she traces between the different ages of children and their relative capacity and willingness to participate in these kinds of decisions.

The two final chapters in Part 1 overtly address a crucial question: Can negotiation with students occur in the context of a school system with a curriculum or syllabus that is laid down by external authorities and which requires students to take a public examination at the end of their studies? In Chapter 6, Pnina Linder describes shared decision-making in EFL classes with students in Israel from their first year of secondary schooling to the age of 18. She exemplifies negotiation between teachers and students from more complex matters, such as the establishment of learning needs and objectives through to the more mundane task of learning vocabulary. Linder illustrates how students' own learning agendas can become a significant contributory element towards their achievement within a prescribed curriculum.

In Chapter 7, Isabel Serrano-Sampedro argues that, working with her secondary students in Spain, 'negotiation seems to enable every student to achieve the aims of the official curriculum by engaging their personal objectives, knowledge and ability with the support of their classmates and the teacher.' Describing shared decision-making with a class of over 30 mixed ability 14-year-old students, she illustrates a stage-by-stage process beginning with finding out as much as she can about her students in terms of previous learning and approaches to classroom work, and helping them become familiar with the institutional require-ments which they will need to meet in relation to their language learning. As the work unfolds, students' decision-making which directly shapes the teaching–learning process gradually increases. After the initial familiarisation stage, subsequent stages include formulating objectives, choosing activities, deciding upon working procedures, choosing materials, and the crucial stage of evaluation of both learning outcomes and the appropriateness of their decisions at earlier stages. Serrano-Sampedro illustrates how young students may be involved in making decisions in relation to every aspect of the language curriculum.

Each of the authors helpfully describes the difficulties they encoun-tered when seeking to engage school students in negotiation whilst learning a new language. They also identify particular advantages to be gained from the joint effort this requires from both teacher and students. All of them suggest that negotiation, even about a single aspect of the teaching–learning process in the classroom, can itself serve as a means for development in the student's knowledge and use of the language.

2 Negotiated evaluation in a primary ESL context

Anne MacKay, Kaye Oates and Yvonne Haig

The working context

Graylands Intensive Language Centre (GILC) is part of a suburban primary school. Between 70 to 100 recently-arrived immigrant students with a non-English speaking background (NESB) attend the centre for four terms (equivalent to a year) of intensive language assistance. These students are aged between five and 12 years. Where necessary, they are transported to the Centre. There are constant enrolments and exits, though the latter are usually at the end of each term. Six classes – two each of junior students aged five to seven years, of middle students aged eight to 10 years and of senior students aged 11 to 12 are organised into Phase 1, for on arrival students, and Phase 2 for students who have acquired 'survival' English and are now ready to focus more on the language of the school curriculum. The centre aims to foster a supportive atmosphere where the students are provided with the time and opportunities to come to terms with learning in a new language and to adjust to a new culture. Negotiated evaluation was begun in mid-1991 and continues to the present. There are differences in how this approach to evaluation has evolved in the various levels and phases in the centre.

What does negotiation mean in this context?

1. It is the teacher negotiating with students about what they know and understand and what they do not yet know and understand.
2. It is the teacher sharing their expectations with students.
3. It is the teacher and the student negotiating learning goals and the means by which they will be achieved.
4. It is negotiating with parents about their understandings of their child's progress and about what progress they see as important.
5. It is encouraging parents and children to negotiate with teachers

what learning is to be valued within the GILC programme, both in terms of future learning and the outcomes to be achieved.

Focus of negotiation

Negotiated Evaluation at GILC evolved from work carried out by Helen Woodward (1993) and was undertaken as a possible solution to the dilemma of finding an effective means of evaluating student learning and the learning programme provided by the Centre.

Woodward defines negotiated evaluation as 'a system of evaluation which helps those with a vested interest in the child's progress to make accurate decisions about that child in order to better accommodate and stimulate his or her learning as well as to record and report the child's progress over time' (Woodward, 1993: 1). It contributes to how the teacher makes judgements of merit and worth, makes decisions about future planning, and informs the student's learning. Woodward believes that children have a right to be involved in the evaluation process and that they are capable of self-evaluation. The teacher therefore needs to negotiate with the student about what is known and what needs to be known.

Parents also share in this process. The method provides an opportunity for teachers and parents to negotiate their understandings of the student's progress and what future learning is to be undertaken. This notion is best represented in a simple diagram (Woodward, 1993: 18), shown in Figure 2.1.

Procedure for implementing negotiated evaluation

In the particular process we are describing, teachers met to discuss what learning would be evaluated. The language content was largely derived from the Western Australian Education Department's K-7 Language Syllabus and material from the Australian Language Levels (ALL) project. The ALL material is a curriculum framework which acknowledges the inter-relationship among aspects such as syllabus content, strategies for teaching and learning in the classroom, learning resources, strategies for evaluation of all aspects of the curriculum and student assessment practices expressed in terms of five integrated goals: communication, sociocultural, learning how-to-learn, language and cultural awareness and general knowledge. The Centre also utilised the organisational framework from the ALL for planning classroom programmes. Methodological issues such as the means of recording and reporting the

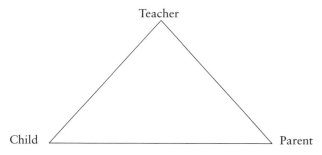

Figure 2.1   The negotiation process

evaluation were discussed by the participating teachers to ensure consistent understanding and practices supported the implementation process.

The processes designed varied between junior and senior grades and between Phase 1 and Phase 2 classes. The overall process was trialled gradually, evaluating only one child in each class at first, then negotiating with the child and only including the parents after the first two steps were well in place. Parents were contacted by letter informing them of what was happening and report folders were developed and translated for them (see Figure 2.5).

The process as designed for the Centre operates as follows:

1. Between three and five nominated students are observed over a period of a week engaging in a number of language activities which are part of the usual learning programme in the classroom.

2. During and after activities the teacher and student discuss and record the student's learning. This discussion is about what the student is able to do and is therefore always positive. Possible areas of future learning are also often discussed.

3. At the end of the period of observation, usually a week, the teacher and student write a report to inform the parents of what the student has achieved in that time. They may also indicate ways in which the parents can assist the student in meeting learning goals.

4. The parents may then respond in writing on the report, commenting on their child's learning or making recommendations about future learning. Parents may also request an interview to discuss their child's learning. Reports are returned to the school and become part of a cumulative record of the child's progress from the various participants' points of view.

5. This cycle is repeated with different students each week. Thus, in a class of 15 students each would receive at least six reports a year.

Classroom record sheets

Teachers note observations of students' learning on a record sheet. The headings on the record sheet are the same as those used in the teachers' planning documents. The four headings are (1) Language, (2) Communication, (3) Learning how to learn and (4) Sociocultural and general knowledge, and are based on the Australian Language Levels goals. Copies of the record sheets are either taped to students' desks or put on clipboards so that both teacher and child have access to them.

The negotiation takes place during or after learning activities. At this time the teacher discusses with each of the children issues such as how the child felt they had handled the activity or what they thought might be the next step in their learning.

The children also record their comments which may include an evaluation of what they have done and/or what they are working towards. These are initially very brief and superficial and in the case of some junior students are in the form of a 'happy face' or a 'puzzled face'. Gradually the comments become more in depth until by the end of the year students are able to make detailed and perceptive judgements.

Over the period of evaluation, which lasts for five consecutive days, approximately 7 to 10 entries are made by the teacher. At the end of the period students are asked to make written comments to questions covering areas such as what they have enjoyed, what they have found difficult, what new things they have learnt and things that they want to achieve in the next week.

The whole process becomes a predictable system for all the students who feel comfortable with it and who share in each other's success. Figure 2.2 illustrates one of the classroom record sheets created during a discussion between a student and teacher.

Reports

Reports are written immediately the period of evaluation ends and at a set time each week. The teacher's comments are very specific and focused on recent achievements. Positive comments are made and areas of learning that need attention are also expressed positively. Comments are made in the same areas as the classroom record and planning headings so that there is continuity for planning, evaluating and reporting (see Figure 2.3).

The student and teacher discuss the comments and the student then writes his (or her) own comments onto the report sheet. These may be anything that he wants to write or may be in response to the teacher's

---

DATE   T1 Wk 4   NAME

LANGUAGE
Some tense in writing e.g. were/went – others present. Uses 'next', 'then' appropriately. Uses 'an' with initial vowel sounds. Uses some past tense orally. Could use correct question formats in group game.

COMMUNICATION
20 questions. Clear questions, correct word order. In spinner game takes turns, adds to dialogue appropriately. Some clarity problems but understandable and will repeat.
Can use written news format to tell and expand.

LEARNING HOW TO LEARN
Writing – Completed 10 days of swimming diary. Good simple sentences. Punctuation, mostly present tense. Spelling good – some inventive e.g. 'chige' for 'change'.
Reading – Collect 14 sentences for recipe and sequence from master copy. Collected 10, struggled with sequence but happy to persevere with some guidance.
Writing – Procedure for recipe. Good sentences. Correctly sequenced. Good spelling. Can read back.
Semantic grid – fruit/adjectives. Completed quickly and correctly.

SOCIOCULTURAL AND GENERAL KNOWLEDGE

FOR ME

> Next time I well do wit I
> remmder my flo stop.
> It was ezy (the semantic grid)

Figure 2.2   A classroom record of a student aged eight years who has attended the Intensive Language Centre for eight months

questions. Figure 2.4 exemplifies the comments of a child who has attended GILC for eight months. The report then goes home to parents in a folder with a translated explanation on the front cover as illustrated in Figure 2.5.

Although written in English, the report is usually translated by

_____ is starting to use good sentences. He can understand tense and can use adjectives.

He has been telling news and can speak clearly using good sentences.

He has been reading the names of food and can read the story we have been writing at school.

In writing he has written a diary about an explorer and tries to use full stops when I ask him to.

This week he spoke very well at assembly.

Teacher Signature

(Student aged eight years who has attended the ILC for eight months)

Figure 2.3   Teacher's comments on the report for parents

I can write very good.

My full stops are all good.

My spelling are right.

Last week we went to assembly and I talked very well.

(Student aged eight years who has attended the ILC for eight months)

Figure 2.4   Child's comments on the report for parents

members of the ethnic community or the student or, in some cases, the parents ask the school to translate it for them. Parents are encouraged to comment on their child's progress on a section of the report (see Figure 2.6). More than half the parents do this, sometimes in their own language and sometimes in English. These comments become more in depth as the parents' trust and understanding develops and as their own English improves. Those who do not comment, sign the report. They are given the opportunity for interviews with the teacher, the child being included where appropriate. During the following week the report is returned to the school where it becomes part of the cumulative record of the student's learning.

Macedonian
Македонски

Родители,

Во Грејлендс се служиме со систем на постојано оценвање во кое што се вклучени учителот, детето и родителот.

Секоја недела ќе бидат одбрани нежолку деца, од страна на учителот, и нивниот напредок ќе биде внимателно набљудуван и забележуван.
Децата исто така ќе имаат прилика да го изложат своето мислење за тоа што го учат.

На крајот од очнувачкиот период (обично една недела) учителот ќе ви испрати коментар. Со тоа ќе ве информира за напредокот на вашето дете. На информацијониот лист постои дел каде што ќе можете да го напишете вашиот коментар. Ве молиме потпишетесе на писмото, дадете ги вашите коментари и вратете го писмото во училиштето.

Доколку ви е потебна помош за да разберете некој од коментарите ве молиме телефонирајте на тел. 384 0047 преведувач ви е на располагање.

Translation

Dear Parents,

At Graylands we are using a system of continuous evaluation which involves teacher, child and parents.

Each week a few children will be chosen by the teacher and their progress closely monitored and noted.

The children will also have an opportunity to contribute their own ideas on what they are learning

At the end of the evaluation period (usually a week) the teacher will send home some comments for you. This will give you information on your child's progress.

There is a section on the information sheet where you can write your own comments. Please sign the sheet and add any of your own comments and return the sheet to the school.

If you would like help to understand some of the comments please phone on 384 0047 and an interpreter will be arranged.

Figure 2.5   Content of the report cover

In order to foster informed communication with parents, every term each class has an 'open morning' where parents spend the time observing their child engaged in the usual learning activities of the classroom. Teachers are available over morning tea to discuss what parents have observed and to answer questions. These are very well attended with all parents attending at least one and frequently all of

We appreciate your commitment to education.

Thank you very much for your comment. We understand the point you touched upon. Sometimes he is reluctant to say his opinion but I don't think it is a good idea to push him hard because of his character. He is really interested in English. He always tries to remember the spelling and read English books aloud. It's marvellous, isn't it? Thanks again.

Figure 2.6   Parents' comments on the report

them. Parent interviews are also held twice a year. Where needed, interpreters are made available for communication with parents.

Outcomes of negotiated evaluation as implemented in the Centre

Over a period of years there has been ongoing dialogue around the many issues associated with the implementation of negotiated evaluation as they have arisen. This dialogue has taken place not only with the teachers involved in the implementation but also with parents, students, administrators and main-stream teachers. Valuable contributions to the dialogue have been made in professional forums outside the centre and by visitors to the centre who have been especially interested in the implementation of negotiated evaluation. In order to consider all of the issues raised by this process, a full-day workshop was organised. Teachers critically examined and made professional judgements on the benefits to the students' learning, the evaluation of learning and relationships between the participants.

The benefits to students' learning

The process of negotiation involves the students in their own learning and allows them to take responsibility for it. Students are given the opportunity on a regular basis to comment on what they know, don't know and would like to know, as well as how they feel about this. This enables the student to set and achieve goals and also makes them aware of the teacher's expectation for them as an individual. All students receive equal time and input, including those who are not as readily noticed in a classroom context.

Students take responsibility for setting their own goals, and these are sometimes more realistic than those of the teacher. Students are highly motivated to achieve these goals. This, plus the added responsibility assumed by the student, improves learning outcomes. They therefore approach learning tasks knowing what to expect and what is expected of them. While the teacher's expectations are conveyed to the students they are nevertheless negotiated and are therefore better understood by the students. All students in the class share in the celebration of learning as these goals are achieved, and this also encourages improved learning outcomes.

The evaluation of learning

The regular negotiation with the child allows a teacher to use both the student's and the teacher's understanding to make valid judgements of merit and worth. 'Merit' relates to the specific outcome achieved by the child while 'worth' refers to the value of that outcome in furthering the developmental process. Previously this had been the role of the teacher only. Teachers are able to design learning activities which will develop specific learning behaviours and skills in such a way as to make these behaviours readily discernible. They feel that they more closely observe how a child handles a variety of tasks and are therefore in a better position to make judgements.

Initially, because they have little English, students go through the motions of self-evaluation. However, gradually their skills develop so that with time they can make pertinent and relevant comments about their learning and needs. Whereas evaluation was once the sole responsibility of the teacher, the student now sees that he or she also has a role in determining how he or she performs. Should negotiated evaluation continue throughout students' primary-school life, they would be in a far better position to make decisions about course/subject choices in their continuing education.

Data on students' use of language and broader learning is collected from a variety of contexts which reflect both the teachers' and students' perspectives. Only the positive is recorded but, by omission, teachers are aware of gaps in the child's learning and in their own planning. Data collection is more systematically carried out and more accurately reflects the circumstances; it can also be used immediately to communicate with student and parents. It doesn't take any less time than other recording/reporting procedures. The advantage is that it is a positive use of time because collecting and analysing data in this way allows teachers to make informed decisions about future planning and to guide student learning. The data is used immediately, not stored away for writing a report several months later. The analysis of the data in the negotiation with the student allows the teacher to look beyond the products to the reasons, concerns and/or expectations which impact on the student's learning outcomes. By taking these into account, teachers are able to make a more accurate assessment. Overall, the process satisfies the need for a relevant, valid evaluation system to inform the student, parents and teacher of learning outcomes.

This process has a very strong influence on future planning. Teachers report that both long-term and short-term planning are altered because of their more focused observation and subsequent negotiation with the child. These influence the choice of future types of activities and content because teachers are made more aware of where the 'gaps' are, both in the student's learning and in the teacher's provision of appropriate learning activities. Students' input into this – when they express opinions as to what they think they want or need to do next – means that they are negotiating the curriculum in an ongoing and genuine manner.

Relationships between the participants

Students appreciate the opportunity for the shared time with the teacher who becomes, in effect, a 'partner' in their learning rather than someone who solely directs it. They feel that they are being specifically and individually noticed, and that their achievements, needs or concerns are recognised. Sharing the responsibility promotes in the students the notion that the purpose for evaluation is to inform the learning process, not to discriminate between those who can and those who cannot.

Parents are involved in regular communication with both their child and the teacher about the immediate learning of their child. Because they are encouraged to be a part of this negotiation, they feel their opinion is valued and that they are partners in the process rather than recipients of the products. These students come from different education systems where different products and learning behaviours may have been valued. The evaluation and reporting of these has also been different, and negotiated evaluation gives parents the opportunity to better understand what behaviours and products are valued in the ESL classroom serving their community. The positive nature of this evaluation, and the students' role in it, encourages them to share their learning achievements with their parents.

The process of negotiated evaluation in the intensive language centre gives rise to increased professional dialogue. Teachers benefit enormously from the opportunity to discuss in depth the implications, the successes and the difficulties associated with the issues of evaluation and its impact on planning and reporting. They receive support and encouragement from each other and feel they are working together to develop a deeper understanding of their role and those of the student and parents in evaluation as an intrinsic part of the learning process.

The conditions which have led to successful implementation

- Staff were provided with time to discuss and resolve issues arising.
- Colleagues were very supportive and encouraged one another when difficulties arose.
- Discussion was open and ongoing.
- The co-ordinator of the centre kept the project moving with lots of encouragement and prodding when necessary.
- There was a commitment to this approach. Negotiated evaluation was not implemented in addition to earlier established methods. It replaced them and was therefore not seen as an extra 'burden'.

In general, therefore, negotiated evaluation has provided all participants in the learning process with positive outcomes. The students have greater involvement in the decision-making surrounding their learning and greater motivation to learn. They establish and take an active valued part in identifying and achieving learning goals and are thus encouraged to take more responsibility for their learning. They are aware of the expectations of others for their learning, and their learning is celebrated. Parents are involved in their child's school education and have their input valued. They receive specific information regarding their child's learning through 'open mornings', interviews and the reporting process. The teacher has an evaluation process which informs planning and teaching and an opportunity to share the responsibility for the student's learning with other participants. The focused nature of the individual assessments of learning encourages the teacher to report on student learning in *specific* terms. The Centre is able to satisfy a need for an effective evaluation strategy. The negotiated evaluation framework provides the means to engage in professional dialogue around a shared concern and encourages collegiate support for innovation. The success of the approach is endorsed by the degree of commitment it has engendered in all involved.

3 Negotiating assessment with secondary-school pupils

Kari Smith

This chapter describes how secondary-school pupils are involved in negotiating the components of their term and yearly grades. The setting is a regional kibbutz school in Israel with about 300 pupils, and the subject of the course described here is English as a foreign language (EFL). English is an important part of the Israeli school curriculum; it is studied for nine years, beginning at the age of nine, for an average of four hours per week. The pupils take an external examination administered by the Ministry of Education at the end of their twelfth and final year, and the mark on the matriculation certificate is a combination of the teacher's mark (50 per cent) and the score on the examination itself (50 per cent).

The negotiation described in this paper takes place in tenth and eleventh grade (age 16 to 17) and partly in twelfth grade. However, in the last year the criteria of the external examination have a strong backwash effect on the teaching–learning process which, to a certain extent, dictates the components of the teacher's mark. However, the learners are still involved in the decision-making process regarding what course components should be included in the assessment and their respective weights in terms of percentage. The learners and the teacher use a negotiated assessment scale for assessment, and the mark for a report card is finalised in an individual tutorial. Figure 3.1 illustrates an assessment by both student and teacher.

The report card is given to the pupils twice a year and reports in numerical form the pupils' achievements in all subjects for that specific term. The report card is meant to be a summary of the pupils' learning outcomes in school and it has to be taken home and signed by the parents. The negotiated assessment is the basis for the marks given on the report cards in tenth and eleventh grades, and in twelfth grade it represents 50 per cent of the final mark the learners receive in English on their matriculation certificate.

ASSESSMENT SCALE

Component	Weight (%)	Pupil's mark	Teacher's mark
Doing homework	10	8	6
Level of homework	20	16	17
Participation in class	10	9	7
Individual progress	10	5	8
Projects	30	26	27
Test results	20	15	15
Total	100	79	80

This assessment scale reflects the importance of ongoing work at home and in class. Tests are part of the assessment but not the only source of information about the learner's achievements and efforts. In this specific case the teacher's mark of 80 was the one used for the report card.

Figure 3.1   An example assessment

Involving learners in assessment

The definition of assessment used as the basis for the negotiation is Nunan's definition: 'Assessment is referring to the set of processes through which we make statements about a learner's level of skills and knowledge' (Nunan, 1990: 12). Nunan talks here about a set of processes for learning which includes activities done in class and at home. Homework, class projects, class participation, portfolio, tests, etc. are examples of activities which can be represented in learner assessment. In most learning situations the teacher or school authorities decide on the components of the reported mark. Test results are generally one of the major elements in learner assessment (Smith, 1993). However, tests cannot replace other learning activities taking place in the classroom. My approach to teaching is based on an open dialogue with the learners regarding the context of learning the language (topics), how to approach the various tasks and what activities to do or homework to assign. The learners are partly responsible for the type of work done in the course, and I feel uncomfortable holding on to the total responsibility for their assessment, which was mainly based on tests. As I understand Nunan's definition, a more valid representation of learning procedures needed to become part of assessment which could be a negotiated agreement between the teacher and the pupils.

I believe the learners themselves can be involved in deciding what procedures are to be included in the assessment, and the relative importance or weight of each aspect of learning. This belief is based on the approach to education which is reflected in Knowles: 'Active learners taking initiative learn more things and learn better than do people who sit at the feet of their teachers' (Knowles, 1975:14). The assessment process can be seen to be part of the learner's responsibility, and they need to be active participants in this decision-making process under the teacher's guidance (Ediger, 1993).

I also believe that the learners' involvement in the assessment procedure cannot be limited to deciding what aspects of learning are to be included in the assessment, but also to what extent they, the learners, recognise and meet the criteria of the specific aspects. Numerous studies have found that there is a fairly consistent agreement between self-assessment and external criteria in foreign-language learning (Bachman and Palmer, 1989; Blanche and Merino, 1989; Oscarsson, 1989; Smith, 1991). In addition, the many educational values of self-assessment are to be emphasised in the approach taken in this paper. Even studies reporting on poor evidence for using self-assessment as an assessment tool see the educational advantages of this type of assessment as outweighing its disadvantages (Janssen-van Dieten, 1989; Heilenman, 1990; Ready-Morfitt, personal communication, 1990). Self-assessment can be seen as an integral part of learning how to learn.

> Students need to know what their abilities are, how much progress they are making, and what they can (or cannot yet) do with the skills they have acquired. Without such knowledge it would not be easy for them to learn efficiently.
>
> Blanche and Merino, 1989: 313

Learners should be critically reflective of their own learning situation in order to be 'in charge' of their cognitive processes. This includes awareness, monitoring and self-regulation, and such metacognitive skills are, according to Rowe, 'a prerequisite for academic and real life success' (Rowe, 1988: 229).

Another important aspect of self-assessment is that it improves teacher–learner relationships (Dickinson, 1987). By understanding each other's problems, the empathy between the two parties grows and this again is conducive to learner autonomy based on independent thinking, the ultimate goal of education. These days, we are talking about ongoing learning or learning for life, both in terms of professional development and also in terms of being knowledgeable and active members of a democratic society. Learner autonomy developed in school is the key to ongoing, independent learning and thinking processes carried out without having the teacher around. Accurate self-assessment expresses learner autonomy and Boerkaerts claims that '[a]ssessment and self-assessment are unavoidable and highly informative components of daily functioning' (Boerkaerts, 1991: 2). However, keeping all this in mind, the teacher is still the authoritative voice in the classroom which means that before being implemented the learners' proposals for assessment have to be accepted and approved by the teacher. After the learners have reached an agreement among themselves, there has to be agreement between them and the teacher.

The negotiation process

Although the process presented here is undertaken with 16 to 18-year-old learners, similar processes have also been carried out in primary school and in higher education. The learners negotiate with each other in order to decide on the components which will serve as the basis for their assessment. The negotiation starts about two months into the course and is an ongoing process; the final decisions are made twice a year in secondary school before the pupils are to be given a mark for each term's work. The teacher becomes involved with the negotiation only towards the end of the process if the learners' assessment scale seems unacceptable or if their self-assessment differs significantly from the teacher's assessment of the same pupil.

The negotiation process has two parts:

1. reaching an agreed assessment scale with the chosen components of the learner's progress; and
2. learners' and teacher's actual assessments using the scale.

In order to clarify the process it is presented step by step as follows. The first step is to remind the learners of the objectives of the course with a course outline including the requirements or objectives. The learners have to know what they can expect from the course and what is expected of them.

The second step takes place when about a third of the course has been concluded. The teacher involves the learners in a discussion of *what* has been taught so far in the course and *how* it has been taught. The preparation for assessment can be done at home by the individual learner who is asked to go through her/his notebook and make a list of course content for the following class. This information is then elicited from the learners in a brainstorm activity in class. The teacher organises the information on the board or on a transparency. This is a useful activity to make the learners review the material and fill in gaps in their notebooks.

The third step is carried out in groups of 4–5 pupils with the task of deciding what learning activities should provide the focus for learner assessment. The lists which the learners produce are usually fairly conventional; they often include homework, participation, individual progress, tests, etc.

The fourth step consists of reporting and voting. The groups report their lists of components, and all the suggestions are written on the board. The pupils vote for the one they prefer to be assessed on, and the suggestion with most votes becomes the only scale of assessment which is applied by the learners and the teacher in that class.

The fifth step is again carried out in groups, and this time the task is to allot a weight to each component, totalling 100 per cent. Once again, the groups report and vote for the proposal they feel best reflects the course work. At the end of the fifth step the class (including the teacher) have a list of components and their different weighting for the final assessment. It is necessary to state (and the pupils expect this) that the teacher has a veto, and she/he can use it if necessary. In other words, the teacher has to approve of the decisions made by the class. From experience I can say that in most cases there is usually strong agreement between the pupils' scale and what the teacher had in mind.

The sixth step is optional, but nevertheless recommended. The learners are asked to assess themselves according to the newly created scale and thereby analyse their own learning based on the main components of the course. The teacher assesses the learners independently. The average mark of the two assessments is then calculated and provides the final mark. If the discrepancy between the teacher's and an individual learner's assessment is 10 per cent or more, the teacher discusses the mark with the learner in a one-to-one tutorial. The purpose of the tutorial is for the teacher and the learner to listen and learn from each other regarding information that might have been unknown. The teacher's view is not necessarily the 'correct' or accepted view. If the process is well planned, however, this does not often happen. In any case, the self-assessment/teacher-assessment serves as an excellent springboard for an individual tutorial with the learners, providing an opportunity to discuss various aspects of the course and to plan future work according to the needs of the individual learner.

Advantages of the process

One advantage of the negotiating approach is that assessment is based on what really takes place in the course and is therefore likely to be valid. The learners are assessed on course components they feel are important and best reflect their effort, knowledge and achievement in that course. The weight of each component is given according to importance as the learners see it and not only according to the teacher's opinion. A secondary-school pupil, Ofra, expressed how she felt about the process:

> I feel that finally we, the pupils, have got a say regarding our own assessment. Usually teachers make all the decisions, and they give us a grade only based on the tests they give us. Nothing else I do in class or at home seems to matter.

The second advantage is that the assessment criteria are clear to the learners and to the teacher. In order to avoid the frustration caused by the receipt solely of a specific grade (number, letter, short statement, etc.) which serves as the information carrier (Dressel, 1983), the teacher, the learner and other parties need to know exactly what information underlies the grade. Tom, a tenth grade pupil, commented on this point when he said:

> I know that I didn't do all the work I had to do in English, and that is the reason why I got an 80, even though I get 90 on most tests. I guess I have to do more work next time if I want a better grade.

The learners are active partners in deciding how to be assessed. This leads to a third advantage: increased empathy between learner and teacher. Assessment is one of the most difficult tasks the teacher has to carry out, and it is often the cause of anger and negative feelings from the students' side. When the learners participate in the assessment process, they get a better understanding of the difficulties and the teacher learns about how the learners see themselves as learners. They can share the responsibility and decision-making with the learners. Roy's comment illustrates this:

> I never knew that giving a grade was so difficult. I thought you just looked in your 'black book' and wrote down a number.

A further advantage is that learners have to face their own reality as learners. They become aware of their weaknesses and strengths. Ella stressed this when she said:

> I know that I was okay in English, but I never really knew where I had to put in more work in order to improve my grade. After knowing how the grade is formed and being asked to give myself a grade, I realised that much more work had to be put into my compositions. I have to structure them more and see too that my spelling improves.

A major advantage of negotiated assessment is that it provides a good opportunity for formative evaluation of the course and for formative assessment of the learners. When the class discusses the course components, they provide the teacher with evidence on the relationship between what has been learned and what she had meant to teach. If this is done during the course there is still time to make changes and reform the course according to the stated objectives. Sometimes there are reasons to change the objectives if they are not in accordance with the learners' needs. The learners are given informative feedback on the learning process and their achievements, not only in order to make judgements about them as learners, but also in order to help them improve their learning. This can be done only if it occurs during the learning process and not at the end, and if they receive sufficient information through communication with the teacher.

Difficulties with negotiated assessment

During my several years' experience using the negotiation process in teaching English to secondary students, the following main problems have risen. First, it is time consuming. The process takes about three to four hours if done properly, and this might be seen as a problem if there is a lot of material to cover in the course. However, much of the time is spent by learners usefully reviewing the material in groups. I try to stress the importance of negotiating using the English language, and this serves as a good oral practice of the language. However, there are cases where the learners get carried away and discuss in their first language. The teacher has to decide how important the language-learning aspect of the process is and act accordingly.

A second difficulty is that not all learners are willing to take on responsibility; neither are all teachers strong enough to share it. Learners and teachers have been given very specific roles in the classroom, and it is difficult for them to change. There are many learners who do not want to do the 'teacher's job', and they prefer being told how they are doing instead of looking at themselves from the assessor's point of view. Teachers often feel the need to use the authority they have been given, and if they give up on it, they feel they are in danger of losing control. However, I explain the process to my pupils at the beginning of the course, and at other times in the course they are given responsibility for assessing their own homework, tests, etc. It is also necessary to inform other parties involved such as parents, etc.

Teachers who already have a fixed picture of their role as teachers have difficulty accepting the idea that the learners are permitted to negotiate their own assessment scale and grade. I therefore try, in my teacher training, to let the participants experience it as learners, hoping they will try it out with their own classes afterwards.

A third issue is that self-assessment is not accepted in all cultures. In cultures where the official authority is clearly expressed and exercised, it is difficult to persuade teachers, principals and, in general terms, the education system that assessment can be done in other ways. Relevant and up-to-date information supplied with evidence of success is needed to convince policy-makers that negotiated assessment is a worthwhile enterprise.

A final difficulty is that marks derived in this process cannot be used for comparative purposes as each group might choose different components and scales. Self-assessment is therefore appropriate for formative purposes during the year, but possibly only useful as a contributory part of external summative assessment and certification.

Conclusion

In this chapter I have described how negotiation of assessment procedures and criteria carries a potential for change throughout the curriculum and in the teaching–learning process. The points made are that assessment has to include a variety of course components, and that the learners, through negotiation, decide on which components should be included in their assessment and the relative importance of these. The learners assess themselves based on the same components and, through negotiations with the teacher, the final mark is agreed upon. Both teachers and learners benefit from the changes by sharing the responsibility of assessment, increasing the understanding of each other's problems. The learners' views are expressed and taken seriously, and they learn to assess themselves according to negotiated, clear criteria. They learn how an assessment procedure is carried out, becoming better prepared to assess themselves in a life-long learning process.

The negotiation process has successfully been tried out in a kibbutz regional high school and at the kibbutz university, both of which maintain a fairly liberal approach to education in general. It is necessary to try negotiating work in more conservative educational settings and learn more about the problems found there. Negotiation work carries a positive change which can be pursued by educational theorists and practitioners.

4 Introducing negotiation processes: an experiment with creative project work

Ramon Ribé

Two sides of a mirror

Any project work, if properly implemented, requires from the student not only a considerable workload, but also a high degree of personal commitment. In addition, project work very often involves the following:

- the unlearning of deeply ingrained preconceptions as to how a foreign language is learned;
- the application of a new set of instruments (such as self-access materials) and techniques (such as autonomous learning and co-operative learning);
- an active assumption of responsibility for both process and product; and
- the acceptance and constant use of negotiation as the axis of all procedural activity.

If we are implementing *creative* project work as opposed to *research-based* project work (for details of the distinction, see Ribé, 1994), we have to add a few extra factors. Among them, the risk involved in the contribution of personal ideas and constructs and of their disclosure in front of an audience, as well as the strain derived from a much higher measure of personal investment in the generation of a new product. If a particular group of students are undertaking project work for the first time, the high degree of language learning and of achievement motivation that is usually the outcome of this long creative process are as yet unexperienced after-effects for these learners. They need to acquire a certain measure of trust in their own capabilities for autonomous work, and of faith in the teacher and in the process before committing themselves fully to this style of work.

A similar measure of personal involvement, risk, and faith in his or her students and in the eventual results is required from the teacher, who negotiates each step and works hand in hand with the students. If unexperienced in these affairs, he or she needs to progress through an educational process that mirrors that of the students. Therefore, certain acclimatisation and adjustment processes, which may start with the establishment of a conducive atmosphere in the classroom and end up with a full initial experience of creativity within a sheltering structure, may be necessary.

At the time the initiation project described in this chapter was implemented, creative project work and other varieties of creative frameworks were being experimented with by more progressive teachers and were shared in teachers' meetings and training seminars, where the main concern was to find a way which allowed both teachers and students to slowly evolve towards this style of negotiated work without traumatic experiences in the process.

This particular experiment confirmed that certain creative frameworks may provide the kind of sheltered environment that is necessary for this type of educational process to take place. In the course of the few weeks of creative co-operation that it takes to complete the activity, both the teacher's and the students' work style and beliefs are gradually modified, and their acceptance of a new style of work and of risk-taking and personal involvement grows steadily.

This chapter describes some of the negotiation processes in a self-contained unit of work implemented in a nine-week period in a secondary-high state school in Barcelona. Students were 16-year-old boys and girls in a mixed-ability class of 40. Their level of English ranged from (post-)elementary to pre-intermediate.

Although told in the third person, this is the account of a personal experience later replicated by myself and by other teachers. Designed as a tool for developing individual creativity and autonomy in a group which had never worked within this kind of environment, 'The land of the green people' was an original story which opened spaces for creative work, for security in taking decisions and for building up the students' own image as successful learners of the foreign language. (For a fuller account and analysis of this experience from the point of view of task structure, see Ribé, 1994.)

Used as a kernel for a creative framework, this negotiation process offered multiple functions:

- It supplied the necessary initial language input.
- It was in itself a starting point for negotiation processes that would eventually lead to a full-blown project.
- A virtual scheme for group and class work was hidden in the initial input so that negotiated choices could, to a certain extent, be foreseen by the teacher.

64

- It provided a permanent and immediate frame of reference to fall back on whenever necessary.
- It provided in-built clues for follow-up work once the project had been completed.
- It created a kind of fairy-tale atmosphere that was captivating for learners living in a diametrically opposite physical environment (dry climate, industrial society, etc.), and that eventually allowed students' creativity to take over from the teacher.
- It offered constant opportunities for the processing of input and output, for classroom interaction in the foreign language, for planning and memorisation strategies, and for assessing and evaluating both process and product.

Implementation of the project in the classroom was recorded by the teacher and by observer trainees taking part in a pre-service course. Both the process and the ensuing product were later qualitatively and quantitatively analysed. In the following paragraphs, diary quotes are marked 'O' for observer's diary and 'S' for student's diary.

In the brief description which follows, negotiation is taken as a generic label comprising a selection of process and product-affecting acts in the domain of content, procedure and language, performed either individually or collectively by teacher, students, small group or class and within a completely shared planning and execution process.

A brief summary of the story:
The story, as told by granddad Fergus to Annie and Andrew, is about an ancient happy valley inhabited by small people. These little beings communicated with plants and animals. Colours and shapes of all existing things were different from our world's. Their whole lifestyle was different, and a few hints about this are given (for example, they did not work, they spoke to the trees, the animals, etc.). They had a mysterious enemy who lived on a mountain. Two children disappeared one day while climbing it. The enemy descended to the valley. The rest of the clan disappeared too. New people came. They looted fauna and flora in order to survive. Big animals fled to other countries. Plants and little animals changed colours to disguise themselves and save their lives. There are clues (for example, eye colour, sadness) that point to a mysterious relationship between Annie, Andrew and Fergus and these strange people.

Description of the task sequence in a project framework

Pre-negotiation

The teacher suggests a game. Each student describes himself or herself using three adjectives. Non-visible personality traits are asked for (for example, 'I am very shy, imaginative and love music', 'I am stubborn, organised and a good swimmer'). The teacher describes himself or herself first. The students love this kind of personal disclosure and gradually overcome their initial shyness.

> The students are eager to participate. They love this kind of attention and many want to say more than three adjectives.
>
> (O: from Maite's observation diary)

> Some students cannot stop talking about themselves. They like being the protagonist ...   (O: from Maria's observation diary)

The teacher echoes each description, offers positive comments, and reflects on how different each personality sounds and on the uniqueness of each of us. He says that similar differences probably exist in our learning styles and preferences. Then he proposes embarking on an experiment ('a collective adventure') in which each student is able to choose things he or she wants to do and how to do them. He stresses the seriousness of this venture and that the students are able to negotiate changes in the experiment and analyse it later.

As a creative framework is a trip into uncharted waters, some recording elements are agreed 'in order to keep the adventure well organised' (in fact, to generate in the students an awareness of the underlying structure – but this is something the teacher keeps to himself). Among other things, daily individual diary writing, and periodic group and class log books, plus individual task evaluation are included as part of an initial contract which goes into the students' notebooks.

Getting the class interested

This is an introductory framework, so the students are not faced with formal negotiation of a topic yet. They are to be conducted through an experience of creativity and autonomous work step by step. The teacher's agenda in these preliminary tasks is to prepare the ground for what is to come: a certain kind of fairy tale. By promoting a special receptive mood, the teacher is alluring them to walk voluntarily into an imaginary world.

> The learners are still excited but the teacher never gets angry.

Instead he tries to relax them by making them breathe deeply and talking to them in a soft voice.

(O: from Núria's observation diary)

This pre-warming activity around story-telling has four phases:

1. A schemata (such as stories they have read, stories they have liked) is activated.
2. The resulting lists are then webbed on the blackboard with lines drawn to link stories of the same type (adventure, sci-fi, magic).
3. Individual resonance processes (where they have heard/read them) are triggered and then listened to.
4. Two of the most shared stories are reconstructed and different versions discovered.

The teacher proposes telling them a magic story and lists some of the possible objectives.

Little by little he is attracting their attention as he is explaining the new activity they are going to embark upon. Now the atmosphere is more peaceful.

(O: from Núria's observation diary)

Briefly, comprehension of objectives is negotiated by means of a matching exercise. The first column contains formulation of objectives ('Learn to describe people'), the second one sentences which reflect their meaning in the simplest language of the students ('She had beautiful blue eyes').

A kernel for negotiation: telling the story

It is important that the spell of the story lasts until the point where the real project negotiation begins, and that the students retain as much of the content as possible. The teacher suggests ways for better listening and memorising ('When the music starts, close your eyes and concentrate on the story. All the details are important. When it finishes, the volume of the music will come up again. Then you can open your eyes.').

Music sounds, then dims. The teacher tells the story slowly, rhythmically, in a soft voice, stressing repetitive chant-like patterns. Before beginning to tell the story, he plays an old Scottish ballad on the tape. The teacher starts telling the tale (you cannot hear a fly in the class!).

Co-operative reconstruction of the story

The events of the story are reconstructed through a process of collective brainstorming. A tree is drawn on the blackboard by two students (and the teacher) who takes down what their colleagues say. The trunk represents the sequence of episodes. Branches and leaves are added which contain all the remembered details. The teacher prompts when the retelling gets stuck. Soon it is realised that some sections and details are incomplete or missing in the original. While identifying the blanks and representing them on the blackboard by means of empty bubbles on the trunk, branches or leaves, the underlying structure of the story is revealed and a framework for possible class and group work discovered.

The teacher reinforces the students' curiosity through the process by acting elusively and not providing answers to questions on missing elements. He also frustrates initial students' attempts to fill in the gaps. He maintains an agile pace, throwing questions around when no suggestions of missing aspects are offered. In this way the excitement of discovery is kept up all the time.

A dual awareness emerges: first, the possibility of completing the story and, second, an idea of what areas to work on. ('We will first complete the story and then each group will decide what to do with it.') Discussion of what kind of final product we will fabricate once we are ready to put together all the missing pieces is at this point unrealistic and is postponed by collective agreement, though hints appear here and there, and some students anticipate possible formats. They begin to see the chain of events as a contingent path towards a final product.

> Now I understand what we are going to do. We are going to invent a magic story. (S: from Jordi's diary)

Group work on negotiated aspects

The tree on the blackboard shows 12 areas of possible topic work. Seven are selected, allowing for seven groups of four members each. The logistics of each task is collectively discussed and suggestions are recorded. Three areas of work are considered specially large and, as Figure 4.1 shows, they are further subdivided and covered by two groups each, making a total of 10 groups of four.

The 10 identified tasks are listed on the blackboard. Students mentally choose at least two different tasks and write in their notebooks one reason for each choice or one particular good idea for each job:

> I am very interested in biology and animals. I know many. I want to learn how to say their names in English.
>
> (A student volunteer for Group 8)

The teacher calls out the title of one task and students raise their hands. If there are more than four volunteers, they read their reasons for that

	Group 1	
	Description of the green men	

Group 2	Group 3	Group 4
Description of the country and map production	Their way of life (description)	Their way of life (description)

Group 5	Group 6	Group 7
What happened on the way to the Big Mountain (narration)	What happened on the way to the Big Mountain (narration)	The enemy (description and narration)

	Group 8	
	Colours and shapes of animals and things in Greenland (lists and description)	

Group 9		Group 10
Annie, Andrew and Fergus (description and narration)		Annie, Andrew and Fergus (description and narration)

Figure 4.1   Tasks for group work

particular choice and, having listened to them, the rest of the students select the four members of each team.

Before starting work, rules are collectively discussed. For example, all groups share the same general agenda, as summarised in Figure 4.2. Different procedural cards, one for each job, have been prepared by the teacher. They contain:

1. A blank grid to be filled in by students with job description, work distribution within the group and the steps to follow individually and by the whole team.
2. Pointers to self-access language cards for consultation and practice, relevant to the specific task of the group (for example, the country and map group (Group 2), need the card with place indicators, prepositions and adverbials; narration tasks involve the use of time sequencers, and so it is suggested that groups 5–7, 9 and 10 go

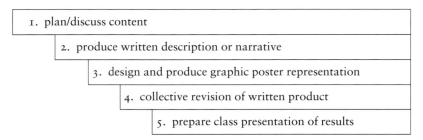

1. plan/discuss content

2. produce written description or narrative

3. design and produce graphic poster representation

4. collective revision of written product

5. prepare class presentation of results

Figure 4.2   General agenda for group work

through the card that contains them). These cards are distributed on request. In this way teacher keeps remote control on each group; if the cards are not solicited, the the teacher checks on the group.

All individual members sign up a copy of the procedural card, thus being responsible for a series of actions agreed within the group. The teacher anticipates logistical needs and wants at the same time to boost language processing:

> If you need to consult the story, the text is on my table. Do not take it. Send a member of the group. S/he finds the information you want and reports it to the group.

The teacher also explains the importance of memorising, scanning and reporting:

> You will need information from other groups. The map group needs information from the group who study colours. The two groups which work on the adventure of the Big Mountain need information about the enemy ... When this happens, send a member of the group to ask for this information. If you have contradictory information or ideas, negotiate a solution.

The groups then meet and work. A list with all the individual and group jobs, as on the procedural cards, is displayed on the wall for inter-group reference. Then over a period of several classes they brainstorm, make decisions, divide up work and produce their results together following the steps described in the procedural card.

> They can use their imagination and relate the story to other things, thus developing other capacities through the language.
> (O: from Glória's observation diary)

> I think that their attitude towards the group was very positive ... Although in most of the groups there was always a leader, I

do not consider it to be negative if this attitude is not too exaggerated and allows other members to bring in their own opinions and contributions. (O: from Roger's observation diary)

Inter-group negotiation also takes place, as suggested by the teacher, and messengers walk back and forth carrying information. Very often they consult the small self-access corner containing grammars and dictionaries which the teacher has set in a corner of the room. Occasionally two groups meet to discuss conflicting solutions to the same problems.

The teacher keeps remote control on work progress and on individual or group difficulties. He walks around, listens, prompts, checks on rhythm, length of product (two to three pages on average). At two points he detects common language problems or requests (for example, sentences have to be shorter and joined by co-ordinators or punctuation marks; correct uses of tenses of the past in cases when students have problems deciding between the use of past continuous and past simple, which is often a major issue). He interrupts group work and asks whether the students need examples relating to these points. Then he explains them. On two more occasions he provides additional language hand-outs for specific needs (for example, information and practice on *used to/would* constructions for Groups 3, 4 and 7; additional vocabulary related to the body for Groups 1 and 7).

When the work is nearing completion, the groups decide on presentation format and on how to share the report.

> I visit the groups while they prepare their report. One group uses background music imitating the teacher's reading of the story, but their music is more lively and modern. Two groups want to mix dialogues and explanation. They imitate voices ...
> (O: from Maite's observation diary)

Reporting is a risky affair and some students feel very nervous. They have to perform in the foreign language in front of an audience. Reading is not accepted (it is one of the agreed rules). They therefore, rehearse (some groups even record themselves) and correct each other. If asked, the teacher listens and suggests, always with encouragement. A procedural card for reporting to the whole class is on the table of the teacher to be consulted if necessary.

Oral group reporting to the class and processing of feedback

This is a big occasion and the students prepare for it. A few rules are suggested. ('Remember that all the groups need to incorporate this information into their final products. So, take notes of what the other groups say.') The teacher has prepared hand-outs with two columns, one for note-taking and the other one for comments and suggestions.

One can judge the importance they attach to this presentation by the self-imposed silence in the class. One by one the groups stand up and report while displaying their poster. A few excerpts of students' statements show the level of creative content and language use:

> They were as short and bright as butterflies. They were half people and half flowers. (Group 1)

> Below the mountain there was a valley. A beautiful river of orange water started from the top of that mountain.
>
> (Group 2)

> Their political system was a certain kind of anarchism ... What we mean is that they lived as friends and rarely had to take big decisions. When they had to, they did it in the community meetings. They lived in complete harmony ... They used to eat dust from plants or trees and drink water from the river, but on Sundays they used to eat pollen. (Group 3)

Ideas are always imaginative, but certain groups excel in this aspect.

> When they reached the top of the mountain it started to rain. It was very cold there. Greenrose and Greenbell spoke to the rain and invited him to come down to the valley where the temperature was more comfortable. When the rain arrived at the valley, green grass started to grow everywhere. Now you cannot see the greenings ... They are still there but you cannot see them, because they are green like the grass and hide from the white man. But if you listen in a quiet night, you will hear them whisper. (Group 4)

Feedback on presentations from students and the teacher leads to strategic changes:

> Students tend to read their compositions instead of explaining ... and when they read, the other students do not understand.
>
> (O: from Glória's observation diary)

> Although they make more mistakes [when not reading] the speech is more natural and they are able to communicate ... The description is nice and detailed.
>
> (O: from Núria's observation diary)

> They do not read. They explain. Some have memorised the text.
>
> (O: from Maite's observation diary)

Adapted explanations included:

> The enemy was an ugly monster. It looked like a red balloon in
> the sky. With him there were two friends.   (Group 5)

> Horses were like snow with black moles. Birds were white with
> brown wings. Mice were purple. Monkeys were the colour of
> the sea in winter. Ducks were light green with silver heads.
>   (Group 6)

> His (Fergus's) eyes had turned green. He was very old. He still
> remembered when . . .   (Group 7)

During the reporting process, elements appear which conflict with
other groups' information. Then students protest. Some are minor
problems:

> One group said that the Green people swam in the lake. For the
> map group the lake was frozen and the ice could be eaten. This
> was important to them, because Group 3 said that the Green
> People fed on pollen.   (O: from Jordi's observation diary)

In two cases the group suggests an alternative. In some others the
teacher opens a debate. When voting does not solve the problem, a
small subgroup is nominated, meets and suggests something acceptable
to all. Students suggest improvements and changes. Notes are taken.

The teacher makes sure that all the reports are successful and that
each group is applauded and derives a sense of achievement from their
contribution. Involvement in the process makes students impatient and
sometimes they discuss ideas and procedural aspects in their mother
tongue:

> He allows his students to express their opinions in English or in
> their mother tongue, but he always uses English, so this
> encourages students to switch over to English again.
>   (O: from Glória's observation diary)

Negotiation of final product and putting all the information together

Incorporating feedback and information from the other groups involves
taking a decision about format for the elaboration of the final product,
as this dictates needs, style, length, etc. Several are suggested in a
brainstorming session, for example a booklet with the whole illustrated
story, a recorded version, a comic book or video-recording of the text
on still frames. Students vote not to change the present group arrangement and to develop group products rather than a whole-class venture.

Once back to their work places they decide the format of the final product. The result will be four illustrated books, two cartoons and one video-recording.

The teacher distributes a hand-out with reminders about style, common mistakes (which were observed during the first group production and report), paragraph-building, and presentation. Decisions on procedure and content are also taken.

> This is based on the notes they have already taken. However, they can add whatever they want in order to write an original and well-organised story.   (O: from Glória's observation diary)

Each group as a whole is responsible for the collation, final production and correction of the text. Concerning format, different individual abilities and strengths suggest areas of personal responsibility. These are negotiated. The information is written down, passed on to the teacher and displayed on the wall.

Once finished, each draft is sent to another group for peer correction before final typing. First recordings are also shared, commented on and improved. In the credits of the bound volume or video-tape, the correctors are acknowledged as group collaborators.

The teacher monitors progress and checks samples of the work done in order to ensure a degree of language appropriacy and, consequently, presentation success. Students sign their group product collectively and their personal areas individually, formally declaring their agreement to public disclosure. The level of content and language creativity, accuracy and lexis is surprisingly high.

Presentation and public recognition

Group presentation includes:

- oral explanation of the product in class: its content, format and authorship;
- display: circulation of illustrated and comic books, and viewing of the video;
- brief explanation by groups of the process: objectives, decisions taken, pros and cons, agenda, language and content needs, difficulties encountered, etc.

Groups decide roles. Besides the main presenter, each member has his or her own share, such as reading one paragraph of the product, explaining a section of it, etc. This time the information from the other groups has been incorporated into a unified account. The following

> Sit with the other members of your team and look at what the other groups have produced. Comment on at least four productions.

Title:	Authors:
About the production	About the presentation
1. One thing I have particularly liked about this production.	1. One thing I have particularly liked about its presentation
2. Name one aspect of the production that may be improved.	2. Name one aspect of the presentation that may be improved.
3. Is the title catchy?* ❏	3. Was the report interesting? ❏
4. Is the content beautiful and imaginative? ❏	4. Was it clear? ❏
	5. Was it well-organised? ❏
5. Is the vocabulary rich? ❏	6. Did all contribute equally? ❏
6. Are paragraphs well organised? ❏	7. Was the length . . .
7. Is it well typed . . .	
* Evaluate from 1 to 4.	

Figure 4.3   Fragment of the analysis card

paragraphs are taken at random from different productions (a longer excerpt can be found in Appendix 4.1).

> The Greenings were dwarves that lived in a big green forest where the sun was white and the moon was purple. In the forest there also lived birds with striped feathers.
>
> Have you ever seen a place like this? I have seen it only in my dreams. The Greenings lived in logs and worked just in pleasant jobs like farming, preparing parties, and things like that. Every full moon . . .
>
> We only know that the Greenings were divided into a million tiny parts which you can still see in the sky at night.
>
> Years later the valley was absolutely impossible to recognise. Many concrete buildings had been made and the landscape was ugly and dirty because the factories expelled black smoke.

During the presentation, students have analysis cards with grids for comments, as shown in Figure 4.3. Each presentation is commented on, celebrated and cheered.

1. I enjoy reading a story.					
2. I can understand stories in English.					
3. I can write a simple story in English.					
4. I can explain a simple story orally in English.					
5. I can describe.					
. . . . .					
9. I have shared work in the group.					
10. I can use grammar cards and dictionary without difficulty.					

Figure 4.4   Fragments from the can-do card

Assessment and evaluation

Individual steps along the framework which has been described so far have been evaluated through questionnaires. Now students make a general appraisal of the final product, the process and the objectives reached. Together, teacher and students make a list of the main language areas (for example, past tenses of irregular verbs, time adverb position, lexical fields), attitudinal aspects and strategies (for example, note-taking, explaining in public) which students put into practice in each of the steps.

The teacher prepares an assessment (*can-do*) card containing these negotiated items reworded into assessable statements. Figure 4.4 illustrates part of this kind of *can-do*.

A second list (a *need-to* list) is copied by each student detailing objectives which were poorly achieved. He or she then writes a letter to the teacher explaining both good and not so good points in their work ('I think I must speak more, because I cannot explain my story very well'). To help in this, a test plus key for self-correction and grading is distributed, containing arrows that point back at the relevant language cards distributed during the process, with indications to revise them if the student's mastery of them is poor.

A formative evaluation questionnaire is handed out by the teacher asking about steps and activities the student has found particularly easy or difficult, interesting and enjoyable, and asking for suggestions for improving group work and language work, etc. It is a negotiation with oneself in an attempt at reconciling the project experience and their beliefs about language learning:

> I like working in this way, especially inventing things. My dictionary is not good and some times I don't find the words.
> (S: from Jordi's answers to the questionnaire)

> I don't like answering many questionnaires, but language cards are very useful.   (S: from Montse's answers to the questionnaire)

> The reports are very difficult. I think they are too difficult.
> (S: from Josep's answers to the questionnaire)

> I think that it is difficult to write a story with the others. We should work all equal.
> (S: from Teresa's answers to the questionnaire)

> I like this project but I want to read articles more scientific.
> (S: from David's answers to the questionnaire)

> The cards are very useful, but I learn more when I read.
> (S: from Reme's answers to the questionnaire)

Follow-up work

The students seemed to need a pause from group work once the project was completed.

> Today we have decided to write our own stories. I am tired of the work in group. I am going to write the story of two girls who went to Africa.   (S: from Maria's diary)

After having decided to spend a few classes writing their own stories, they selected their own individual input readings from a list of graded and non-graded books available. Diaries showed increasing concern for accuracy and a steady sense of progress. Once the stories were finished, read and celebrated, the class decided to work on a new project. They had gone through a first experience of negotiated creativity and this time they wanted a topic of their own choosing.

Some outcomes

Evaluation cards showed a high degree of acceptance (more than 80 per cent of students) of this way of working ('I hope we continue this style of work'; Joan) and a preference for this kind of activity over previous ones (73 per cent). Being responsible for decisions was felt to be a crucial factor ('I liked planning my work' was the most often selected statement on the card). A few unexpected facts were observed: for example, negotiation towards group formation had resulted in some of the weaker students volunteering for some of the more difficult tasks; conversely, the best students had not always taken excessive risks at the beginning. Being adolescents, a few felt the story was a bit childish (four students), but nevertheless enjoyed taking part and creating their own products. Re-addressing some aspects of group work negotiation (such as equal sharing) was considered an objective for the following project. The sense of achievement was equally high:

> I have learnt a lot in this month. More than all last year.
>
> (from Mary's diary)

> I think now I speak better when I explain my work to the others. (from Montse's diary)

Experience of success was for some something totally new:

> This activity is good. I think I can learn English some day. (Pere)

The English class and teacher's prestige soared, in spite of his up-front teaching having diminished:

> I think he is a bit crazy but he knows a lot. We are learning many different things which are not in the book.
>
> (from Joan's diary)

Involvement could be seen in the quality of the products. Not only were their content and pictures very beautiful, but syntactic accuracy and text organisation were higher than in any previous activity. An analysis of the lexis (with a concordancer) in the different final-group outputs showed a range of 685 to 946 words each with a very low index of redundancy (3.3 per cent). When analysed together, word type went up to 1390 with a ratio of 4.0 per cent. Compositions on different topics and of similar length from a non-project control group of the same level showed word type at 702 and a ratio of more than 9.0 per cent when computed together. Retention was not measured, but simple *use* of this quantity of lexis was very high compared to any other activity in classes of the same level. They were conscious of it ('I must use the dictionary all day. I am learning many new words'; Joan). After a short spell, the students decided to continue working in this way.

The framework for project work described in this chapter has consequently also been implemented with other groups. It has also been used as a blueprint for generating similar creative structures. Groups have included teachers in several teacher training events where it has served a demonstration function (steps, techniques, etc.). They have rarely felt this kind of practice to be threatening and the results have almost always been good in terms of creating an awareness of what steps and techniques are involved in implementing a creative framework in the classroom, of generating self-confidence and enthusiasm, and of generally helping the students/trainees evolve towards more complex forms of experiential learning.

A final word on tasks and frameworks

Major foreign-language learning objectives are context bound. Focus may range from basically linguistic goals in the language institution, to broader language-education goals in the school system. Language education requires the opening of 'spaces', not only for language processing, but also for whole-person involvement. The implementation of such 'spaces' (for example, space 'for risk-taking processes', 'for formal instruction', 'for pleasure in the use of the foreign language', 'for cognitive strategy development', 'for creating motivation towards the foreign language', 'for developing the student's self-image as a foreign language learner') should correspond to the variables operating in each context, as I have described elsewhere (Ribé, 1994).

Language tasks, like larger project work of the kind described here, 'create spaces' for negotiated interaction. Different tasks open different spaces. This allows us to establish a pedagogical classification of tasks and to draw correlations between task, spaces and context (see Ribé, 1994).

From a perspective of language education we can differentiate three generations or levels of task. This is a classification teachers usually understand and accept as it is directly related to their own experience and relevant to the educational objectives in the curriculum (for a succinct and clear description see Ribé and Vidal, 1993). The first level includes most of those currently described as focus-on-form tasks (see, for example, Long and Crookes, 1992; Pica *et al.*, 1993; Nunan, 1989a). Although variously described and categorised, most of these (whether simulations, role-play or problem-solving activities) share a few common traits: they are basically mono-episodic, specialised (directly subordinated to a linguistic objective) and therefore easily sequentiable within a language syllabus which becomes a constellation of them (see Candlin, 1987).

Second- and third-level tasks are better described as *frameworks* (Ribé *et al.*, 1997). These are in themselves curricula or constellations of tasks. They generate their own syllabus and fall well within Breen's description of process syllabuses (1984; 1987). Whatever their implementation, and project work is one of them, (published examples abound; see, for example, Edelhoff, 1981; Vidal and Farrando, 1987; Enright and McCloskey, 1988; Vidal, 1989; Carter and Thomas, 1990; Legutke and Thomas, 1991; Paretas, 1991), they are multi-episodic structures which, like a novel, unfold into a series of linked but autonomous events, each of them a task. They also have multi-level designs; the focus is not just on language, but on the learner's cognitive development (second level) and on attitudinal change (third level). Second-level tasks are research-based frameworks whereas third-level tasks are essentially creative frameworks. Frameworks can therefore be described as networks of tasks expandable in many directions (see Ribé and Vidal, 1993). They usually produce good language learning results and high indexes of positive attitudinal change, while providing an interface between the learner and the new language.

Whether class-brainstormed, teacher-induced, text or context-derived, the initial class-negotiated kernel of a creative project ('an intergalactic trip', 'a new world', 'a science-fiction project', 'a new school', 'an alternative town', etc.) starts growing through negotiated processes into an integrated and organised interactive network towards a final group or class-shared product, or towards a series of interlinked products.

This accepted or self-imposed environment becomes surprisingly alive in the following ways:

- It is learner-controlled and constantly modifiable in a process of day-to-day recreation.
- It is regulated by its own internal needs concerning language, content, interaction modes, organisation, skills, strategies, next step planning, etc.
- It constitutes an alternative syllabus, with language, content and educational objectives being discovered and constantly evaluated along the process.
- It is a whole communication system in itself; language flows constantly between individual, group and class.
- The learners carry out work which is totally self-generated and within which they accept responsibilities.

Some teachers and students evolve naturally from the simplest to the more complex forms of experiential learning work. However, we have found that certain varieties of creative framework are especially apt at introducing students and teachers alike to more complex forms of experiential learning. These frameworks usually present a structure that opens spaces for creativity, autonomous work, co-operation, and global processing of input and output, within a sheltering structure that offers a protected environment and thus a degree of security.

Appendix 4.1
Some fragments from final products and follow-up stories

Fragment 1

Once upon a time there was a magic country in the middle of the golden mountains and red lakes of Scotland. In this land the Greenings lived.

They were peaceful creatures who communicated with nature. They never ate. They were born fat and as time passed they got thinner because in their body there was enough food to live on. In winter they lived in logs and in summer they lived out in the country enjoying the good weather. For these creatures, family was very important. They all belonged to the same family and they were always together. They helped each other and when somebody was in trouble the family used to gather and they tried to solve the problem. The oldest members of the family were the wisest ones and so they could give advice to the other members. In general they lived in happiness and harmony.

But one day, little Greenbell and little Greenrose went to the white mountain because they wanted to reach the top. Once there, they wanted to see the beautiful landscape where they lived. It could be wonderful! But as they climbed something strange happened. A big red balloon appeared in the sky and it was approaching them quickly. At first they were shocked . . .

Fragment 2: 'The immortality bank' by Anna Llácer, Sonia Riu and Ana Serra

– It's two o'clock. I'm sorry, but the bank has just closed.
– Please, please. I need some checks. If I don't get them soon I will die! Please, please!
– You know that the bank closes its doors at two o'clock. Not a second earlier or later.

Forty-seven hours later a man was lying on a lonely long bench. His face showed desperation, his hands were tense. He was dead.

Near the bench many people were walking but they didn't notice the real situation of the body on the bench. Among the crowd there was a special couple. The man was young, tall, about ninety-seven years old. The girl was younger, about ninety, and her blonde hair contrasts with that of her friend.

– Poor man, he is dead – said Sheila.
– But it has nothing to do with us. Forget it – Mike replied.
– For us it's really easy to avoid this kind of situation and just because we have enough money to buy those life checks, but what about those with no chance of choosing between life or death? What happens when they die?
– I don't know, Sheila. But don't worry about it! I remember that many years ago people thought there was another life after death, but this theory has been totally dismissed. Hey! Let's have a 'Hot Tuna Melt'.

– Yes, thanks. Let's go to 'Mario's'.
...
Ring, ring, ring. . .
– 317045, hello?
– Sheila?
– Oh! Hi, Mike, where are you right now? ...

Fragment 3: from 'Dr. Ameinsanhaven's fauna' by David Arrufat, Xavier Heredia, Carlos D. Fernández, Guillem Formiguera

Let *me* explain a curious event. It was February sixth at five o'clock. I was working in the garden when my father called me. I went to him and he gave me a box that had been posted in Germany. I was very surprised. I went to *my* room where, immediately, I opened it. In the little box there were three packets. Each one had a number written in red colour. I took the first. It was a letter. I opened it. It was an English letter, I gave it to my father because I had never studied English, I prefer German. My father started to read it.

'On February first, 1988, Dr. Peter Ameinsanhaven has died.'

My blood stopped, but in a moment it started running again. Peter was my old and favourite uncle. He lived in Germany and I visited him every summer. He was a slightly crazy scientist. This year he should have celebrated his ninetieth birthday. My father continued the horrible letter.

'I, public prosecutor of Gelsenkirchen, communicate to you that your uncle in his will, has left you these two packets. Nobody has opened them because this was your uncle's desire'.

5 'We do what we like': negotiated classroom work with Hungarian children

Marianne Nikolov

This chapter is intended to provide insights into the day-to-day implementation of the process syllabus in the teaching of English as a foreign language to children between the ages of six and 14. Because of this wide age range, a focus of the chapter will be some of the changes in negotiation due to age. A further focus will be on how aspects of classroom procedures and content are negotiated and how feedback from the children is obtained and acted on.

Subjects

The study which this chapter builds on was conducted over the last 20 years. It involved three groups of children from the age of six up to 14. The children were learning English at a primary school affiliated to Janus Pannonius University, Pécs, Hungary. The first experimental group of 15 six-year-old children started in 1977. After an eight-year pilot period the second group of 15 learners started in 1985. Another 15 children were involved in a third group between 1987 and 1995. Altogether 20 girls and 25 boys have participated for the full length of each of the eight-year periods. Five children out of the first group came from disadvantaged families and the parents of only two had learnt English. In the second and third groups two and three subjects respectively came from disadvantaged families and five and six parents respectively had some background in English. Most of the children came from middle-class families and their parents wanted them to study English. The school is situated in a not very well established neighbourhood in the city centre of Pécs, Hungary. Most of the students live in the district but many of them commute from other parts of the town for the sake of the English programme. Children had two classes per week in the first two grades, three classes in the third and fourth grades, and four classes between the ages of 10 and 14. The teacher, syllabus designer and researcher was the same person throughout, viz the author.

This account is based upon reflective research as I have worked through and developed the programme for the whole period.

Background to the study

Teaching English as a foreign language to young learners was introduced in an experimental class in 1977. The programme was initiated by the Ministry of Education, but their support was withdrawn after three years. At that time Russian was the compulsory foreign language; all children were supposed to begin Russian at the age of 10. However, a few specialised schools introduced English or German at the earlier age of eight.

Recently, the general situation has changed: Russian is no longer compulsory and English programmes have mushroomed all over the country (for a summary, see Medgyes, 1993). Schools are required to develop their own curricula based on the New National Curriculum but, to my knowledge, syllabuses are rarely negotiated.

In most cases syllabus design means the adaptation of published teaching materials, spiced with some supplementary materials, and children are not involved in any kind of decision-making. Teachers tend to stick to their syllabuses because they see them as prescribed documents and learners' expressed needs are not usually taken into consideration. The same syllabus is used with gifted, mixed-ability and low-ability children but the achievements of each group are different.

Teachers are required to assess children from the very first school year. Hungarian children are graded on a system of 1 to 5: mark 5 is the best and mark 1 means complete failure. Most teachers of younger children develop cumulative systems of assessment in which children receive small rewards, such as red points and, after gaining five such points, students are awarded a mark 5. Negative feedback accumulates along the same principles: lack of homework, inattention and a high number of mistakes in tasks result in low marks. Good marks are extremely important both to children and parents as these represent progress in studies and determine access to different types of secondary schools. Formal testing is, however, generally infrequent; consequently a few test results determine the final grade at the end of the term. As a result of these facts, children hate and fear tests.

Negotiation in the classroom

Two reasons are mentioned by Breen for the introduction of the process syllabus: '[It] provides the framework within which either a predesigned content syllabus would be publicly analysed and evaluated by the classroom group, or an emerging content syllabus would be designed (and similarly evaluated) in an ongoing way' (Breen, 1984: 55). In this study the aim of negotiation with the first experimental group was the design of an emerging story-based syllabus; in the second and third groups this syllabus was evaluated and further developed.

The purpose of the early English project was to develop and pilot materials, tasks and teaching techniques for children between six and 14. As no ready-made materials or teaching techniques were available, the most appropriate way of developing the syllabus, for me, was negotiation with children.

Another reason for negotiating the syllabus was my own inexperience as a teacher. It was my very first teaching experience after graduation from college and, although I had never heard of process syllabuses or negotiation in the classroom, I relied on the children involved as much as possible since the syllabus was to be designed for them. I felt it a personal challenge to find out about children's likes and dislikes, and how they acquired English in the classroom. Negotiation is not used in Hungarian schools and my inexperience turned out to be useful: I found that the usual rigid teacher-directed, classroom routine could be avoided. As a result of inquiring about children's attitudes, a story-based content syllabus with playful language-teaching techniques was developed.

Decisions are usually taken by teachers: they determine what students do and how they do it, and evaluative feedback is also provided by the teacher. Children have only one choice: whether they participate or not. Breen (1984) identifies three major elements of classroom work where decisions have to be made: participation, procedure and subject matter. I describe below the procedures I adopted with the children with reference to these three areas of decision-making. Student assessment is not usually explicitly negotiated in school, but I have seen it as having an important role in my own work. These four aspects are explored across the different age ranges.

Participation

Issues related to participation relate to two questions: 'Who wants to participate in a particular activity?' and 'Who wants to work with whom?' With respect to the choice of participation, young learners often feel shy and would like to see first how the activity goes, or they are unhappy and would like to withdraw. Most of the children have special favourites, while some of them particularly dislike one of the activities. There were several boys who never wanted to play singing games as they thought 'Lucy Locket' was only for girls, but they always wanted to play 'What's the time, Mr Wolf?' and other games with a lot of physical movements. After introducing the activity the teacher can ask children whether they want to participate in that particular game or task. One way of doing this is asking for volunteers, children who want to join in, while the others may choose to do something else, e.g. observe, colour or draw pictures. The other way is voting on the activity. Children are asked 'Who wants to do it?' and, if the majority votes for it, they are all asked to do it. At first this rule does not work very well with young students but after a few months they understand it and they start persuading each other to vote for what they want to do. The most democratic outcome is usually suggested by the children themselves: 'Let's do this first, and then what the others would like.' I adopted this principle from their suggestion and in most of the cases it works.

The situation is fairly similar up to the age of 12, children rarely choose not to participate but in such cases they like peers to invite them. There are no children who regularly withdraw, except for team competitions. Children who are chosen last by captains develop inhibitions and do not want to participate. An eight-year-old boy suggested that the ones chosen last should be the captains the following time. His suggestion was adapted and this way uncomfortable situations could be avoided and students did not mind being last.

Around puberty some girls develop inhibitions and they always choose not to participate in any role play if they are to be watched by the others. I asked them for suggestions and they came up with two rules:

1. only volunteers act out, and the ones who don't feel like performing need not;
2. if they still feel they want to be marked on the role play they may choose their audience for the break, sometimes only the teacher.

In these cases before or after classes, while the other students are out of the classroom, these students would perform in front of the limited audience of their own choice.

As for who works with whom, children in all three groups liked to choose their partners and after the age of eight or nine they hardly tolerated pressure. Due to aptitude differences and discipline problems, sometimes low achievers or aggressive children are not chosen. Two ways of avoiding embarrassing situations have been developed. Children volunteering to tutor a classmate who has fallen behind get a reward every time their partner improves a subskill. They fill in missing letters, dictate to one another, play guessing games, act out, develop puzzles for partners and are motivated to collaborate. Sometimes children find this patronising or irritating, mostly boys with girls, but several girls have developed long-lasting friendships through this technique. When two more gifted girls have worked with a less gifted one, over the years the differences may disappear.

The other way of avoiding embarrassing situations is based on coincidence or chance; for example, with a counting rhyme, or numbers picked at random from a hat, or ends of strings taken without seeing who the one holding the other end is. Young children enjoy these solutions but with adolescents it may cause trouble when one or more children decide not to participate after finding out who they are supposed to work with. In these cases they usually choose to do another activity by themselves or the group persuades them to join in. After such occasions they tend to vote for choosing partners on their own and they come to class with decisions made among them.

Procedure

Several aspects of procedure have been touched upon in the previous review. In what follows some further information will be provided concerning how tasks and activities are negotiated and in what ways students contribute to the choices.

Young children are usually offered choices: 'Would you like to play the card game with the animal cards or the clothes cards?'; 'Shall we sit on the floor or do you want to sit on your chairs?'; 'Would you like a guessing game or a puzzle'; 'Shall we play "Simon says" now, or do you want me to go on with the story first?' This way they feel involved in decision-making and in most of the cases they vote for both; in this way negotiation influences the sequence of activities. Around the age of eight some children come up with suggestions: 'Let's go on with the story'; 'I have a puzzle, can I put it on the board?' In these cases we usually strike a bargain: they would like to do something and I say 'Yes, we can, *if* we do all I think we need to do first.' That way we can save time for the desired activity, which is the best way of avoiding discipline problems due to boredom.

Children often contribute by bringing favourite animals, toys or books, drawing pictures, developing crossword puzzles, fill-in-the-slot tasks, jumbled words or sentences, or by writing their own stories. The only drawback to using materials supplied by children is that the others sometimes find these tasks unclear or misleading so they argue and may disappoint each other. This difficulty can be easily avoided by consulting children before they present tasks for the others. Some children develop special expertise in some areas. One girl in the first and second groups produced a crossword puzzle for each class from the second grade up to the last class in the eighth grade. Another girl in the third group became hooked on word chains and produced half a page of them for each class in the last four years. Children automatically receive rewards for these extra tasks, although not all of them are aware of the possibility. A problematic boy in the seventh grade realised only after almost seven years that he could also gain rewards in this way. He developed 11 puzzles within two weeks, and later he prepared one every week to ensure a regular good mark.

Up to the age of 10 children have rarely turned any of my offers down. After this age they sometimes vote against my suggestions and they are even more critical of peer suggestions. In the fifth grade they tend to decide not to sing songs or play games with physical movements. In the seventh and eighth grades they do not want to play 'Bingo' through guessing meanings of words from contexts to be written in a chart, but want synonyms and antonyms instead. They suggest doing writing and reading tasks either in pairs (when it is meant to be an individual activity and vice versa) or as homework so that they can go on with the classroom activity instead. Sometimes they ask for a copy of the next chapter of a story and choose to read it themselves instead of listening to it, or they don't want to elaborate on a prediction task as they are too eager to know more of the story. Negotiation in these cases is usually triggered by my offer of options on which all children are asked to vote. Sometimes one or more students suggest an activity and they want to involve the others in the decision-making by asking for voting. In all cases the wish of the majority determines what should happen.

Subject matter

Students have been involved in making decisions on the content with which we work. The story-based syllabus is built on a sequence of rhymes, songs and stories, together with games and tasks associated with them. The most important reasons for the development of the story-based syllabus are the following. Children find rhymes, songs, picture stories, fairy tales, adventure stories and thrillers intrinsically motivating, thus these authentic English sources offer relevant content areas for an EFL course. Children are familiar with similar materials, sometimes even with the same story, in their mother tongue. Tasks associated with stories are cognitively familiar, meaningful and context embedded. All language functions and formal aspects of language are available in stories from authentic sources. Stories lend themselves to adaptation easily and contribute to the development of both the receptive and expressive skills. As the syllabus is based on stories, children have contributed by suggesting stories (such as their own picture books which can be told as a story), by suggesting new story books and by choosing from my offers. In the first two or three grades they enjoy listening to the same story several times and they vote for their choice and we retell the ones most of them want. In the fourth, fifth and sixth grades they still feel happy with the teacher's choice and suggest their own books less frequently, mostly because they realise that the books should be in English and they have limited access to them. When a story is finished, children are asked how much they enjoyed it and why. As for the next choice, they either want something exactly like the one we have just finished or something completely different. Sometimes they suggest a pop song or want to do a project on a particular topic. I need to make sure that wishes of both boys and girls are granted: after 'Cinderella', 'The Wizard of Oz' or 'Babysitting is a Dangerous Job' – which are considered 'girlish' stories – they tend to vote for a story considered more 'boyish', like 'Pinocchio', 'Doctor Dolittle' or 'Run for your Life'. As negotiation becomes routine in the classroom the teacher has to be prepared for the possibility of her or his offers being turned down. I have tried to read 'The Hound of the Baskervilles' to all three groups in the seventh grade without success. Every time I offered it in a choice of three novels, another story was always chosen.

Sometimes children suggest the *type* of story they would like: in the third group in January they wanted a horror story, so they chose from 'Dracula', 'Frankenstein' and 'The Canterville Ghost', but after that story they voted for a detective story rather than either of the other two.

Once you start negotiation on likes and dislikes you cannot stop, and sometimes this can lead to unexpected issues being raised by children. In the sixth grade we worked on 'Jack and the Beanstalk': we dramatised it, put it on stage, and parents came to watch their children. After this success it seemed the right time for evaluation and I asked learners for their opinion concerning how much they had benefited from the experience. All the children sounded enthusiastic until one of the boys, a very scholarly one, raised his hand and said in Hungarian, 'I wonder how useful Jack and the Beanstalk is going to be if I want to travel to the USA?' All the students gaped at me and I asked him what suggestion he would like to make. He wanted 'proper' grammar instruction, like the other grades in school. I was still thinking about the most relevant answer when the other children commented, 'When Jack went up to the other world and asked the way, it was like in New York.' And another one added, 'If you don't like Jack and the Beanstalk you can join the other group and do Project English.' I asked the children how many of them wanted more explicit grammar explanations and exercises. Two girls pointed out that it might be useful in secondary school. Since that time we have been doing some follow-up tasks on grammar points; however, this poor boy still received the blame every time, even when some of the other children ask for them, because these kinds of tasks are not among their favourite activities.

Role of mother tongue

As negotiation is almost impossible in the target language, in the initial stages Hungarian is used. Children will understand the routine questions in English after one or two times but they will answer in the mother tongue and this second phase lasts two or three years. In the last three grades most of the students are able to discuss, bargain and argue in English, and this is clearly a part of the language syllabus. If they cannot express what they would like to say, they switch back to Hungarian, however, I always answer in English. If they try to say something that they should be able to express in English, they are asked to do so. In problem situations I ask fellow students what they think the other person is trying to say. They either help the student out in English, or offer their own opinion on the topic. In some cases students who want to avoid English are asked to postpone what they want to say, and they can always speak Hungarian in the break.

Assessment

As children are to be given marks, they are involved in the negotiation of assessment procedures as well. First of all they need to assess themselves. At the age of six they are asked after each class whether they think they have deserved a reward. They look at each other, and then the ones who have considered it and still think they deserve one draw the reward (red points, little hearts) in their own notebook which is used for drawing and keeping track of rewards. Each child is responsible for the 'book-keeping' of his or her rewards or, in the upper grades, their marks. In the first grade sometimes a child gains so much pleasure from drawing rewards that they somehow multiply. The others usually notice it and then I ask this person to count carefully and keep as many as he or she is sure to have deserved. In the case of some children not behaving appropriately, a boy suggested they should lose one of their rewards. If they feel it is just, they need to cross off one of their own red points. Sometimes they ask me to allow them to keep the red point and promise to deserve two the following time. Usually it works out well.

Every month children are asked in Hungarian how they assess themselves, and they like to comment on each other as well. They are to tell us if they are trying hard enough and where they feel their strengths and weaknesses are. Generally they tend to underestimate their own work and like to hear remarks of praise from peers and encouragement from me. This is part of the general evaluation procedure when they are asked for their views about classroom activities, materials and the teacher. As for testing, they can suggest the time of testing, and they can ask for more practice in certain areas; they often suggest what should and what should not be included in the test. I always give them a mark on their first trial, and if children feel they would like to give it another chance they can try again, self-correct, and the better result is the one recorded. From the very first moment of writing they are asked to check their own work and self-correct. I indicate how many problems there are and in which areas, and they have to find the mistakes and correct them. Sometimes they ask to be allowed to use sources and in most of the cases they can do so, except for tasks when they need to remember accurately; for example, in dictation or a test on vocabulary. Tests are evaluated on the spot and children check their own results in a different colour. This is very useful for sorting out misunderstandings or solutions which I had not thought of but which are nevertheless creative and acceptable. Final marks at the end of the term are also negotiated and individual children are asked to suggest them; the others are also asked their opinion. Children are to tell us what final grade they think they deserve and why. Their suggestions are very often realistic and relevant.

Negotiation on assessment is based on trust. Children know that they are trusted and they try very hard to come up to expectations. Whenever it occurs to any student that one of them may have cheated, I emphasise the importance of trust and ask the particular child if we still have a reason to trust him or her. Another strategy is to take the responsibility myself. In a case where I feel dissatisfied with learners and they also feel slightly guilty, I always try to take the responsibility by asking them what I should have done differently or how I could help in the future.

Formal feedback

Towards the end of each school year children are asked to fill in a questionnaire in Hungarian, anonymously. The following six questions are asked:

- Why do you learn English?
- What are your first three favourite school subjects?
- What are the school subjects (if any) you dislike?
- What do you enjoy doing the most in the English classes?
- What do you dislike (related to English)?
- If you were the teacher what would you do differently?

The first three questions are meant to tap attitudes towards and motivation for English, whereas the other questions aim at eliciting concrete information on what activities children like, dislike and in what ways the teacher should adapt to their needs.

Detailed analysis of the findings can be found in Nikolov (1994); here only findings relevant to negotiation are mentioned. One of the reasons why children think they study English is that they feel they do what they like. As for the question inquiring about concerns and suggestions, results differ according to age. In the first two grades very few children gave an answer and all of them indicated everything was good the way it was. In the third, fourth and fifth grades about half of those questioned were pleased with everything, whereas some would not make children write tests, and others would send children who misbehave out of the class. In the last three grades, half of the students would not change anything, some would punish the ones who have not done homework and the misbehaving children, and many would not require a home assignment. All of the children in the third group in the study would do more grammar and have more horror stories, and some would allow eating during class.

Conclusion

What are the outcomes of this project? First, negative outcomes should be mentioned. As English was the only school subject where negotiation was integrated, children often faced rejection as they tried to come up with suggestions in other classes. Some parents criticised the 'non-traditional' approach, wondered if 'freedom' is not harmful, and worried that the children may not learn English 'properly'. After eight years, most of the children went to different secondary schools and their new teachers perceived their suggestions as irritating or cheeky, and their behaviour as conceited. It may be fair to say that some of the children grew too critical of their new circumstances.

On the other hand, the children became self-confident and responsible for their own learning. In the first and second groups more than half of the students passed the state intermediate-level proficiency exam by the age of 16. Four students from the first group of 15 graduated from university as English majors, and nine others are using English daily for professional purposes. All learners involved in the project are still studying or using English, and most of them have studied other foreign languages as well.

As a result of the negotiated syllabus, children have acquired a lot of language, have developed a favourable attitude towards English, the teacher and language learning in general. On the whole, negotiation can be successfully applied in the teaching of English as a foreign language to 6 to 14-year-old children if the teacher is willing to take risks.

6 Is a negotiated syllabus feasible within a national curriculum?

Pnina Linder

Our interest and concern with process syllabuses and teacher–learner negotiation stemmed from the desire to improve learning and to establish a more democratic framework of relationships within the school. We were confronted with a seeming contradiction: on the one hand, a wish to introduce negotiation which entails that the syllabus or many of its components should not be pre-determined whilst, on the other, working in the context of a centralised educational system which prescribes curricula, authorises textbooks and sets external exams.

Our pupils are in a compulsory educational framework which includes obligatory study of EFL for about nine years of their schooling (ages 9 to 18). There is a set national curriculum culminating in a matriculation exam, which has a pronounced washback effect on programmes and procedures in the classroom. Pupils at the secondary school have been generally geared to an exam culture and summative evaluations assessed by the teachers are the norm in much of the country.

Our motives for classroom negotiation

We sensed the beneficial effect on learning that student decision-making, options and choices, awareness of learning procedures and co-operative learning could have. We believed it could develop more responsible learning. The premises we had for exploring and opting for elements of negotiation, even within the constraints we were working under, were both educational and practical. Our objectives were, among others, for our pupils to become life-long, independent learners and crucially, to have positive experiences in the process.

Furthermore, we viewed negotiation as an important component central to the language-learning process itself, involving, as it does, interacting through language while negotiating meanings in a shared context. We concurred with Curran, who expressed this as a belief that 'people learn best from utterances in which they have a strong personal stake or "investment"' (1968, cited in Stevick, 1976: 42). And Allwright (1979) also reflected our sentiments when he claimed that effective learning depends on what happens in and between people in the classroom. He went on to suggest that responsible teaching entailed the sharing of that responsibility because the organisation and management of classroom work are too much for any one person to bear and that assuming management responsibilities have a very important contribution to make to the learning process.

Ours being a regional school catering for a largely kibbutz population from generally egalitarian communities, we were concerned to provide for as democratic a setting as possible. The motivations and beliefs justifying our opting for elements of negotiation in our EFL programme can be summarised as follows:

- Learners' personal investment in the learning process can enhance motivation and learning.
- Negotiation can generate an atmosphere of trust and mutual respect which the typical teacher-fronted and teacher-directed arrangement does not necessarily succeed in achieving.
- It can assist in attending to different learning styles, levels and needs within the single classroom.
- Sharing and co-operation are cornerstones of an egalitarian society, the basic ethos of our communities.
- The actual process of negotiation is congruent with and integral to a communicative approach to language learning.
- Practising negotiation can lead to learner independence, learner assumption of responsibility for learning and potential for life-long learning because negotiation entails not only discussing subject matter to be learned but also the awareness and application of particular capabilities needed in processing and applying one's knowledge.
- Negotiation can lead to the acceptance and appreciation of differences central to the successful operation of mixed-ability classes because negotiation, in our situation, implies that the same stipulated content and the same prescribed materials can be worked through in a variety of ways inviting diversified contributions from learners.

Though the curriculum is prescribed by a central educational agency, the Ministry of Education, teachers with their classes *can* determine the pace of the work, design tasks, suggest a variety of approaches to the materials and add supplementary materials of their own choice.

Have our hopes, beliefs and procedures been justified? We would like to show that our experience supports the claim that negotiation *can* be congruent with a prescribed syllabus and that it can be applied to 'any content because it would directly address the shared activities of selecting, focusing upon, subdividing, and sequencing appropriate subject matter – activities which could be desirably and publicly undertaken in the classroom itself' (Breen, 1984:54). We also believe that learning is enhanced by such negotiation.

Examples of negotiation within the programme

What follows is an attempt to illustrate some of the actual classroom practices adopted in our school in terms of both the content and processes of negotiation within the classroom.

Initial questionnaires

At the start of the school year, most of our EFL teachers present some form of questionnaire to the class to aid in getting to know the attitudes, experiences, needs and wants of the different pupils. Figure 6.1 illustrates the kind of questionnaire which teachers designed and used. (Appendix 6.1 provides other examples of the questionnaires designed by staff members for different classes in the junior and senior high school.) The questionnaires engendered a climate of sharing and thinking about learning and a climate of trust.

These questionnaires were then analysed, the findings presented to the class and then agreed procedures of work were drawn up. The questionnaires provided for collaborative thinking about ways of implementing programmes, making decisions as to procedures and for ongoing self-evaluation.

As part of the procedures for classroom working, one objective was to provide for different ways into and through a topic of study for the individual's contribution to his or her own learning and to that of the group. We found that this enhanced the learning process as well as that of broader socialisation, believing as we do that school is not merely a preparation for life but the actual living itself.

The extensive reading programme

In our junior and senior high school we have an ongoing extensive reading programme and pupils are encouraged to make individual book selections according to the level and interest of each. In any one class, a wide range and level of English is read at any one time. Class time is allotted for the reading session, thus emphasising its high priority. No

MAKING SUGGESTIONS AND ASKING FOR HELP

A. What would you like to have happen in the English class this year?
Make some suggestions by completing as many of the following sentences
as you wish.
1. I think we should_____.
2. I would like to have _____.
3. I hope we will _____.
4. It would be a good idea if _____.
5. I suggest that we _____.

B. What types of activities did you benefit most from/enjoy most in your
English class last year?

C. What types of activities did you least enjoy/benefit from?

D. Which of the following areas do you feel strong in and which do you feel
you need help in? Rate them from 1 to 5, where 1 is VERY GOOD and 5
is HELP!
1. reading and understanding _____
2. listening _____
3. speaking _____
4. writing _____
5. spelling _____
6. doing homework assignments _____
7. understanding instructions _____
8. other? _____

E. How do you like to work in class?

	often	sometimes	never
a. alone	_____	_____	_____
b. in pairs	_____	_____	_____
c. in groups	_____	_____	_____

Figure 6.1   A questionnaire for students

texts are set and learners, therefore, choose their own books from
among the resources available in the school English library. It has come
to be understood by the children that they select for themselves the
reading matter most suited to them. They may ask their teacher and
librarian questions and receive their guidance, and they can also obtain
the recommendations of their classmates.

In addition to our concern for advancing the knowledge of English
and for individual choice and decision-making, we found that the
extensive reading component of our programme led to more effective

work in heterogeneous classes. Children came to realise, through the experience of individual selection according to personal interest and ability, that they can study together regardless of different ability levels and that not the whole class is required to perform the same tasks at the same time and in the same way. The children have learned to accept and appreciate differences in addition to appreciating the value of processes as well as outcomes.

Negotiating ways of revising a story studied by the whole class

The Ministry of Education's curriculum specifies contents and skills objectives but does not prescribe the routes one must take nor the classroom organisation and procedures one must follow to achieve the specified final objectives. A teacher, for example, asked the class for suggestions for alternative ways of working through a unit. Once the suggestions were listed, the class and the individuals decided upon which options to select and in which participatory framework they chose to complete their tasks (alone, in pairs or in a group). Their decisions could also be about the quantity of tasks undertaken. The products of work from these alternative routes were then shared by the group.

One particular example of this negotiation procedure is how a class chose to work through a short story that was one of the required selections for the matriculation exam which learners sit at the end of their senior high school at age 18. Below are some tasks for in-depth study and revision which were suggested by the students themselves once the story had been read through for the first time:

- Extract and study some of the vocabulary items and how they express the central meanings of the story.
- Go through and list all the different words used to suggest the colour 'red'.
- List the cliches and suggest what they may indicate about the speaker.
- Extract the descriptive phrases relating to the main characters.
- Find comparisons and contrasts between two central characters.
- Find any grammatical forms that appear to be more prevalent than others and copy the sentences you found.
- Suggest reasons why the author chose these forms so often.
- Select scenes for role play; list appropriate scenes and role-play them with a partner.
- Write your own scene or ending, or a short story of your own with a similar theme.
- Select examples of irony.

- Prepare questions of your own for the class as revision of the story.
- Read the story again, straight through.

The tasks themselves were not unique nor especially innovative but the list was elicited so that both student and teacher suggestions were captured. The content – in this case the story read together – was common for everybody. Likewise, there was a stipulation agreed upon at the onset of the unit that everyone selected a task, decided the framework of study (to work alone, with a partner or to join a group) and each person was to be responsible for the task's completion. Therefore, although the content was prescribed, the learning procedures were negotiated on the basis of the their initial brainstormed suggestions.

The prepared talk

A further example of a required feature of the curriculum was, in this case, the *task* of presenting a talk while the content and form it took became the negotiable features. Pupils chose a topic of interest about which they had information to impart. It has been our experience that, when youngsters have something to say with which they are personally involved, they almost inevitably find ways to formulate and express it even if the language is a bit halting or faulty. The key element of the task was the communication of information, ideas and experiences. Pupils, in turn were assigned or could select a time slot as the due date for the presentation. Though most accepted the challenge, there were some who were hesitant or shy of an audience. For some the emotional burden and anxiety aroused at the prospect of speaking in front of the whole group was too daunting. The class was therefore asked to recommend alternative options for the presentation. In addition to presenting directly to the class, which was the option most often selected, suggestions ranged from preparing a cassette recording of the talk, simulating a radio programme presentation where the pupil does the speaking but is hidden from view, or reporting in private to the teacher who would then relay the contents to the class. In a number of instances, the class also chose to set some rules pertaining to their responses to the talks. These included:

- The speaker may invite questions for further clarification.
- Members of the class may add information or express opinions about the contents.
- Members of the class may not criticise the actual performance.
- The teacher and pupils may point out instances of faulty use of language, but only if the speaker requests this.

Learning vocabulary

Even regarding the very traditional curriculum specification of spelling and the learning of vocabulary items, negotiation and individual responsibility for one's own learning were found to be very beneficial. Here a procedure was suggested by the teacher but the contents were left to the decision of the learners. Rather than continuing the well-worn pattern of simply presenting the new words to be learnt the teacher shared the following thoughts with the class:

> I cannot know nor profess to know what elements are new to each of you. You have various knowledge and language sources and your English is not only determined by your textbook and your teacher. Therefore you can prepare your own new-word and spelling list, choosing those items each week that you have decided to learn about and to spell from the materials studied and from problem areas you encountered in your assignments. You will check yourself at the end of each week be exchanging your list with your partner, reading out and checking one another's achievements on that skill for that week.

This procedure proved effective in the following spheres, some of which were quite unforeseen:

- the development of peer co-operation;
- awareness arousing of problem areas that could be tackled independently;
- built-in revision of previous assignments;
- personalisation of learning;
- improved handwriting (their word list was meant for the eyes of their partners, not for the teacher!).

Pupil contributions

An English teacher of an eighth grade class (consisting of 28 pupils all 14 years old) undertook a particular negotiation process with her class related to a unit in their prescribed textbook. The content of the unit focused on discoveries and inventions. The teacher asked the class to recall the various inventors, discoverers and explorers they had read about. She listed them on the board and then asked the children to think of ways to revise the unit itself for a review test. They formed groups of three or four and, for a few minutes, negotiated ways of doing revision. Each group then presented their deductions. Among the suggestions which were all listed were the following:

- List some of the items discovered or invented under the chart of names of famous discoverers and inventors (designed by the group) and match the items to the appropriate person.
- Choose any of the names of the people and tell something about them.
- Divide the people into groups according to any idea you have (the children's wording for classifying the people into groups according to a particular criterion).
- Match any two persons and be ready to tell what they have in common.
- Open the book and find sentences that mention any of these people or discoveries; copy them into your notebooks.
- Explain in Hebrew details of the different inventors and ask your neighbour to repeat in English.
- Decide with your partner who is going to find out details of the different people; divide the inventors/discoverers between you.
- Ask each other questions in order to find out/check who invented/ discovered what.
- Prepare a list of questions in order to find out 'who I am', such as: 'I flew over the Atlantic; I discovered radium; I invented the airplane'; etc. Ask your friends the questions.

Each group designed a different set of tasks from these ideas which they exchanged with another group. The groups then decided which options to select for their revision. The teacher also told them that their designed tasks would be used by her as the basis for a worksheet and summary exercise which became the review test.

In the same class pupils were regularly invited to bring materials to class for the class to study and work on. Song cassettes, puzzles and games brought in by members of the class became part of the work activities of the class with the pupils, aided by the teacher who prepared additional materials related to these items.

Exams and assessment

In a senior class, preparing to sit their English matriculation exams, the teacher conversed with the pupils about their specific strengths and weaknesses relating to the exam requirements and held lessons in a workshop atmosphere, setting up a stock of materials – based on the various elements that appear in the matriculation exam – from which the students selected. These materials were often accompanied, where appropriate, with self-check keys, thereby freeing the teacher to be available to provide more guidance where needed. This teacher observed the improved atmosphere and the reduction of anxiety related to the exam.

Another teacher reported presenting time options for sitting for review tests. Pupils were free to determine when they were ready to sit these exams and set the date with their teacher. Criteria for assessment and grading were also negotiated. Decisions reached included basing the individual's grade on the following components: participation, effort and progress, home and class assignments, classroom deportment (including co-operation), and results of quizzes and exams. The weight given to each component was also determined by a class decision based on the individual responses to questionnaires. Figure 6.2 illustrates this kind of questionnaire for younger pupils, with their views on the weighting of assessment referred to in the last section. A similar self-evaluation questionnaire for older students is shown in Appendix 6.2.

Exams, which the authorities require teachers to administer, can become an effective and enriching learning experience when composed and compiled from questions and tasks prepared and revised by pupils. We have also attempted to devise exams which include elements of choice and a variety of task types.

Future directions

These and other instances of negotiation at the onset of studies and negotiation of content, procedures and assessment have become a fairly general practice at our school. It has developed through constant and consistent staff reflection and sharing. The negotiation process experienced by the teachers among themselves in these sessions has encouraged them to initiate such practices in their classrooms.

We have not yet come to terms with a systematic evaluation of the effects of our endeavours in negotiating aspects of the curriculum. We haven't yet achieved, nor is it feasible to achieve, the same intensity of commitment by all teachers to pupils sharing in determining aspects of the curriculum. We haven't systematically recorded student reactions to these processes but have observed the positive impact in terms of increased participation, increased use of the target language, and the generally more satisfactory assignments submitted (these were higher in both quantity and quality). Furthermore, pupils have reported their appreciation of their greater involvement in and with the programme. The atmosphere in most of the EFL classes is generally positive, and you hear less teacher-talk and less teacher-lecturing in the EFL area at school.

However, the reporting of our work in this chapter is mainly

HOW WELL DO YOU DO?

RATE YOURSELF BY WRITING 1–5 BESIDE EACH OF THE FOLLOWING:

1 = not at all;   2 = poor;   3 = get by;   4 = well;   5 = no problems

LISTENING
Listen to the teacher's instructions ____
Listen to the news in English (TV or radio) ____
Listen to other students ____
Listen to movies in English ____
Listen to words in songs ____
Learn new words by only hearing them being used ____
Listen to people conversing in English ____

READING
Read books ____
Read newspapers ____
Read instructions ____
Read a letter ____
Read signs/advertisements ____
Read short stories ____
Learn new words by 'seeing' them in print ____

WRITING
Write a short paragraph ____
Write a letter ____
Write a composition (250–300 words) ____
Write out a joke or story (100 words) ____
Write an essay (500–1000 words) ____
I need to write out new words to learn them ____
Spell accurately ____
Write grammatically correct sentences ____

TALKING
Answer questions in English ____
Ask questions in English ____
Give directions to someone who is lost ____
Describe my kibbutz to someone ____
Talk for some minutes on a subject of my choice ____
Describe a movie I have seen ____
Learn new words by using them when I talk ____
Conversation with English speakers ____

IN MY OPINION, A FAIR MARK FOR THE END OF SEMESTER IS BASED ON:

____ %   Classroom behaviour (you come on time, participate well, can listen quietly, work well alone and with others, bring your books, paper, pen, homework)
____ %   Homework (quality, neatly done, handed in on time)
____ %   Small spelling/grammar tests
____ %   Exams
____ %   Effort (you know your weaknesses and try to overcome them; your homework shows extra thought, care and work; you ask questions in class, also help others)

Figure 6.2   A self-evaluation questionnaire

impressionistic. We wish to refine and improve our work and develop better instruments with which to evaluate our efforts. Although national exams may not be an accurate measure of success or failure of our programme, those who sit for the matriculation exams generally perform well and often above the national average.

We have undertaken to work more intensively with the pupils on 'learner training skills'. By this term we mean, for example, how to read and follow instructions, how to use a dictionary effectively and how to find information in a text index and table of contents. Likewise we have incorporated in our teaching ways of co-operating, forming groups and dividing up responsibilities.

We plan to embark upon a staff-based, in-service programme which will focus on two components, both related to negotiation processes in the classroom. First, it will focus on the sharing of experiences which will involve collaborative joint mapping of procedures and their application. Second, it will focus on action research in the classroom which will follow through the implementation, observation and recording of outcomes of the various procedures and will analyse in detail the results obtained. For the teachers, this is to be both an individual and collaborative undertaking by incorporating peer observation and peer consultation along with regular staff study sessions. Teacher participation in our staff in-service work was originally entirely voluntary, and took place outside the ordinary working day. More recently, we have managed to pursue our staff sessions within the timetable and not in addition to the school day.

Overall, we feel encouraged and sense that we have chosen an important route towards the goals of effective learning based on shared responsibility.

Appendix 6.1
Questionnaires for different classes in the junior and senior high schools

A short letter to my English teacher

Dear _____,
    As I walked into the English class I quickly chose a chair near _____ because _____. To tell you the truth, I feel sort of _____. That's due to the fact that _____.

    Actually, I really _____English. I _____ listen to songs in English. (My favorite groups/singers are _____.) If you ask me to read _____ then I do just fine. But if I had to _____, I'm not sure I'd succeed.

    This year, I would like to improve my _____.

    I can do this if you _____, and if I PROMISE MYSELF _____.

    I am the kind of student that other teachers usually _____ because_____.

    You will probably soon notice that I rarely/often _____ and that is because _____.

    A class which is _____ really disturbs me. On the other hand, if there is _____, _____ and _____ then I can concentrate on what we are doing.

    I like to work with other students who _____ and who can_____.

    Hopefully we will all have a good study year. I wish you a good year with our class.

    Sincerely,

A letter/questionnaire to pupils

Dear pupil,
Please read and answer the following to help us plan together with you the term's work. Remember: there is no one right answer! The answers relate to your own feelings and position regarding your English studies.

1. If I have to write something in English:
   a) I'll have no problem writing it.
   b) I'll ask someone else to write it for me.
   c) I'll write it even though I know there will be mistakes.
   d) other? _____

2. When I speak English, I feel:
   a) ok.

   b) confident/comfortable.
   c) foolish.
   d) other? _____

3. If an English-speaking tourist stopped me and asked me for information I would (tick off as many as are right for you):
   a) try to listen and understand the question.
   b) tell the tourist I don't speak English.
   c) try to give the information with gestures and a few words.
   d) smile and walk away.
   e) explain as well as I could.
   f) find someone who speaks English to help him/her.
   g) other? _____

4. There's an interesting article in the daily English-language newspaper. I:
   a) would look for a similar article in the Hebrew language press to read.
   b) would try to read the article with the help of my dictionary.
   c) would read to get the general idea.
   d) would ask an English-speaking friend to read it to me.
   e) other? _____

5. Please tick off the statements that are right for you!
   a) I'm afraid to speak English.
   b) I feel that my English has improved.
   c) If I had an English-speaking friend abroad, I would write to him or her in English.
   d) Reading an article in English is impossible/very difficult/manageable for me.
   e) English is one of my favorite subjects.
   f) We should not be required to study English.
   g) I hope to improve my English this year.
   h) I am ready to spend time doing English assignments if I know it will help me progress.
   i) I am planning to sit for the matriculation exam.
   j) I enjoy/don't enjoy reading library books in English.

GRADING: In my opinion, a fair grade is based on:

__ % Classroom behavior (come on time, participate, listen quietly, work well alone and with others, bring your school things, etc.)
__ % Homework (quality, neatly done, handed in on time)
__ % Short quizzes (grammar, spelling, comprehension)
__ % Exams
__ % Effort (you know your weaknesses and try to overcome them; your assignments show thoughtfulness, care and work; you ask questions for clarification, help others)
__ % Individual progress

Appendix 6.2
Self-evaluation/course evaluation

Name: _____ Home room class: _____

1. My progress/achievement in: (excellent; very good; good; fair; poor)
   a) understanding conversational speech   _____
   b) speaking   _____
   c) reading   _____
   d) structure of English/ grammar   _____
   e) independence in working in English   _____

2. The following contributed (+) did not contribute (−) to my progress:
   a) Reading passages   _____
   b) Class/group discussions   _____
   c) Library books/extensive reading   _____
   d) Writing tasks/exercises   _____
   e) Language study   _____
   f) Individual journals   _____
   g) Pair/group tasks   _____
   h) Literature study   _____
   i) Individual homework assignments   _____
   j) other? _____   _____

3. I would like more of _____.
   I would like less of _____.

4. a) Do you think we have enough oral/aural activities? (yes/no)
   b) Do you find it hard to speak/express yourself in English? (yes/no)
      If your answer is 'Yes', how can I help you?

   c) What helps you most in understanding speech? (teacher talk; pupil
      conversations; taped readings; TV programmes; conversations with
      English speaking young people, etc.)?

   d) Do you feel we have (too much; sufficient; not enough) homework?

7 Refining negotiated classroom work in a Spanish secondary school

Isabel Serrano-Sampedro

My concern with trying to involve learners in decisions related to their learning process in the classroom goes back to my first years as a teacher. My efforts stemmed from a deep dissatisfaction with the methodologies I had experienced, first as a student of foreign languages and later as a teacher. Such methodologies seemed to me too directive, since they proposed the same treatment for obviously diverse people with different learning needs. At the same time, they seemed to foster the idea of the teacher as 'actor' and of the learners as a captive audience that has to be engaged in a timed sequence of teacher-directed activities, whose purpose students often cannot see. This seemed to me to be at odds with some of the stated curricular aims, namely those concerned with the development of learners as critical, self-sufficient, but co-operative people.

However, it was not until 1986 that I started involving learners in negotiation across all aspects of the curriculum. The experience as such started in the form of negotiated project work, and later developed into a more flexible framework.

On the theoretical side, I was influenced by the concept of language learning as the development of communicative competence (Hymes, 1971; Canale and Swain, 1980) and of learning as learner construction (Ausubel, 1963; Novak and Gowin, 1984). I was also influenced by the findings of studies on factors that may foster the development of such competence in the classroom (Varonis and Gass, 1983; Long and Porter, 1985; Pica and Doughty, 1985; Porter, 1986; and later M. Long, 1989; Pica *et al.*, 1989).

On the practical side, I saw the need to facilitate the development of learners as communicators in a context where success and teacher survival depend on his or her ability to cope with the following contextual constraints:

- A foreign language is a compulsory subject in Spanish schools; its importance for communication across cultures and for their professional future is acknowledged by most learners. However, in reality few are willing to invest the necessary effort. This is sometimes aggravated by a story of failure in language learning.

- Classes have an average of 30 or more pupils, although occasionally groups of 20–25 are possible.
- In addition to diversity in cognitive abilities, even in a single first-year class, it is quite common to find students with a range of proficiency that goes from no knowledge of English to a pre-intermediate level.
- Lack of a good working atmosphere and resulting discipline problems mainly derive from an interaction of the above factors.

My objective was to create a framework that allowed for more effective learning, through learner participation and the attention to learner diversity within the context of the official curriculum. At the beginning, I borrowed and adapted different ideas from different approaches: Counselling Learning, Villégier and Gauthier's Expression Libre, the Silent Way, the Bangalore project, general humanistic pedagogy, teachers of other subjects working on learning through discovery, classroom projects, etc. However, the most direct and decisive influences on the experience in its latest form were the process syllabus (Breen and Candlin, 1980; Breen, 1984; Candlin, 1984; Breen 1987) on the theoretical level and, later, Leni Dam's work with Danish secondary students, on the practical level (Dam and Gabrielsen, 1988; Dam 1995; 1999). Reading about the process syllabus provided me with theoretical support for my views, and a framework for classroom planning where my ideas and personal aims could be easily accommodated. Watching videos and reading about Leni Dam's experience, and later direct contact with her work, provided lots of information and ideas on how to implement a process syllabus in the classroom. It provided an important direction for me and a source of ideas that I could try and adapt to my own teaching environment.

The concept of negotiation and the curriculum context

I see negotiation as a basic tool to create learning opportunities, and it functions as a catalyst for the development of the learners' communicative ability since, from the beginning, the negotiation is attempted in the target language. For me, negotiation takes place within the context of the official exam at the end of studies at the upper secondary level. Negotiation seems to enable every student to achieve the aims of the official curriculum by engaging his or her personal objectives, knowledge and ability, with the support of classmates and the teacher.

The curriculum in its official form identifies as the main purposes for the teaching of foreign languages the development of the students as communicators in written and spoken language and as language learners, as well as for their personal growth. Some detailed specifications (fewer than many teachers would like) are given in the curriculum in the form of topics, functions, morphosyntactic elements, types of text, skills, attitudes, etc. but it leaves some space for the learners' individual needs and interests, and it mentions learner autonomy as something to be developed.

The negotiation takes place within this framework. The official specifications are always taken as a point of reference, either as the starting point for planning classroom activity ('What aspects of this are a priority for me/us at the moment? How are we going to work on them?') or as a checklist for evaluation at the end of it ('Which of these aspects have we covered? How well have I grasped them? Do I need to work further on them?'). Negotiation is also used as a tool to solve any problems that may arise during the whole process, such as keeping to deadlines, quantity and quality of work, group conflicts, or a fair and organised use of the limited resources available. The evaluation of the process and learner assessment also involve a substantial amount of negotiation.

My role in the negotiation is to provide the learners with various types of information regarding objectives, activities, materials and ways of working – or any other aspects they may need – and to support them in their reflection process by highlighting possible priorities, alternatives, consequences of certain decisions and so on. Both my learners and I argue our positions, but it is the learners who decide in the end what is going to be done and how; they then have full responsibility for their decisions.

The procedures and rhythms in introducing negotiation have been many and varied, both through time and across groups, adapting to different needs and situations. They have been determined by factors such as age, whether the learners have had previous experience with the approach and for how long, their disposition to learning, previous knowledge of the language, the particular group dynamics, group size, specific curricular aims and, very importantly, my own learning process and evolution.

The process

There is insufficient space to give a detailed account of all the procedures employed in my classes. Instead, a description of those used with a typical first-year group is provided. Such a class is usually made up of 30 or more 14 to 15-year-old mixed-ability students with a varied knowledge of English and with no experience in a negotiated curriculum.

At the first stage, my classroom aims are:

- to find out as much as possible about the learners' previous experience and knowledge, about their characteristics as learners and the group dynamics in the class;
- to allow the learners to become familiarised with:
  - the curricular aims and criteria for evaluation (institutional requirements);
  - alternative types of activities, which are of a more communicative nature than those they might be used to;
  - alternative ways of going about learning a language;
  - the different resources available and their effective use;
- to encourage the learners to get involved in a process of decision-making about what to learn when and how, and of evaluation of both processes and products of their learning.

At the beginning the learners are engaged in one or several activities to get to know each other, to reflect on their previous experience in language learning, and to identify some of their needs and interests. Then they are provided with a simplified version of the curricular requirements. Once these have been briefly discussed, a series of preliminary general agreements are made concerning the general approach to assessment, resources available, materials they will need to bring, etc.

From that point the procedure varies. For example, if there is a majority of zero English students/false beginners I may start with simple activities, often games they play in their native language (for examples see Figure 7.1), which allow them to communicate what they know, think or feel with very limited linguistic resources, sometimes single words.

If the group is mainly composed of false beginners or above and they are not unfamiliar with a more communicative methodology, I may start by asking them to decide which topic of those proposed by the curriculum they want to start with and then proceed in a way similar to the one illustrated in Appendix 7.1. In all cases, after each activity has been completed, learners are asked to reflect on what they have done, what it has been useful for (for them personally and with respect to the demands of the curriculum), what difficulties they had, how such difficulties have been or could be overcome, etc.

If, on the other hand, they are used to depending almost completely on the teacher, I may give them a written text or a recording and a series of related activities they can choose from, depending on what objective

---

- **A traditional game**

Learners are asked the following three questions. They use their dictionaries, classmates and the teacher to find out the equivalent English words and their pronunciation.

  – Which is your favourite animal? Think of three characteristics of that animal.
  – Which is your second favourite animal? Think of three characteristics.
  – Which is your third favourite animal? Think of three of its characteristics.

Learners share their choices. After the first learner has told the class / small group, learners are told what each animal corresponds to:

  1st animal: how you see yourself.
  2nd animal: how others see you.
  3rd animal: what you are really like.

Then the rest of the learners share their choices.

- **What things are in fashion and what aren't? (Girls' magazine).**
- **Your dream boy or girl. (Teenage magazine)**
- **What makes you afraid? (Sunday colour supplement)**
- **What makes you feel happy / angry / uncomfortable? (Young people's magazine)**
- **Do boys have the same rules at home as we have? (Girls' magazine)**

Figure 7.1   Examples of initial activities for real beginners

they want to focus on. On another occasion I may suggest an objective, a task and a procedure and let the learners suggest a topic or select one from a given set. Later, I may ask them to choose the objective and task, and negotiate the procedure (see Serrano-Sampedro, 1992; 1993). In all cases tasks are followed by a joint evaluation of the decisions taken in relation to the objectives proposed.

Learners are also encouraged to bring to class examples of English-language texts of recordings (T-shirt messages, labels, instructions, slogans, magazines, books, songs, etc.). If this appeals to a particular class or group of learners, it is also used as another means to introduce learners to decision-making, by asking them to think what this material might be good for, and to decide what they want to do with it.

Alongside this process, I gradually introduce new ways of working and using the resources available by drawing on the students' experience as learners and by suggesting that they try alternatives provided by other learners or myself. As learners progress in their knowledge and understanding of the alternatives available in what to work on and how to work, their freedom of choice increases. They become used to handling different types of decisions that are normally in the hands of teachers and textbook writers, they become confident and experienced, and they proceed to design their own learning plans using the official curriculum as a point of reference (for an example of such a plan, see Appendix 7.2). The structure of these plans is suggested by me at the start, but as time passes it may vary to suit the needs and preferences of different groups of learners.

My experience has benefited from the assumption that for the learners to be able to plan their own learning they require not only the opportunity to do it, but also information on how to design their plans. This information guides each of the following key phases in the whole process:

- How can students select and formulate their objectives, and what the alternatives are.
- What activities can, in principle, help them reach those objectives.
- What procedures can be followed to carry out those activities, and how best can they choose among those procedures according to their aims.
- What materials would be most appropriate (having their availability as one more factor in the negotiation) and how can they select an appropriate level of difficulty (conceptual or linguistic).
- How can they evaluate the efficiency of their decisions and the outcomes of their work.

It is the teacher's job to help the learners uncover this information and to support them in their decisions by pointing out factors to keep in mind, formulating questions they should ask themselves at each stage (if they do not yet do it spontaneously), and suggesting possible courses of action, alternative solutions to a situation or sources and resources that they may find useful. I now briefly describe each of the above phases in turn.

Formulating objectives

In my opinion, learners need to know at least three things in order to be able to formulate their objectives:

- What is required from them (achieved through the analysis and discussion of the official curriculum, both in large and small groups).
- What that involves (through the ongoing joint reflection on what 'knowing a language' means and how it can be learned).
- Where they stand with respect to those requirements (through reflection, self-evaluation, peer-evaluation and teacher-evaluation).

As a result of this process of reflection, my students take different starting points in designing their plans at different times. Figure 7.2 illustrates these alternative starting points.

- **Something they want or need to learn, improve, or develop.**
  Such as language skills, grammar points, vocabulary areas, formulaic language, spelling, pronunciation, intonation, discursive, strategic or sociolinguistic aspects, sociocultural knowledge, learning strategies, working methods, study skills, etc.
- **An activity or task they want to be able to carry out.**
  For example, to phone some institution asking for information or to write a report on a lab experiment.
- **A topic they want to do some research on.**
  Such as what people in the class spend their pocket money on, what values American TV series reflect, or how optic fibres work.
- **A piece of written or spoken English they want to understand, or something they want to communicate.**

Figure 7.2   Different starting points learners use in designing a plan

Students may start by looking at the curriculum and identifying a specific objective they need to work on (for example, learning to talk about relationships). Alternatively, they may decide to focus on an aspect they feel they have to improve (for example, text organisation or word order) after having received feedback on their recent productions. Instead, they may simply choose to work on something just for fun (for example, transcribing and translating a song or finding out what their schoolmates think about a particular issue). Later in their evaluations they analyse the learning outcomes of the chosen activity.

The objective they select is only a starting point. In reality, each plan necessarily works towards several objectives, either communicative or formal aspects of the language. If the activity chosen involves real communication, orally or in writing, specific objectives will appear integrated and several may be achieved at once. Figure 7.3 shows an example of this kind of activity.

On the other hand, learners may decide to work consciously and specifically on formal aspects as a preparation for or follow-up to a chosen communicative activity. I suggest to learners that even formal activities should be communicative to some extent. Figure 7.4 provides an example of a more formal activity.

Choosing activities

After formulating objectives, the next step is for the learners to find out what types of activities might help them better achieve these, being conscious that they cannot always expect immediate results.

This particular first year class has a link with a class in a Danish school. They received a letter asking them to send Information about a series of topics. This is the way we proceeded:

- Groups read letter.
- Class decide what they want to know about Denmark and the Danish students.
- Class write letter (simultaneously they find out how to write an informal letter in English).
- Topics are distributed among groups (groups negotiate who is going to do which).
- Students agree to display all the information in the form of a magazine.
- Each group decides how they are going to collect the information required by the Danish students, and how they are going to work. For example: the group in charge of 'Smoking and alcohol' decide to write a questionnaire and pass it around their friends and schoolmates, the 'Music' group choose oral interviews, the 'Indurain' group use Spanish magazines to document their essay on the Spanish cyclist, and so on.
- They all read all the productions and share views on them and how to improve them.
- The magazine is put together and sent to their correspondents.
- Groups reflect on what they learnt from the activity, what did and didn't work and why, and what can be learnt from that.

Figure 7.3   An example of activity around a communicative objective

Through the teacher's corrections of their drafts learners agree that although they *know* the Simple Present, they keep making mistakes all the time and they decide that they need some *practice*. After discussing with the teacher a series of alternatives, they decide each member of the group will write a series of questions like the ones illustrated below, they will exchange them and try to answer them.

Examples:

What happens in films when. . .
. . . a boy meets a girl?
. . . a door opens slowly?
. . . you see a wagon train going through a narrow pass ?
. . . the RAF pilot tells his girlfriend 'I'll see you this evening after the mission'?
. . . they think they've killed all the gremlins?
What does Tarzan do when a violent tribe kidnaps the girl?
What do you do when your father tells you you can't go out?
What does Madonna do at night?
. . .

Figure 7.4   An example of activity around a formal aspect

Each class gradually builds up a bank of types of activities and tasks formed by the kind they were familiar with before the experience, new activities suggested by the teacher and other sources, and those produced by the learners themselves. I encourage learners to choose, combine, adapt or design those they think more appropriate (for an example of learner designed activity, see Appendix 7.3). I also suggest that they choose activities that reflect real-life activities, although at the beginning they may be inclined to select those that have a more textbook style.

Working procedures

Two main types of procedures are considered. First, the actual steps that might be followed in order to carry out an activity. Alternative sequences are discussed first by the group members and then with the teacher; finally a decision is agreed on. Second, how to work on different aspects of the language in order to promote effective learning.

Each class gradually builds up a bank of ideas on working procedures with my help. The process of formation of these banks of 'Tricks', 'Tips to learn', 'Tips to improve', etc. starts when a need is detected, either by the teacher or by the learners, and it varies according to the origin of this need. For example, the starting point may be:

- A whole class reflection on possible ways of improving the ability to write or speak, to take part in conversation, to learn new vocabulary, etc. (What can you do in order to improve X?). This usually takes place at my initiative, as a way of involving learners in a revision of their current ways of working, and of providing them with alternative suggestions. It usually follows the observation of not very effective working methods on the part of a considerable number of learners.
- Learner difficulties detected from the evaluation of a particular activity. After a learner or group of learners have analysed their work and its outcomes, they may realise (spontaneously or with my help) that they need to modify their way of working.
- The search for solutions to a concrete problem a learner or group of learners meet in the implementation of a plan. Sometimes in the process learners come across a problem that has not been foreseen; for example, as a result of their work, they find themselves with more new words than expected, and they need to find out ways of storing and learning them that are effective and economical.

The result is a heterogeneous range of suggestions that learners are encouraged to try out, adopting those they consider most appropriate to their particular way of learning. Those suggestions come from a variety of sources: the learners themselves, the teacher or books they use for reference. Figure 7.5 provides an example of such suggestions.

Choosing materials

Learners are prompted to choose any piece of spoken or written English they find interesting or that suits their purposes. The materials they have access to are often of the kind addressed to a native audience of similar age and interests.

It is obviously very difficult to predict or grade the language the learners may find in such texts. The aim is to help them develop strategies to cope with materials not designed for the EFL classroom. A few teenage and general magazines, textbooks of different subjects for English teenagers, reference books, video and audio recordings are usually enough. The bank of materials is gradually increased, including contributions collected and produced by the learners.

Evaluation

Evaluation is a fundamental part of the learning process. However, procedures used for evaluation also constitute learning activities. They contribute to the development of the students as learners by helping raise their awareness of their own learning. They are also communicative activities in themselves, with a real purpose and a real audience.

Evaluation consists of the description of what the learners can or cannot do and to what degree, and of the analysis of the factors that may have contributed to speed up or slow down their progress. It involves reflection on the learning process and covers such issues as:

- Whether the chosen objectives, activities, materials, procedures, time distribution, personal strategies, etc. have been the most appropriate to the needs of the moment.
- Difficulties arising, their possible causes, and strategies used to overcome them.
- Whether the outcomes correspond in quantity and quality to what was planned.
- The role played by each of the participants (including the teacher).
- The possible incidence of external factors.

The degree of detail and the depth of the analysis learners undertake once they have implemented their plans depends on factors such as age or experience in working with this approach, among others; the type of questions that they try to answer also depends on these factors. However, they all respond to three basic questions: 'What worked

---

Tips for developing your listening comprehension ability
1ST RULE: DON'T GIVE UP!

- Relax.
- Closing your eyes may help you concentrate.
- Give yourself time to think / understand / remember:
  < Use the PAUSE button.
  < Replay as many times as you need.
  < In conversation, ask your interlocutor to repeat / explain / speak up, more slowly, etc. and check that you have understood correctly.
- Lip-read.
- Whatever you are doing, pay attention to pronunciation (e.g. check in the dictionary, take note of the pronunciation of difficult words, repeat to yourself, etc.).
- Listen to songs / recordings following the words in silence, focusing on how they are pronounced.
- Listen and imitate the sounds, rhythm, intonation.
- Try to visualise what you hear.
- Listen with a friend. (It's fun and you can help each other!)
- At first, listen to topics < you know a lot about.
                        < you are familiar with.
                        < that interest you.
- Focus on key words and try to imagine what it is about.
- When watching a video, try to deduce what they are talking about from what you see / hear:
  < the situation
  < who is speaking (relationship/age/clothes/attitude/feelings/. . .)
  < body language
  < tone of voice
  < intonation
- Find out what helps you most at each stage:
  < To read the transcript
      – before you listen.
      – after you have listened.
      – while you are listening.
  < Not to use the transcript at all.
  < To read a summary of what you are going to listen to.
  < To find out about the situation first.
- Borrow subtitled films from the library.   . . .

What other things can help you understand spoken English better?

Figure 7.5   An example of a bank of suggestions for developing listening comprehension skills

well?' 'What could be improved?' and 'How could it be improved'? The information collected through such questions informs future decisions. Later in the process learners are encouraged to design their own evaluation questionnaires. Periodically the general classroom process is also analysed, mainly through questionnaires, recordings, group and whole-class discussions with the teacher, and individual interviews.

The learners' satisfaction with their progress should be a valid enough criterion for success. However, in the context of Spanish secondary education, learners have to be assessed and given a mark three times a year with reference to a set of external criteria. This is ultimately inconsistent with asking students to take responsibility for their learning, and it is often felt so by the learners. I attempt to minimise this inconsistency by trying to involve learners as much as possible in all aspects of the process of assessment, from the identification of what to assess, how to assess it, through the process of test design and correction, to mark allocation.

Daily classroom interaction and work diaries (see the next section for details on these) often provide enough data to be able to allocate a mark without having to resort to tests. However, tests of different types and content are used for different reasons and purposes.

Class, group or individual tests are used to cater for the teacher's or the learners' psychological need to know where the students stand at a given time with respect to other learners, an external exam, or certificates issued by other institutions. For example, a test may be used as training for an external exam, and taking such an exam is often one of the learners' objectives.

Class tests (mostly teacher designed; mainly in student classes of 25 or more) are given to the students at my initiative or at their demand. Learners often show a preference for being assessed through tests rather than through self-evaluation or direct observation by the teacher or others. This is frequently justified by inertia ('That's the way it's always been done'), analogy with other subjects ('All the other teachers give us tests') or mistrust of the objectivity and reliability of other methods of assessment.

Group tests (teacher or learner designed) are given at the learners' demand at the end of one or a series of group plans (see Figure 7.6). The purpose is to find out how effective the plans have been, that is, whether the students have achieved their learning objectives and whether their working methods need to be improved. Students may or may not ask for this to be taken into account when their mark is allocated.

The introduction of self-assessment and peer-assessment is a gradual process whose rhythm is determined by the learners' response at each particular given moment. Figure 7.7 illustrates one of a variety of

This particular group had been working on the topic *Education*. They had decided to write a leaflet describing the ideal school. Later they had presented it orally to the class. They further agreed that at the end of the activity each member of the group would write questions for a test to be exchanged amongst them. These are some of the questions they came up with:

Mathematics is a very difficult school . . .
We can't swim here because this school hasn't got a . . .
Every two lessons we have a 20 . . .
If you don't study you get bad . . .
Which is your favourite subject? Why?
Who is your favourite teacher? Why?
Describe the ideal teacher.
What do bad teachers do?
What subjects should the ideal school have?
Who should be the boss in the ideal school? Why?
Give me three rules for teachers.
Describe your ideal classroom.
Give me three reasons to ban examinations.
Homework is rubbish. Explain that.
. . .

Figure 7.6   An example of a group test

Stage 1:   learners are asked to provide a global mark based on partial marks allocated by the teacher to each section of the test.
Stage 2:   learners give partial marks to each section of the test, and then a global mark, applying teacher adaptations of the official criteria.
Stage 3:   learners are involved in the design of the criteria and apply them to provide both the partial and global marks.

Figure 7.7   An example of one approach used in introducing self-assessment

techniques used. The aspects that are usually taken into account in such assessment are:

- the progress of learners with respect to their starting point;
- the level of proficiency reached by the learners with respect to the official requirements for each year/cycle;
- the amount and quality of learner work and participation.

The weight given to each of these elements on the mark is also a matter of negotiation, although constrained by the official requirements (for example, the second point is given more importance in the end-of-studies exam than in compulsory education). The final mark therefore usually reflects a combination of self-evaluation, peer-evaluation and teacher-evaluation.

Other resources in the process

Two important resources are group work and work diaries. Group work provides the learners with an opportunity for verbal interaction and peer help and for collective reflection on the language and its learning, among other things. Work diaries act as field logs that support students in their exploration of the new language and of their ability as language learners.

Grouping is flexible in the sense that it responds to different criteria depending on different purposes, at different times. Group changes may take place at the learners' request or at my suggestion, but they always have to be justified and it is for the learners to decide the course of action.

Learners are asked to keep a work diary in their notebooks; this is complemented by a cassette that contains oral productions. Work diaries have a double purpose: to serve as a useful learning tool and as an important source of data on the individual and group process. It is supposed to include their plans and agreements plus anything they do to learn the language. A common structure for the diary is provided at the beginning, but the students are encouraged to modify that structure according to their individual needs. Figure 7.8 illustrates one such common structure (for a page from a learner's diary, see Appendix 7.4).

The number of learners I am responsible for determines the frequency with which I have access to the diaries. Parts of them are revised during normal classroom activity, such as when I am called by an individual or a group to discuss their plans, to solve a doubt or to provide feedback on their productions. When time allows, the notebooks are collected periodically in small numbers; otherwise this is substituted by group sessions with the teacher where diaries are jointly analysed. In both cases the learners receive feedback not so much on their production as on the way they seem to be working. All work diaries are also collected three times a year before assessment is due. This review is not as detailed and it aims at getting an overall impression of how the learner works and whether there has been an improvement.

The difficulties of the process

The main difficulties encountered over the years have been those derived from administering the introduction of change. Sometimes it is

Date
(Other information is sometimes included, such as the weather, class news,
  personal news, . . .)

Plan for today
(What are they going to do, what for, who with, on what materials, etc.)

Class work
(Their written work, a summary of or a commentary on what they have listened
  to, etc.)

Class notes
(Notes on the vocabulary, grammar structures they found, pronunciation, etc.)

Evaluation (at the end of an activity)
(The answer to some of these questions or similar ones: What was good? What
  was bad? Why? What difficulties did I have? Why? How did I solve them?
  What can I do to solve them? What did I learn? etc.)

Plan for homework
(What they are going to do and why)

Homework
(What they have done, notes or comments on it)

Doubts to refer to the teacher
(Those for which there was no time during the lesson or those that arose from
  their homework and they could not solve by themselves)

Figure 7.8   Work diary: a suggested structure

difficult to determine whether these difficulties derive from the approach
itself or from the teacher's lack of experience. Introducing negotiated
work in the classroom is necessarily a slow process in which teacher and
learners become familiar with their respective functions in constant
interaction. Some of the difficulties I have encountered are briefly
summarised below.

The learners' preconceptions of language and how it is learned

> I prefer having things explained and exercises set.
>
> (First-year student, aged 14 years)

This is one of the first things my learners and I have to cope with.
Previous language teaching may have led them to think that learning a
language consists of memorising a number of question–answer exchanges and/or a list of structures, and a list of vocabulary. This idea

seems to have been conceived not so much through the way they were taught as through the way they were tested.

For many of them 'passing' is equated to 'learning', so making the effort to develop their ability to communicate in the classroom does not seem to them as profitable initially as learning by heart the night before a test.

The new way of working breaks the rules of the game. The teacher does not do what she or he is expected to do, and students may refuse to adopt an active role in their learning simply because it requires more effort. They are satisfied with the way things were before and still are in other school subjects.

The tension between choice and a sense of direction

> I never know what to do next. (First-year student)

The freedom to choose is a challenge to learners who depend upon the teacher to provide a sense of direction and a feeling of progress. This was a big problem at the beginning. As I became more experienced in supporting learners in their decisions, it almost disappeared. Now only occasionally does a learner claim to be adrift, usually as a justification of his or her opting out at the beginning.

Knowing when to intervene

> Sometimes I would like the teacher to impose more things.
> (First-year student)

Perhaps one of the biggest challenges for me has been to find the appropriate rhythm, in different cases, in the introduction of negotiation and increased autonomy for the learner. This is again an area that improves with experience. Teachers have to learn to accept the learners' refusal to work in the way they propose and be ready to provide them with what they need and/or demand at each stage but, at the same time, introducing them gradually into the new ways and ideas.

Evaluation

> I enjoy working in groups and choosing what to do, and I think I'm learning a lot, but I hate doing evaluations.
> (First-year student)

The more my younger learners enjoy what they are doing, the less ready they seem to be initially to look back at what they have done or to think about what they are doing. Helping them to focus on reflection and evaluation of their learning process was a hard job at the beginning of the experience. It had to be approached from the point of view of helping learners realise its usefulness and find their own ways of doing it.

Coping with large numbers

> The teacher cannot always give the attention we need. Too many groups, too little time. (First-year student)

This way of working certainly allows the teacher to pay much more attention to individual needs than more teacher directed approaches. However, the follow-up of and attention to each learner is still difficult in a class of 30, especially with younger students. With time I have found out ways of maximising the time available so that it is still possible, if not easy, to keep a balance between self-direction, support and control.

One such way is involving learners in the development of class norms, aimed at a more effective use of time and resources. For example, solutions can take the form of peer correction or not calling the teacher every time they have a doubt, but trying to solve the problem by consulting reference books or asking other learners; if it is still un-resolved, to take a note of it and carry on working till they have accumulated several doubts or have finished their work. Another way is to develop more effective and economic follow-up techniques on the part of the teacher, such as group analysis of work or carrying around the class all the original group plans and writing quick notes on the process and performance of each group and its members on the back of those plans.

The advantages of the process

I have found that the degree of acceptance of the approach by the learners was quite satisfactory from the beginning of the experience. However, the learners' reaction (collected through direct observation, questionnaires, interviews, class and group discussions, written reports, etc.) has ranged from enthusiastic acceptance to blunt rejection.

The latter cases have been few and have almost disappeared in the last few years. This may be explained partly by my improvement in introducing negotiation and helping learners to act in more autonomous ways in the classroom. The gradual incorporation of the other teachers in the department into the scheme, assuring a certain continuity in the approach, may have been another important determining factor.

The advantages of working within the framework of negotiation are acknowledged by the clear majority of the learners and by fellow teachers who have tried to apply it. Advantages that have been identified include the following:

- It allows learners to work in different ways and at different rhythms in accordance with their needs and interests. As a consequence, their sense of progress and achievement increases and so does their motivation.
- While learners work in groups the teacher can give more individual attention. This facilitates the attention to learner diversity: learning styles, rhythms, needs, interests, etc.
- Both teacher and learners feel more relaxed in class, and a better atmosphere for learning is created.
- The learners' self-confidence increases. They show more initiative in communication and in organising their work.
- They learn from their classmates and a variety of sources, they co-operate with other students to learn better.
- They learn to learn a foreign language. They solve problems, foresee them, identify advantages and disadvantages of alternatives, take into account contextual limitations (for example, suitability of available recorded material) and act to overcome them. They work harder and more effectively (which usually results in better learning).
- They show more curiosity for the language and its learning, and more interest in being precise.
- They show more awareness of their learning process, including the relationship between what they do or do not do and their progress and what they need to do next. They evaluate their own and their classmates' production, and the teaching–learning process itself.
- More direct interaction allows the teacher to obtain a great quantity of information on the learning process in the class.
- There are more opportunities for 'real' interaction which favours a holistic approach to language learning.

(for some examples of learner feedback comments, see Appendix 7.5)

Some broader considerations

The outcomes are many and difficult to report and can only be summarised in this chapter. From my point of view, especially interesting have been those outcomes derived from attempting a negotiated syllabus within the framework of an institutional curriculum.

In primary and secondary schools

All the apparently limiting factors – such as the existence of an official syllabus, or the need for final-year students to prepare for a university-entry exam – have, in practice, had a positive influence upon the negotiation process. Apart from providing learners with a sense of guidance, a map in which they could draw their own learning route and a checklist for self-evaluation, they have contributed valuable learning opportunities for both the learners and myself. These were derived, for example, from the attempt to solve conflicts between the aims and content of the curriculum and the needs and interests of particular learners at a given time.

The experience also suggests that, in Spanish secondary schools, a negotiated classroom process can help in ways that are more effective and less exhausting for the teacher dealing with endemic problems such as large classes, diversity of student levels and lack of motivation. Its suitability to meet the new curricular demands has also been probed and found to be very appropriate.

Finally, such negotiation has proved to have enormous potential as a classroom-research and teacher-development tool. The approach sheds light on many aspects of the learning process – both individual and collective – which are usually hidden under uniform, teacher-directed instruction. This allows for the development of more realistic learning plans, and the parallel development of the teacher as facilitator. I am encouraged to look at the teaching–learning process from a different point of view and, like the learner, I get involved in constant problem-solving activity. The permanent need for refinement and adaptation of procedures creates a certain habit of flexibility which I believe is beneficial to a teacher's own professional development.

Note on appendices

The examples are a selection from a group of first-year students during their first term.

Appendix 7.1
An example of a learning plan jointly developed by learners and teacher starting from one of the topics suggested in the official curriculum

- Learners select topic: family relationships.
- Brainstorming: What do I want to be able to say/write about that?
  In this case, learners suggest three aspects and agree that different groups will work on different things and will share their findings:
  - Members of the family;
  - What they are like;
  - Family problems.
- Brainstorming: What do families argue about?
- Learners suggest the following (when learners do not know how to say it they ask 'What's the English for . . .?' or 'How do you say . . . in English?' When they do not understand they ask 'What does that mean?' or such like):
  - Doing the housework;
  - Money: unemployment, pocket money, price of things, inheritance;
  - Who your friends are;
  - The time to be back home in the evening;
  - Relationships among brothers and sisters;
  - Using the telephone;
  - Choosing TV programmes; zapping;
  - Loud music;
  - Keeping your room tidy;
  - Drugs and alcohol;
  - Parents' arguments; divorce;
  - Using the bathroom;
  - Clothes you wear;
  - Grandparents living in the house;
  - Where to sit at the table, in the living room, etc.;
  - Opening the door, answering the phone, putting the rubbish out, etc.
- Groups are formed around their preferred topics.
- Brainstorming: What are we going to present to the class?
  - an essay
  - a news item
  - a letter (to a friend, advice column, . . .)
  - a page from a personal journal
  - a leaflet
  - soap opera (a scene from . . .)
  - an interview
  - a report (fireman, police, social worker, . . .)
  - a poem
  - a phone-in programme (radio)

  . . .
- Groups do their detailed planning.
  - Group A: My family.
    Oral presentation based on family photographs at weddings (who they are, personality, etc.). Improvised from notes.

- Group B: Arriving late at night.
  A sketch. Written, recorded and played to the class.
- Group C: Parents' arguments; divorce.
  Phone-in programme. Recorded and played to the class. Improvised from notes.
- Group D: Zapping; drugs; loud music.
  News items. Written and read aloud to the class.
- Group E: Brothers and sisters.
  Survey in the class. Questionnaire, interviews and oral report. Improvised notes.
- Group F: Avoiding problems.
  Leaflet ('30 ways of avoiding opening the door, answering the phone, taking the rubbish out, . . .'). Read by the class, then oral discussion.
- A deadline is agreed.
- Learners implement their plans.
- Decisions and outcomes are evaluated.

Appendix 7.2
A learner-designed plan

First-year students, 14-year-old, beginners; first plan, after twenty lessons.

GROUP 3D   DATE November 9th
GROUP MEMBERS' NAMES: Mario
                        Noemi
                        Vanesa

- What do you want to find out about, improve, develop or learn?
    we want to learn to talk about travelling

- What are you going to do to achieve this? Who is going to do what and when.
    we are going to write a leaflet
    we are going to record a Radio programme
    – choose one city, Paris
    – we are going to speak about Paris
    – about tradition and its hotels
    – we are going to write texts
            Mario: hotels and introduction
            Vanessa: places you can visit
            Noemi: travelling to Paris

- What do you need to do this?
    we need brochures about Paris

- How are you going to share your work with the rest of the class?
    we are going to play the cassette and give them the leaflet

- How many lessons do you need?   six lessons

- What deadline have you set?

Appendix 7.3
A learner-designed activity

First-year students, 14-year-old beginners

Names:	Santi
	Jesus
	Jorge
Activity:	A radio interview to a football supporters and hooligans
	— Jesus will be the interviewer
	— He will write the questions
	— Jorge will be the hooligan
	— Santi will be the supporter
	— We will answers Jesus' questions
	— We prepare the questions and the answers together
	— The teacher revises
	— We rehearse pronunciation
	— We record the interview
	— We play it to the class

Appendix 7.4
A page from a learner's diary

First-year student, 14-year-old beginner; English words in brackets are the learner's own additions.

Date: Monday, 6th May

Today is cold
It's very windy
Class news: A good new: we hadn't class of Spanish Personal (class) news: I am going to buy a present for Sylvia tommorow

PLAN: We are going to record a story of love because we (are) won't learn to speak

HOMEWORK: I am going to do the evaluation of my plan for today.

Evaluation. This activity (is use) has been useful because we will wan to speak in English. Today we had recorded 'To our way', and the next day we correct the pronunciation.
This activity has been very nice because we have participated well. (My) I like this activity.

           VOCABULARY
Way → manera   Part → papel (en teatro)
Participate → participar
  I am going to revise my part of the story
  I had ingestivated the pronunciation of the difficults words.

Date: Friday, 10th May

I feel tired because I have sleep and I feel happy because tomorrow is Sarturday and is a holiday.
PLAN:
    correct the story
    pronunciation the story
CLASS NOTES:
    Pr – do/does   A Jewish man (adjective)
    Past – did   A Jew (nombre)
    Fut – will + inf   She guessed, she thought she knew (ella adivino)
      Youcan't deceive me → no puede enganarme
      Don't try to deceive me → no trate de enganarme
      TO → 'a' → direccion
HOMEWORK: I'm going to do the conclusion of correct and pronunciation of story.

Conclusion. These activities has been useful, because I learn my mistake and try of correct. Pronunciation is useful because I improve my speak English.

I'm going to write a fine copy of the story '(One) Impossible love'

Appendix 7.5
Learner feedback comments

Translated from Spanish. First-year students, aged 14 years.

- We learn having fun instead of learning sentences by heart.
- I am more relaxed speaking English with my group mates.
- Being able to work in groups we learn what each of us needs.
- I learn in a different way without so much dependence from the teacher.
- We learn more, and more useful things.
- The teacher is really interested in our learning.
- I've learned more than last year. Last year I knew some ready-made sentences. This year I know how to form them myself, although I have grammar mistakes.
- Now I read quicker and better, and I have improved my writing a lot, although I still have many mistakes . . . I think I've learned much more because with this system you learn from your own mistakes, because with the book you swot, you learn the units by heart without knowing how to use it.
- At the beginning of the year I found this system a bit strange an I thought I would not learn much . . . As time went by I realised it wasn't a bad system and that I was learning new things. I think the whole class had that problem. With the systems I had followed before in French, I think I wouldn't have been able to express myself or read books, but of course I would have memorised more content.

Part 2 Accounts of practice in tertiary institutions

Overview

In this part of the volume, the focus moves from demands of working with children in schools to the very different arena of introducing negotiation with adults in the context of tertiary education. The chapters as a whole relate to different aspects of this: fulfilling academic course requirements in university settings (Chapters 8, 10 and 12), addressing the demands of what are most usually known as courses in English for special purposes, including academic purposes (Chapters 9, 10, 11 and 13) and language courses in language institutions (Chapter 12).

In Chapter 8, which opens this part of the volume, Stefaan Slembrouck provides a frank and honest account of what happened when he endeavoured to introduce negotiation into a final-year university course at the University of Gent, Belgium. Despite initial scepticism and opposition from his colleagues, Slembrouck was given carte blanche to develop a new approach to a course which had failed badly the previous year. In many respects, Slembrouck reports, the course seemed an ideal candidate for successful negotiation: it was the final language course the students would take, it had been created upon the demands of the students, and the course was to be short and therefore necessitated a focus directly relevant to the students. In reality however, Slembrouck experienced numerous problems in introducing negotiation with the students – and his analysis of why this is the case – is a salutary reminder of the complexities of any teaching–learning situation which need to be borne in mind.

Slembrouck discusses in particular the notion of a dominant educational culture and how this served to undermine his plans for negotiated work. Part of this was the institutional culture, as initially evidenced by the reaction of his colleagues when he expressed the desire to negotiate the course structure and content. More significant for Slembrouck, however, was the educational culture of the students which, he says, favoured a more conservative approach. Slembrouck traces the origins of this to a number of factors including the demands upon students to find their way through the examination system, the apparent conflict in the roles of the lecturer as evaluator and co-participant in the classroom and a closed world of peer relations. More profoundly, however, Slembrouck argues, the manner in which youngsters are progressively silenced in the classroom as they move through the various stages of their educational career means that many learn to adopt a position of 'comfortable safety' in silence. For Slembrouck, therefore, one of the major challenges of introducing negotiation is the need to take account of the students' preconceived views of appropriate classroom behaviour. Slembrouck's account is a timely reminder of the significance of unseen elements in education: the culture of the institution and the culture of the students, both of which frame their interpretation of educational experience. His account also underlines the essential requirement of creating a sense of trust in a situation where, due to the nature of the institution, power imbalances are built into the very fabric of classroom work.

Part of the problem which Slembrouck faced may have been ameliorated by a more gradualist or a more selective focus in initially introducing negotiation and this may explain why the remaining accounts in this part describe more successful, though no less challenging, outcomes for introducing negotiation.

In Chapter 9, Elaine Martyn reports on introducing negotiation into her work in designing a language course for a school of nursing in Pakistan. Her account details how, over a three-month planning period, the proposed content of the course was negotiated through three-way discussions with three stakeholders who had an interest in the outcomes of the course: herself as English teacher, nursing professionals and the nursing students. The initial impetus in doing this derived from her realisation that negotiation was the only viable way forward, as she would be running a course to meet communication needs in an area she knew little about. Negotiation, however, proved not only to be the key to developing a richer, more appropriate course design, but also had an impact in enhancing the status of nurses through a realisation on the part of senior medical staff that nurses were capable of producing, for example, high calibre reports. Martyn's account shows how respect for the differing realms of expertise and rights of all participants is important, and how all participants in negotiation must be working towards the same goal: to accomplish what is wanted and what is achievable.

The next three chapters in this part all focus on a detailed description of a practical approach towards working with negotiation. Each chapter shows how negotiation is selectively introduced into one aspect of the course design: defining purposes (Chapter 10), defining contents of an assignment (Chapter 11) and defining evaluation criteria (Chapter 12).

Working in Brazil, Eddie Edmundson and Steve Fitzpatrick address in Chapter 10 the difficult area of assisting students in expressing their wants and needs at the start of a course in a language centre, in this case with learners at an elementary level of English. The 'Learning needs Analysis through Pictures' or 'LAP' procedure which they describe is an innovative device, reminiscent of Freire's (1970) seminal work in using icons in the development of adult literacy. Here, however, pictures are used as a flexible tool to help students articulate their perceived reasons of difficulty, feelings, wants and needs in English. Edmundson and Fitzpatrick suggest that the procedure is an important element in creating a sense of community and trust in the group and in building feelings of self-esteem, which in the case of many adult learners has been severely bruised by previous 'failure' in learning.

Chapters 11 and 12 both report on work in institutions of higher education in the United States. Wendy Newstetter's account in Chapter 11 describes a procedure for identifying a focus for classroom work, although in this case it is the course assignments which are of concern. Echoing Martyn's worry about her lack of expertise in the students' area of work, Newstetter describes a procedure she uses to enable students to research the types of writing they will need to do in their work as engineers, and then to argue for a particular piece of writing to be used as a basis for their assignment. We also find echoes in her account of the dominant culture which Slembrouck describes and students' previous learning experiences as a constraint in introducing negotiation. Newstetter reports that one of the greatest difficulties she has faced is simply in 'getting the students to hear': that is, in getting the students to grasp the concept of negotiation and to realise that they have a voice in shaping their work. Newstetter's strategy in overcoming this seems, however, to be to make negotiation and shared decision-making a *requirement* of the course, that is it is simply not possible for students to complete the course without taking direct responsibility for their own learning. This, she reports has led to positive gains in three major aspects: quality of the students' work, variety of work and student response.

In Chapter 12, Margaret Sokolik also focuses on the development of writing abilities but this time in the context of academic literacy and the evaluation of student coursework. Sokolik outlines a practical approach to evolving a shared understanding of the criteria for the evaluation of student written work, and a means by which a grade can be negotiated and assigned. Through this procedure, Sokolik argues, her students develop a greater sense of personal investment in their work and a deeper understanding of the requirements of academic work. Sokolik also refers to the 'hidden messages' that may be present in students' self-evaluations, which may be illuminated through the discussion surrounding the determination of a grade. Once again, a key contribution of the negotiative process may lie in bringing to the surface differences that may exist between the perceptions of teachers and students over the value of classroom work.

The theme of the cultural context for negotiation returns in the final chapter in this part (Chapter 13). Like most of the writers so far, Lucy Norris and Susan Spencer recognised heterogeneity in course participants' experiences and learning needs as inevitably entailing the need for explicit negotiation about course content and classroom activities and tasks. As organisers of a course providing pre-departure English for academic studies in Australian universities, they felt that the experience of negotiation would also prepare participants for some of the expectations they would confront as students in an essentially Western academic context. The challenge for them was to facilitate such overt participation in the teaching–learning process on behalf of teachers whom they knew to hold views on the authority status and role of the teacher that were distinct from assumed 'western' notions of the facilitative, decision-sharing and interdependent teacher. They identified the issue of mutual respect among the participants for their own prior knowledge and competencies in such fields as mechanical engineering, Balinese dancing, domestic architecture or organisation management as the springboards for open and willing negotiation about the course. They therefore opened the course with a significant amount of time devoted to the sharing of skills across the group. In essence, the teachers provided classes for each other on whatever interested sufficient numbers of people.

In addition to this initiative, Norris and Spencer adopted the ongoing strategies of providing choice in classroom tasks authentic to the academic context to which the participants were going, forming study groups which designed language-learning tasks for their colleagues on identified areas of difficulty in English and maintained regular evaluation of how the course was unfolding through participant journals and personal interviews. A major outcome from the experience was the participants' recognition of themselves as having significant competencies and the capacity to learn in autonomous ways as opposed to their initial self-perception as language learners with problems.

For Norris and Spencer, the opportunity to negotiate during the course was significantly facilitated by its initial emphasis upon what the participants brought to it in terms of knowledges and capabilities. They also felt that the challenge of negotiation, once explicitly related to and identified with significant cultural values of the Indonesian participants, did not appear to be alien to their ways of acting. The writers identified the Indonesian teachers' beliefs in the importance of self-esteem and self-reliance, freedom of choice and co-operation through mutual respect as authentic foundations for the kind of teaching–learning process they wanted to occur in their course. This insight reminds us that negotiation is not merely a process aimed at facilitating learner engagement in the language class but is also a form of cultural action that may enable students to become more open to discovering how to be a member of another language community.

8 Negotiation in tertiary education: clashes with the dominant educational culture

Stefaan Slembrouck

In this chapter, I want to offer an account of implementing a negotiated syllabus at the tertiary level, in the context of a Belgian university. My aim is to examine the relevance of certain factors in the institutional and wider educational context, in an attempt to account for transformations in student practice when responding to the introduction of a negotiated syllabus. The course in question was a recently-introduced follow-up course in 'practical English' for third year undergraduates in the Germanic Languages degree scheme at the University of Gent.

Negotiating negotiation: the institutional reaction

To begin, it is important to give an account of what happened before the course began and why I had insisted on negotiation. I had recently joined the department and had been assigned to teach the course for the following academic year (1991–92), when it would be running for the second time. When asked for my entry for the student brochure, I proposed not to set any course content or methodology in advance. My assumption was that this particular course was ideally suited for a negotiated syllabus. This decision was partly informed by three institutional factors which, I felt, spoke in favour of negotiation.

First, the course was the only remaining practical language course for third-year students and virtually inconsequential in terms of educational selection processes. It fell outside the language-acquisition and language-testing part of the degree scheme. Belgian universities require only a diploma of secondary education, and a university cannot impose a limit on the number of students. As a result, selection takes place mainly at the end of the first year. English is a very popular option, with 250 to 350 students in the first year. On average, slightly less than 40 per cent of registered beginners go on to the second year. For the English-language courses, selection is based on an assessment of students' actual performance in the foreign language and their mastery of a number of linguistic-descriptive skills. At the time (but less so now) 'English Language: Part I' at Gent University was based on a fairly traditional type of syllabus, inspired by Latin–Greek models of language learning. The first year programme consisted of a grammar–translation syllabus (including a vocabulary-acquisition component) onto which a descriptive linguistic component had been anchored (i.e. phonemic transcription and the description of English grammar). Despite the inclusion of a descriptive orientation in Part I, the overall approach was, and continues to be, very normative. This is partly a result of dominance of perceptions of 'correctness' in the Belgian (and, perhaps, western European in general) foreign-language context, and partly the result of the student-selection procedures which are based on an assessment of language performance. In contrast, Part II (third and fourth year) of the degree scheme has always tended to consist almost exclusively of specialised courses on various topics in linguistics and literary study. The third year 'follow-up' course in practical English which I had been assigned had, therefore, all the prerequisites for a different kind of approach. It was an isolated English as a foreign-language slot in the curriculum, with only two groups of about 20 students each, and no implicit selection goals.

Second, given the limited number of teaching hours ($22\frac{1}{2}$ hours) any choice of curricular contents would be arbitrary. For me, it was obvious that the best thing to do was to consult the students about their learning priorities. I could easily come up with specific activities that students would find attractive and important (e.g. academic writing in English in view of their BA dissertation, vocation-related uses of English such as subtitling, translation in an administrative context and so on).

Finally, the introduction of the course into the degree scheme had been the direct result of strike action from students. Hence, one could expect that they must have had fairly strong ideas about what it is that they wanted. Students had demanded that Part II of their degree scheme should also have components in 'practical language use'. This had led to the formal introduction of a 30-hour course in the study scheme (two thirds were assigned to the language department and one third to the literature department). Nevertheless, during the previous year, when the course had been taught for the first time, it had been perceived as disastrous by nearly everyone involved: lecturers had dreaded it and students had failed to attend the sessions. An approach based on classroom negotiation, I was convinced, could mean a 'fresh start'.

The plan I had in the back of my mind was that I could start off with a bold observation: 'This may well be your last English-language course in life and it will last only $22\frac{1}{2}$ hours; how can we make it useful to what you're doing at the moment, or to what you want to do after you've graduated?' After long discussions with a sceptical departmental head I was given carte blanche to try out a negotiated syllabus. It is worth looking into the arguments which were voiced against my proposal:

- 'Good' students and motivated learners will thrive irrespective of the actual methodology of teaching or learning. 'Weaker' and less motivated students, on the other hand, will take advantage of learner autonomy to lower the level of activity or to opt out from activities altogether.
- Some students are likely to resist a classroom situation in which some of their more opinionated and outspoken peers decide on the contents of the syllabus or the nature of the classroom activities. Will all students equally be heard?
- It is possible to negotiate with students over the contents and the adopted method of a particular course, but a lecturer should set a number of general constraints in advance and outline the course's methodological contours. What's more, how well equipped are students to make curricular decisions? After all, isn't the teacher the pedagogical 'expert' and shouldn't he or she know 'what is best for the students'?
- There is the organisation of the examination at the end of the course to consider. As the student population is to be divided over two groups, the chances would be considerable that, in the end, the course trajectory of the two groups would be very different. Yet, the prospect of a formal examination at the end of the year requires that all students are tested in the same way.

In response to these objections, I argued the following. I expressed my conviction that learner autonomy would inevitably increase motivation on the students' part. I argued that, while initially there may be imbalances in students' contributions to the decision-making, these imbalances would soon enter the scope of the negotiation process itself. I also maintained that we know that students do form opinions about and have preferences for certain methodologies, activities, etc. These opinions and preferences may not be conceptualised in the same way as applied linguists perceive them, but at least they can be a starting point for a process of negotiation. Finally, I questioned whether rationally-based democracy in education – and in other institutions – is a matter of uniform and 'objective' treatment. I saw no problem in working with two or more different examination formats, as long as these adequately reflected the course trajectories of the two groups or of groups-within-the-group.

My own methodological preferences

My own methodological commitment to classroom negotiation stems from a political conviction that 'critical goals' are very important in education. For me, at the time this meant the desirability of:

1. fundamentally democratic forms of classroom interaction and decision-making; and
2. 'critical' syllabus content which is maximally enabling for students in terms of its potential for sociocultural self-awareness.

One important goal I set for myself was that classroom activities should be methodologically truthful to the experience of a language learner/ user. For instance, I thought about the possibility of using the occasion of a particular language activity – say, a language quiz in which participants have to detect and correct syntactic errors – as a preamble for addressing questions such as: how well does a normative view of language learning/use based on 'correctness' accord with the experience of being a bilingual speaker? My assumption was that, rather than simply subscribe to a correctness-based view of language, students should be aware of its explanatory limitations, as well as become aware of the possibilities for alternative characterisations of processes of learning and teaching. I felt uneasy with a purely practical, utilitarian outlook on foreign-language learning: for me, the acquisition of any type of skill/practice should not be isolated from an analytic reflection on the nature, the desirability and the origins of the skill/practice in question. This is the only way to safeguard choice and to preserve the potential for conscious change which is analytically informed. Needless to say, my two-fold orientation was not free from paradoxes as there are, for instance, the tensions between the importance of the outcomes of the negotiation process itself, on the one hand, and the ways in which a teacher, lecturer or course co-ordinator may be grading activities and methodologies in a language-teaching context. The hidden assumption here was indeed that a negotiated syllabus must ultimately lead to methodological growth and perceptual refinement on the part of the students. For instance, the assumption that students will eventually themselves grow to prefer a task-based approach over, say, a grammar–translation one, and that they will eventually prefer to shape practices consciously, rather than simply learn 'how to do things'. In partial contrast with this, it cannot be denied that negotiation can also mean that it is perfectly possible for students to resist change (curricular or otherwise), and that a course convenor should respect this.

I was very aware of this latter possibility, but since I was one of the participants in the negotiation process I assumed that negotiation did not mean that I could not contribute to the construction of a list of priorities/activities. Initiating the process, I captured my idea of a worthwhile course orientation in the concept of an 'English as a foreign language Do-It-Yourself survival kit' – with a view towards useful insights into any learning/use situation which students would be involved in after they graduated, as teachers, as self-study learners or as professional users. This concept entailed two principles which reflected my own methodological preferences:

1. To use the classroom not exclusively for practice, but also to plan and assess what happens in the classroom;
2. To use the classroom to analyse and reflect on the nature of various experiences of foreign language use in real life situations.

Principle 1 was targeted at self-awareness about the nature of ELT activities and methodologies, socially current assumptions about language learning, etc., whereas Principle 2 was targeted towards self-awareness about processes of language use. (For instance, in the space of one or two sessions one can do subtitling as a translation activity, follow this up with a comparison between the students' subtitles and the ones actually used on television, and then discuss the question of actual versus desirable subtitling practices.) Let me now look in greater detail at some aspects of the course.

An account of the course

Quite interestingly – and, on reflection, as was to be expected – my own proposal for an 'ELT DIY survival kit' was thrown out during the first session. I had presented it in the form of a single-page document for discussion in smaller groups at the onset of the first session when students were asked to suggest a pool of priorities and units for the syllabus. None of the items on my list of possible priorities and activities was taken up, with the exception that both groups put a language quiz and subtitling on their agenda as attractive classroom activities. However, they rejected the idea of a cyclic movement between doing complex language activities and analysing these afterwards to reflect on the nature of the processes of foreign-language learning and use. Quite predictably perhaps, students showed most interest in activities which enabled them to refine and improve their language use further. They showed interest in continuing mostly in the vein of the courses of the first two years (e.g. a priority on acquiring new areas of vocabulary) and rejecting anything that would go in the direction of what they labelled as 'theory', something they considered out of place in a practical language course. I did not give up hope at this point, as I was privately convinced that some of my proposals would eventually be taken up in the process of syllabus accomplishment. This, however, did not ultimately happen, as I will explain below.

After the first session, the course followed a fortnightly structure: one week was used to decide on a theme, plan an activity, discuss the roles and make available the necessary resources, etc.; the next week was used for the activity itself. With each group, some of the activities from the initial pool were eventually included in the resulting syllabus, but new activities also emerged in subsequent weeks. I will now focus on two of the activities which took place, in order to examine the impact they had on the nature of classroom interaction and the negotiation process.

The recipe book: diversity in student reactions to negotiation

One of the early activities involved the individual, oral presentation of international dishes (a suggestion made by the students), followed by the compilation of a recipe book with a number of four-course meals (my suggestion). In the course of the session, it became apparent to me that the involvement of the students in the oral part turned out to be quite uneven, even to the extent that certain asymmetries were so obvious that they were perceived very negatively in the group. One student, a history student who had lived in Scotland for a year, took the course as an optional unit. He presented a recipe for haggis in such an eloquent and entertaining fashion that it effectively stopped some other students from presenting their menus. Here was an outsider who 'beat' the insiders at their game, partly because he did not share their collectively understood 'norms' of classroom involvement. Rivalries are not uncommon in classrooms. Nor is it uncommon that some students out-perform others. In a teacher-controlled classroom, phenomena like this perhaps do not surface so strongly, but once the floor is open to anyone who wants to voice suggestions about what to do and what precisely it will involve, imbalances in student expectations surface more easily and so do the relationships between groups-within-the-group. Equally, it became clear very quickly that the dropping of teacher-controlled turn-taking also led to some students taking the floor more often than others, with other students apparently silently under-going the flow of negotiation.

The written part of the activity was also interesting. As I was to be responsible for compiling and word-processing the booklet with recipes, it was agreed that the students would submit their texts in writing and that I was to produce the book without further ado. I edited the texts, as minimally as possible, as I knew that the recipe book was eventually to be read by other staff in the department and that this could well be a critical moment in deciding the fate of the course and its approach. When the printed texts were handed out, I could sense resentment among some students when they noticed some of the changes in their texts. With hindsight, the proper thing to do in this case would have been:

1. for me to insist on a discussion of editing and proof-reading in the classroom, and
2. to be explicit about the role which the 'published text' could play in the department.

Option 1 was a feasible one and I regret the fact that I had not been more careful in negotiating this aspect of the activity, but Option 2 would certainly have been a risky one to take. It raises an important question: To what extent can a lecturer afford to let students be aware of factors of an intra-departmental nature which affect the flow of events in the classroom?

'A for language': other opting-out phenomena

Another activity which both groups had on their list was modelled on a television quiz in which each week a Dutch and a Flemish team of a particular professional group (e.g. journalists or politicians) competed in a series of folk-linguistic tests (detecting spelling errors, multiple-choice questions on the etymology of certain idioms and so on). The idea was to transfer the game into an English context. The student group was divided into two teams who each designed the question–answer pairs for the other team. The game itself was to take place the following week.

Quite to my surprise, a number of students who had taken part in designing the quiz materials did not show up for the game itself and some of them had also failed to pass on their set of questions to the other members of their team, thus preventing part of the game from taking place, which, in its turn, gave rise to voices of protest in the teams. This was the case on both occasions of the game. This experience was quite disorienting, as the questions it raises can be said to virtually undermine the whole approach: Why did these students not turn up? Should one conclude from this that, although this was an activity which had arisen from their suggestion, whose proceedings had been carefully negotiated, and which they had actually helped to prepare in detail, this made no difference to their actual commitment to the course? Attendance checks are fairly common in Belgian universities. I had dropped them, because they are of little value. The difference that negotiation should make is that students attend sessions because they feel motivated and involved and not because university regulations stipulate that they must attend classes.

However, this was not the only blow to negotiation. One of the two language games were also video-taped. I had proposed to tape the session with a double purpose in mind. First, I wanted to use the recording for my own research purposes. Second, the tape could be used in the classroom itself. Significantly, the group agreed immediately to the taping for research purposes but the second option of using the tape in the classroom itself was rejected. Note that I had explicitly asked for the students' permission to tape the session even to the extent that I insisted that any objection from any one of them would be enough to drop the idea completely. Nevertheless, the actual effect of video-taping on some students was that they simply passed their card with a question on to the other team, thus departing from the spoken part of the activity that had been agreed beforehand. Apparently, the effect of the camera was that some students became very reluctant to speak. This seems to indicate that some students at least were very keen to avoid an assessment of their language performance (given that they assumed that this would be one of the purposes of the recording). In this respect, it is also paradoxical that my initial suggestion to follow up the game with an analysis of the assumptions about language use which underlie games of this kind had also been rejected. Something similar occurred a couple of weeks later, when subtitling was the activity. At that point I repeated my suggestion from the very first session to discuss the issue of desirable versus actual practices of subtitling. It was rejected a second time. A professional subtitler came into the classroom to compare the student-made subtitles with the ones produced by the broadcasting corporation but, after this stage, the students expressed their preference to move on to something entirely 'new'. Yet, most puzzling of all in the case of the quiz game was that none of the students had voiced their reluctance to be recorded in the negotiation stage, where there had been room for them to negotiate their way out of an assessment of correctness (if they assumed this was my intention), or to negotiate their way out of recording altogether. Nor did they take up the offer to analyse the activity, even though that would have allowed them to voice some of the fears and anxieties that go together with language assessment. Why?

The course ran on to its conclusion with many hitches, with student attendance varying greatly, and with students who insisted that something different should be done than had been decided on by the others the week before, in a session which they had not attended. Finally, when student representatives put the course on the agenda of the board of studies, and the head of department deemed that the department's face was at risk, it was decided to run the course the next year using a different approach.

Further analysis

When trying to get a clearer insight into these experiences, it is important to realise, first of all, that the introduction of classroom negotiation brings about a number of changes in behaviour at peer level which can only be understood in the context of other local institutional and educational pressures. For instance, how can one explain the persistent methodological conservatism in students' curricular decisions? First, students who are taking a degree in English are in the process of establishing their membership of a relatively exclusive group of users (and teachers) of English, who are likely to occupy gate-keeping positions of language expertise later on in their careers. The dominance of a 'correctness culture' in language learning and use accords more easily with this role identity, yet, at the same time, this culture is apparently also something they dread, as is shown by their reactions to the video-taping. Apparently, voicing such fears is seen as threatening to the self.

The latter, however, is probably not sufficient to explain the students' persistent objections to a reflexive component in the course. One additional factor here may be the making of 'safe' decisions in view of the examinations to come at the end of the course, especially as an unfamiliar type of curriculum or a problematising approach to methodology carries with it an element of uncertainty. It is not unrealistic to assume that some students in a negotiated course will try to see to it that courses remain not only manageable, but also conventional to a degree that it accords with the kind of course contents, structure and assessment they are already familiar with and can routinely deal with. This is a fairly pessimistic conclusion for an approach involving negotiation. What can negotiation offer to avoid it?

One possibility might have been to have insisted more on the negotiation of role behaviour in the classroom as a basis for evaluation. For example, to use an assessment of an activity as a way of planning the next activity. However, this is not an unproblematic proposition. For instance, if lecturers raise for discussion the issue that some students who had helped to plan a session did not show up for that session and also failed to pass on their work to the group, then they are likely to be interpreted as disciplining the students. This may be the case even if they disclaim any such intentions or are simply responding to reactions from students who think it unfair that their session was, as they put it, 'sabotaged by careless and irresponsible negligence'. The point is that it may be very difficult to bring down the wall of 'confrontational silence' which is so characteristic when judgemental issues are raised in a classroom. The same applies when students are invited to assess the role of the lecturer, which they were at various points during the course. Apart from a few students who continued to voice the opinion that they really preferred me to take all curricular decisions and that I should be the sole assessor of the activities, most students appeared to be extremely reluctant to comment on my role in the classroom or to make suggestions about what it should be. Needless to add, it is even more difficult to raise 'the wall of reservations' itself as a topic for discussion.

Yet, we all know from experience that students do talk intensively about classroom events outside the classroom. Ideally, negotiation brings this talk into the classroom and to the forefront of events. But only very few students made use of the classroom floor for the purpose of planning (what to do next?), let alone evaluating (was a session worth attending or not, and why?). The formal introduction of a negotiated syllabus does not guarantee that all students will make their views known about any of the things that go on in the classroom. One particular side effect of this is that silence on the part of some students may create the illusion that everyone is equally happy with the flow of 'negotiated' events. Certainly, it seems that the 'pupilling' side of peer-relations in classroom interaction (Pratt, 1989: 51ff.) remains largely a world inaccessible to teachers or lecturers. In other words, it is something which many students prefer to keep outside the scope of the classroom, where the lecturer would be co-participant. Even a lecturer who claims the best of intentions is unlikely to be allowed to enter their world of peer relations. With hindsight, I do not think it wise even to see a change in this situation as desirable. The challenge here seems to be how to bring about a form of classroom negotiation which is not felt to be intrusive or face-threatening to those involved in it: students and lecturers alike.

A second problem is that the success or failure of negotiation in the classroom may tend to be measured only in terms of the quality of the product: the nature of the language activities, the sophistication of the underlying methodology and observable degrees of student commitment. Throughout the course I had been assuming that complex language use and an increase in the demands of classroom activities were more valuable, and were to be taken as positive indicators of a successfully negotiated syllabus. One can look, however, at this differently. Belgian universities trade on a 'cramming' culture with low levels of classroom participation from students. Therefore, a basic form of student behaviour is to restrict one's efforts to the collection of all the necessary materials for the big examination effort each year in June. This dominant frame of reference generally influences students' judgements about the relevance of activities, including whether or not a lecture or seminar is worth attending at all. It also affects students' decisions when they are offered the chance of negotiating the contents of a syllabus and their involvement in a particular course. Some students have, indeed, responded to classroom negotiation as a chance to narrow the scope of language activities, rather than enlarging it. Similarly, in an institutional context where attendance checks are very common, my shift towards voluntary involvement was interpreted by some as time off for other worthwhile activities (e.g. some students used the course hours to complete their required in-service training in a secondary school; others used it as time off from classes to make progress with the writing of their dissertation, etc.). The rather obvious conclusion from this observation is that one cannot afford to ignore a level of negotiation which transcends one's own curricular responsibilities. Put more strongly, should negotiation in one particular course also take account of students' rights in deciding the proportion of schooling in their daily lives?

Third, and finally, I am inclined to advocate – however paradoxical this may sound for a negotiated approach in a language class – that one may have to think seriously about reducing the significance of language in the classroom context, primarily because it is discredited in a number of respects. As Ehlich *et al.* (1993: 11ff.) point out, educational practices are responsible for gradually silencing youngsters. Although children in their first years at school speak excessively and enthusiastically, gradually all pleasures that may go together with speaking, with listening and with curricular involvement tend to disappear. This situation leads to a vicious circle, where teachers find it much harder to opt out of doing all the talking as they continuously confront 'silence'. This is one reason why some teachers impose interaction on the classroom in the hope of securing a minimal – be it fairly tokenistic – degree of interaction, often in terms of the pattern of teacher initiation, student response and teacher feedback. When youngsters progress to university, one can perhaps expect a partial restoration of curricular commitment, but the speech–silence regime does not really disappear. Of course, the role of language in a course varies but, needless to say, language classes are particularly prey to the dominant discourse regimes of the classroom, basically because nearly all activities centre on language use or have language use as their process and/or their product. Classroom negotiation entails that one seeks to restore the speech of the students by re-introducing their right to plan and assess the educational process. To achieve this, one has to make use of one of the most discredited elements of the classroom: language used to discuss and evaluate. Note that in a teacher-controlled classroom, silence is not just a disadvantage, it is also a position of 'comfortable safety'. The effect of classroom negotiation is that the disadvantage of not being given a chance to speak may disappear, but the position of comfortable silence is also put at risk. Some students nevertheless try to maintain this position of silence or they are silenced by others, who jump immediately on the renewed opportunity for speech. The point is that it is not sufficient for a lecturer to announce that the planning of the course is itself seen as valuable language practice if some students continue to think that any language they produce may be graded on a scale of performance. Nor is it sufficient to proclaim the students' rights in determining the flow of classroom activities if subsequently their suggestions are interpreted by others in the classroom as 'giving in' to 'co-operation' with the party on the other side of the fence, or as complicating the course structure with an extra workload as a result. Paradoxically in the case of the course discussed here, students continued to resist a reflexive component in the syllabus which would have brought any of these problems to the forefront. My suspicion is that they did not interpret negotiation as a device for transforming classroom culture and practice, but looked at it more as a way of adjusting classroom activities to what they felt like doing at a particular moment. Therefore, one rather urgent question which we need to address is: What is required in a negotiated syllabus to avoid the trap of reinforcing the existing speech–silence regime and, with it, students' preconceived views of classroom behaviour?

9 Syllabus negotiation in a school of nursing

Elaine Martyn

The feasibility of implementing a negotiated syllabus in a tertiary environment has been seriously questioned by Clark (1987), Bloor and Bloor (1988), and Clarke (1991). While not the best option in all circumstances I would argue that a negotiated syllabus is quite manageable, and even the most appropriate approach to syllabus design and implementation in certain situations. This is illustrated by an account of a high level of negotiation which developed in a course on English for professional communication in a post-diploma Bachelor of Science Nursing (BScN) degree programme at the Aga Khan University School of Nursing in Karachi, Pakistan.

After a brief background section on the BScN programme, the students and the role of English in the curriculum, this chapter focuses on the meaning of negotiation and how it was manifest in this context. I describe the three phases of negotiation which occurred during planning, implementation and evaluation, and which involved nursing students, advanced nursing professionals from the school of nursing, hospital and community health, as well as English teachers. The concluding section returns to the question of the feasibility of a negotiated syllabus in a tertiary institution and, in particular, some constraints and facilitating conditions for its implementation.

Background

Being the first nursing programme at degree level in Pakistan, a country where nurses are generally held in low regard, the Aga Khan University School of Nursing aimed not simply to upgrade the nursing skills of participants but also to produce leaders who could enhance the role and raise the status of the profession within the health-care system and the community. The situation was described by the Director of the School of Nursing as follows:

> Nursing is seen in Pakistan as a menial occupation and therefore unsuitable for the daughters of middle- and upper-class Muslim families ... Many women are not socially or culturally prepared to assume the roles of decision-makers, risk-takers, or change agents; all of which are needed by nurse leaders to develop the profession.
>
> (Herberg, 1991)

To make such a role shift possible, students needed to develop competence and confidence in professional communication in English. English is not only the medium of instruction at the university: it is also the main language of professional communication within Pakistan and abroad, although Urdu is the main medium of direct patient care.

The students

The 15 students involved in the syllabus negotiations were mature qualified nurses enrolled in the first BScN class at the university. They ranged in age from 23 to 45 years and had two to 24 years of nursing experience. All of the students were Pakistani and most were women (only two students of the fifteen were men). The students were highly motivated in their studies and committed to the professionalisation of nursing in Pakistan, as was evident in the needs analysis and throughout the course of studies. Prior to this course, students had participated in self-directed learning in their nursing studies, some as work-study students and all within the BScN programme. Thus, the concept of syllabus negotiation was generally accepted as appropriate to adult learners by the students and by faculty members teaching in the programme.

English in the curriculum

The development of English academic and professional communication skills was an integral part of the BScN curriculum. Table 9.1 shows how communication skills play a significant role in the development of baccalaureate-level nursing skills. The major elements of the BScN programme are given in the left-hand column. The contributions of English to the curriculum in Years 1 and 2 are given in the next two columns.

While first-year English classes focused on academic communication and study skills, second-year courses targeted professional communication. The 36-hour course, described in this paper, was the third of four English courses. Its purpose was the development of professional communication skills to enable graduates to function effectively in

Table 9.1   *English in the BSc Nursing conceptual framework*

Major elements of the BScN	Contribution of English to the curriculum	
	Year 1	Year 2
Health assessment	Interviewing	
Culture		Report writing
Primary health care; Community-health nursing		
Adult/child health nursing		
Management/ leadership	Time management	Report writing; public speaking
Education	Academic and study skills: reading, writing, researching	Public speaking; Individual learning needs
Professionalism	Academic skills: reading, writing, researching	Public speaking; publishing
Research	Academic skills: reading, writing, researching	Writing for publication

Adapted from Martyn and Husain, 1993: 291

teaching and management roles in nursing education, administration and community health.

Syllabus negotiation

Bloor and Bloor (1988) provide a useful definition of negotiation in the context of English language teaching:

> [Negotiation] involves two parties (teacher and student(s)) attempting to establish consensus regarding what is wanted and what is attainable ... There should be no conflict between the goals of the two parties, the teacher's aim being to achieve what

is best for the students ... Thus it is not a bargaining process that is involved here but a joint exploration to which the two parties bring different specialist knowledge. By 'negotiation' we mean a process of reaching agreement through discussion.

(1988: 63)

In describing the process of negotiation, Tompkins and McGraw, two faculty members in a school of nursing, emphasised 'mutuality in decision-making and student self-determination in relation to learning outcomes' (1988: 173). Clark (1987: 136) further stressed the 'quality of relationship between participants and the sharing of responsibility'. In fact, equality of participants must be accepted so that 'the diverse strengths, energies, and personalities of those involved are harnessed and forged together harmoniously' (Clark, 1987: 136). More specifically, as proposed by Parkinson and O'Sullivan (1990: 114) 'each individual's experience, knowledge, skills, expertise, energy, commitment and motivation' can be used within the group community to negotiate the learning process. In summary, process negotiations recognise and involve the whole person (Clark, 1987).

In brief, these writers have highlighted the key aspects of the negotiation process: joint exploration, consensus building, the difference between what is wanted and what is attainable, renegotiation, equality and mutuality in decision-making and student self-determination. In the context of professional communication, and this chapter in particular, however, the negotiators must be expanded beyond English teachers and students to include a third group of stakeholders (as defined by Nunan, 1989b) in the learning venture, in this case advanced nursing professionals.

A negotiation triangle, as shown in Figure 9.1, best demonstrates the relationship of stakeholders described in this chapter; it consists of nursing students, advanced nursing professionals (faculty members and hospital/community-health managers) and myself as the English teacher. The negotiations brought together the needs, interests, knowledge, skills, commitment and enthusiasm of all three parties. Besides these factors, willingness to share responsibility for learning was grounded in each individual's educational philosophy and views on appropriate and effective teaching–learning processes. Students' uptake of responsibility related to their learning styles and developing skills in negotiation of learning. The advanced nursing professionals as a group had a vested interest in the outcome of the students' learning, but their willingness to negotiate and take responsibility for outcomes was based on their perceptions of their role in developing neophytes in their field. My

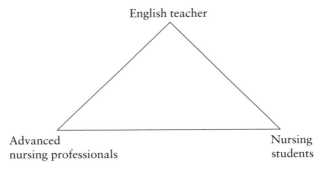

Figure 9.1   The negotiation triangle
(Adapted from Martyn and Husain, 1993: 297)

acceptance of responsibility for negotiation arose largely out of my perception of a need for graduates to meet professional expectations in a field in which I was only able to enter based on the willingness of nurses to share knowledge, processes and needs. The nursing expertise of both students and advanced nursing professionals were essential to me in developing this course.

In fact, the complementary sets of expertise of these stakeholders virtually necessitated a three-way negotiation of syllabus. As few of the other stakeholders were both Pakistani and nurses, the students had valuable insights to offer in terms of their English professional communication needs in an Urdu-speaking country. The advanced nursing professionals brought to the negotiations a broad range of international experience at the target professional level of the students upon graduation. My contribution was based on linguistic knowledge and language teaching–learning experience in Pakistan and abroad.

An account of the negotiation process

The unique contributions of each of the three groups of stakeholders may be illustrated by tracing negotiations of the class through the three phases of the negotiation process: planning, implementation and evaluation, as shown in Table 9.2.

Planning

Initial course discussions were held one year prior to implementation, when the writer met with students and faculty members in order to prepare short course descriptions. Negotiations quickly led to an

Table 9.2   *Contributions to the negotiation process*

Advanced nursing professionals	English teachers	Nursing students
Planning • Identify expectations of graduates • Suggest readings and tasks • Provide samples • Suggest course/topic for joint assignment	• Identify students' language strengths and weaknesses • Synthesise needs/wants analysis and negotiate with other parties • Prepare syllabus and materials, etc.	• Identify own interests and needs based on experience • Suggest topics, tasks and resources
Implementation • Suggest tasks and resources • Provide samples • Clarify points for English teachers • Suggest meetings, provide minutes • Identify visitors to the institution • Suggest speakers • Act as guest speakers • Advise students/give feedback on work in progress	• Develop materials and activities • Manage course logistics • Develop human resource contacts and co-ordinate activities • Conduct classes • Assist students and give feedback as required • Develop and share evaluation criteria • Ensure negotiations continue along all three sides of the triangle	• Suggest tasks and resources • Contribute articles and ideas • Select meetings, topics, etc. • Plan process of work • Seek assistance from faculty, locate resources • Suggest speakers and venues for public speaking • Give feedback on work in progress
Evaluation • Contribute to evaluations of student work • Co-assess public speaking	• Give regular feedback to students • Collect and collate feedback from advanced nursing professionals • Provide ongoing evaluations to students • Prepare final assessments and grades	• Provide feedback to classmates • Evaluate course and faculty • Make recommendations for future offerings of the course

Adapted from Martyn and Husain, 1993: 298

emphasis on professional tasks, as evidenced by this course description written at that time:

> This course will focus on writing and speaking tasks relevant to the role of a professional nurse, such as public speaking, report writing, and writing for publication.
>
> (from the course outline, *English III: English Skills for Professional Nurses*, 1989)

This general statement left the design of the syllabus quite open though with a clear focus on 'real' professional tasks (as defined by Nunan, 1988b: 45). Subsequent negotiations went even further in the direction of real world tasks. As far as possible, assignments were implemented within a 'real environment' so that students participated in and contributed to their local professional community as part of the course.

During the main planning stage (the second semester of Year 1), views of participants were solicited by surveys, interviews and conversations with students, nursing teachers and managers. As negotiations moved from expectations of graduates to more practical aspects of implementation, the significance of a truly negotiated curriculum – involving all three sets of stakeholders – became apparent.

Some of the tasks, identified by both students and other nurses, such as writing minutes, memos and reports, were ones that the students had already done, but which required improvement. Tasks targeted more at nursing leadership, such as public speaking and writing for publication, were suggested by nursing faculty. Students also wanted to improve their oral communication in less formal circumstances, for example, in meeting and interacting with 'higher officials', such as a past president of the World Health Organisation or national nursing leaders. This concern, which led to the development of a unit entitled 'meeting, greeting and conversational etiquette', raised issues of language, cross cultural communication and social etiquette.

As the overall framework was being clarified, further specific tasks were identified and their inclusion negotiated. Students requested impromptu speaking and the writing of covering letters and résumés (curricula vitae). A director of nursing in the hospital suggested that completing the new hospital report forms should be included in the course as well as practice in the writing of letters of apology. One nursing teacher suggested that the report-writing assignment be based on data collected during her community-health nursing course, and be jointly assessed for both courses.

Throughout this three-month planning stage, I synthesised the input from the other stakeholders with my knowledge of the students' language and learning skills (based on having taught the group for over one semester), and my perceptions of the ongoing commitment to be expected from the other stakeholders. A complete course syllabus was prepared with objectives, teaching–learning strategies, evaluation, a schedule of classes and a basic bibliography in time for curriculum committee approval near the end of the semester. The course included six units:

1. introduction;
2. meetings and minutes;
3. meeting, greeting and conversation etiquette;
4. writing for publication;
5. public speaking; and
6. writing reports, letters and memos.

(from *English III: English Skills for Professional Nurses*, 1989)

Implementation

A high level of commitment of stakeholders continued throughout the implementation stage. While the level of responsibility in negotiations varied among students, they were required to negotiate certain aspects, such as topics, planning of learning processes, project preparation and peer feedback with their classmates, nursing advisors and the English teacher. During implementation, nursing teachers (including some diploma nursing teachers who had not been involved up to this stage) negotiated with students in their role as advisors to public speaking and writing-for-publication projects. Nursing managers collaborated with the English teacher in the preparation of materials and feedback to students, especially by clarifying the purposes and requirements of various types of report. Negotiation between all types of stakeholders was significant in co-ordinating oral communication experiences for the units on 'meeting and greeting' and 'public speaking'. A number of the advanced nursing professionals also acted as guest speakers on topics such as 'how to prepare and present a formal paper' and 'opportunities for publishing in nursing'.

As an English teacher in this situation, I was not only responsible for preparing materials, conducting classes and making assessments. I also became a manager responsible for negotiations, bringing together the talents and creativity of the other stakeholders, and co-ordinating logistical arrangements and human resources. The arrangements were fairly complex; for example, each student attended a committee meeting, wrote a paper with the support of a nursing advisor, met a visiting official and made a public presentation. Table 9.3 summarises the range of activities and stakeholders with whom I negotiated during the implementation of three of the units.

Table 9.3   *Negotiations in the implementation of course activities*

Units	Negotiations	Activities
'Meetings and minutes'	with students and committee chairs (AKUSON, AKUH and AKUMC) about meeting times, previous minutes and review of student minutes	AKUH committee meetings: • head nurses • nursing management • quality assurance AKUSON committee meetings: • BScN admissions • Year 2 diploma faculty • AKUMC: committee meetings: • paediatric interest Other hospitals: • head nurses
'Meeting and greeting'	with students and directors of AKUSON, nursing for AKUH and community health	• met nurses and medical doctors, well-known in their fields • conversation at a conference • tour of AKUMC or community health site • interview of candidate for dean (on a student panel) • work at conference registration desk
'Public speaking'	with students and directors of AKUSON nursing for AKUH and other SONs, and AKUSON faculty	• spoke on panel at SON open house • presented at Nursing Grand Rounds (AKUH) • made speech at another SON on further education • spoke at another SON diploma graduation ceremony

Notes: SON = school of nursing; AKUSON = Aga Khan University SON; AKUH = Aga Khan University Hospital; AKUMC = Aga Khan University Medical Centre (AKUH and AKU)

Evaluation

While the responsibility in this area remained primarily with me as the English teacher, input for final student assessment incorporated evaluations from the advanced nursing professionals. Students, although not involved in formal assessment, offered feedback to one another during the preparation of assignments and during in-class activities; they also completed end-of-course evaluations.

The advanced nursing professionals also gave feedback to students during preparation for their two major projects for the units, writing for publication and public speaking. They contributed to final assessment on four assignments: committee chairs commented on student minutes, nursing advisors offered evaluative comments on the articles, a nursing teacher assessed the joint community-health/English field reports for grades in the nursing course and offered input to the English course assessment, and at least one nursing teacher co-assessed each public speaking presentation with me. I offered feedback on all assignments throughout the course, and incorporated the comments and ratings of the advanced nursing professionals in the final assessments. (Course grades were determined by continuous assessment with no final test or examination being held.)

Outcomes

Student response was very positive as evidenced by high ratings on the course evaluation. Negotiations and the reality of the tasks took students beyond the level of skills acquisition to experiential learning, involving, for example, tears before a presentation at Nursing Grand Rounds (in front of nurses and medical doctors from the hospital) to pride in successful accomplishment of the professional task. The significance of the assignments for students was also greatly enhanced; students aimed at excellence, not simply to meet course requirements, but also to make a positive impact, both personally and professionally, on their community. Thus, they actively sought out assistance from both nursing teachers and myself. Both co-operative and autonomous learning skills were developed through the experience.

Informal interviews held two years later, after students had returned to work, showed an extended positive rating on the course and reconfirmed the suitability of the negotiated tasks. Almost all had been involved in writing minutes, memos and reports, in chairing meetings and in meeting 'high officials' in their work. They felt they approached these tasks with greater confidence and competence than they would have without participation in the course. Some had written résumés and applications for new jobs and advanced studies; none had published but a few had made presentations at international conferences.

One interesting outcome related directly to a key objective of the BScN programme: the enhancement of the role of nurses. Students' community-health field reports were viewed by the head medical doctor and nurse as 'prototypes' for a valuable new nursing field report. The assignment proved that nurses were capable of producing high calibre reports, and raised the possibility of instituting regular nursing field reports in the community-health department.

The advanced nursing professionals and English teachers (myself and two others who took over responsibility for the course the following year) appeared to have gained awareness of and respect for each other's areas of expertise. English teachers' contributions to the development of professional communication skills were demonstrated in a very concrete way. Through close collaboration, English teachers were able to enter more fully into the culture of nursing and thereby better address the students' needs.

Conclusions

Syllabus negotiation began in this course simply because it appeared to be the most appropriate way of meeting communication needs in a field in which the English teacher truly had no background. It proceeded successfully with a high level of negotiation due to the co-operation and commitment of all stakeholders to the new learning venture.

A few years later, when I had the opportunity to read and reflect on this issue, I was surprised to see the rather negative responses to and restrictive views of negotiation in the literature, particularly the views of Clark (1987), Bloor and Bloor (1988) and Clarke (1991). While seemingly interested in the notion of a negotiated syllabus, Clarke, for example, described it as 'radical' and 'for all practical purposes unworkable in any other circumstances than with a very small group or in a one to one situation' (1991: 13). Clark (1987) and Bloor and Bloor (1988) similarly questioned syllabus negotiation in any other than a very restricted context. Both the experience reported in this paper – and Simmons and Wheeler's (1995) longitudinal case study of 'The process syllabus in action' in a professional English context – demonstrate that rather than being radical and impractical, a process syllabus may be very practical. Their study 'revealed that the students were 100 per cent in favour of the opportunity to get involved in their own course management' (1995: 63).

What are the constraints and facilitating conditions for syllabus negotiation in a university?

It is important to view constraints as simply a realistic part of any negotiation. Constraints are thus not a cause for rejection of this type of syllabus but rather simply a part of the process. Major constraints seem to be ultimately based on perceptions of non-equality of teachers and students, and a restricted view of the process of syllabus negotiation.

Non-acceptance of equality of participants in the negotiation by teachers and students is a major road block in any course negotiation. Rather than seeing the teacher as choosing to 'confer' power on students (Bloor and Bloor, 1988: 72), as a superior granting something to an inferior, both groups may be seen as equals with differing expertise and experience. A lack of faith in students (and other stakeholders) to participate effectively in setting goals, planning learning, etc. denies their personal expertise and potential. While the teacher clearly has power based on institutional sanction and tradition, students may be seen as having a right to negotiate their learning. This is a right which in a very traditional course may be given up when students join a class and which is exercised only through non-cooperation or non-participation. The students in this course were of a similar age to me, were qualified and experienced as nurses, and had some experience in self-directed learning. Ultimately, however, equality of participants need not lie in such specifics; the equality may be restricted to only the shared learning experience or be very broadly based as human equality.

An absolutely 'designless design' in which 'no decision is binding' (Clarke, 1991: 14) may make a fully negotiated syllabus difficult due to institutional constraints in some universities; however, negotiated agreements between teachers and learners may form a solid basis for process negotiations at a more specific day to day level during any course. Nonetheless, as the above description illustrates, it may well be possible in many circumstances for a teacher to hold pre-course negotiations and meet the requirement of approval by a curriculum committee in a university. Also as argued by D. Long (1990: 135), it is essential from the beginning of a course of study that there is a clear task orientation and commitment from all parties involved in the negotiation.

Key facilitating conditions for syllabus negotiation for this course included institutional acceptance and support, mature and highly motivated learners, a task-based professional syllabus and a perceived need for collaboration. Without institutional support, negotiations are likely to be limited to consultation with 'advanced professionals' or colleagues from other faculties and the offering of limited specific choices to students. While such activities may form a part of a negotiated syllabus, it seems to me that on their own they are insufficient. While learners in this course were generally mature and motivated, it also enhanced their motivation by its focus on their professional needs; these views are similar to those expressed by learners as key reasons for the success of the process syllabus in Simmons and

Wheeler's (1995) study. The final factor which drove this negotiation was my belief in an absolute need to integrate the expertise of others and to discuss and present English-language teaching and learning in terms which were orientated around the conceptual framework of the nursing programme.

Any experience of a syllabus negotiation is not completely replicable as each negotiation depends on the specific participants and environment. However, the principles and processes may be tried, tested and refined in each new environment.

10 Negotiating the syllabus: learning needs analysis through pictures

Eddie Edmundson and Steve Fitzpatrick

This chapter describes a procedure for using pictures to negotiate ongoing learning needs with learners of English at the British Council Centre in Recife, north-east Brazil. The procedure consists of a simple artifice that prompts negotiation at the level of the group and encourages a shared sense of commitment to content, procedures and results, giving motivation and substance, as shall be seen, to individual reflection by the learners.

The British Council Centre was established in November 1986, and it specialises in EAP/EOP (English for academic/other purposes) to adult learners who intend to study or train abroad using the medium of English. All learners study intensively, two hours each weekday, and most students prepare for the International English Language Testing System examination (IELTS) to meet the language requirements of scholarship awarding agencies. The majority of learners pay for their courses, but in some cases the British government's Department for International Development (DFID) covers the costs of pre-sessional study.

Negotiation with learners over many aspects of the syllabus has been a hallmark of the approach adopted throughout the history of the Centre. This approach is learning-centred and strongly influenced by such ELT commentators as Breen (1984), Hutchinson and Waters (1987), Nunan (1988b), Johnson (1989a) and Campbell and Kryszewska (1992). Important contributions have also been made by Tony Dudley-Evans of the University of Birmingham on two consultancy visits to the Centre.

The emphasis on negotiation with the learners arose naturally from the initial decision not to use a set coursebook nor to give internal tests, and from the adoption by all tutors of ongoing retrospective accounts of the syllabus. These accounts detail the objectives agreed at the beginning of each monthly block of studies that focus on learning priorities in terms of macro and micro skills, learning preferences, and group expectations (including the tutor's) as regards methodology, content,

Day	Theme/ activity	Reasons for choice	Tasks	Specific objectives	Focus [language function/skills/ learner development]	Daily evaluation
1.						

Figure 10.1   Daily retrospective accounts

topics and outcomes. These outcomes are evaluated daily, weekly and monthly in the retrospective accounts, to which the learners contribute by means of feedback discussion normally held at the end of the block.

The daily retrospective accounts have the format shown in Figure 10.1. The retrospective accounts are regarded as public documents open to everyone concerned in the teaching and learning situation. Making the document public is justified on three counts. The learners and the tutor can return at any point to the written account to see whether 'we are doing what we set out to do'. Second, the tutor and the learners can use the unified account to try to untangle the typical ambiguities and contradictions present when the participants reflect on what is happening and what is being learned. Third, the accounts help vindicate an unusual approach to EAP/EOP in the eyes of outside visitors.

Tutors feel intuitively that if the learners participate actively in the decision-making process this is likely to help inculcate an awareness of both individual and group wants and needs, and learning strengths and weaknesses. Such collaboration also tends to promote intra-group respect for each other's opinions and individual agendas, or at least provides an outlet for the expression of dissent. Furthermore, the tutors believe that the sharing of expectations of goals and responsibility for outcomes is likely to foster the growth of trust and authenticity, since the potential exists for promoting a genuine sharing of power – unconditionally – in the classroom.

All adult learners bring a great deal with them to the classroom in terms of experience of the world, but tutors at the Centre are particularly fortunate in dealing with students who, on account of their sophisticated professional and academic backgrounds, generally respond positively to the invitation to articulate their opinions and feelings about what happens in the course of their learning, and recognise the relevance of being invited to collaborate on decisions affecting their learning. We also feel that promoting negotiation in the classroom builds up self-esteem, which in the case of many adult learners has been severely bruised by previous 'failure' to acquire any practical competence in the foreign language.

Nevertheless, the full affective and cognitive involvement of the learners in this process at the Centre is not immediate. There is in effect a cline that starts from the kind of syllabus which contains several pre-designed elements at the most elementary course level, leading to syllabus statements that are arrived at almost wholly autonomously by learners at advanced course levels. The approach has been influenced by the view that pre-determined syllabuses 'gradually render themselves redundant as they are replaced in their implementation by that syllabus which is jointly discovered, and created in the classroom' (Breen, 1984: 53).

The particular focus of this chapter is an attempt to facilitate the formulation by the learners of ongoing learning aims and objectives. The procedure pays special attention to possible reasons for the learning difficulties identified by the students. We see this innovation as a natural consequence in the evolution of the Centre's experience with a negotiated syllabus.

The instrument developed for this self-diagnosis purpose is called Learning needs Analysis through Pictures (LAP). It is possible to describe LAP as a kind of questionnaire. Most surveys, however, are intrinsically inflexible, and do not permit the user to elaborate on the answers given or offer opinions on topics that have not previously been predicted by the person or institution that designed the questionnaire. LAP, in contrast, invites the active participation of all learners in the formulation of the questions as much as in the elaboration of the answers.

LAP consists of sets of specially designed cartoons. Different sets correspond, respectively, to:

- the four language skills, (listening, speaking, reading and writing);
- 'communicative acts' (an open set of sub-skills, language functions and affective purposes which has been intuitively arrived at);
- 'reasons for difficulties';
- 'learning preferences' (in terms of activity types); and
- themes/topics.

There is a deliberate avoidance of complicated terminology, and experience has shown that students are content with these labels. In courses at a more advanced level, both 'skills' and 'communicative acts' are subsumed under the heading of 'training priorities'.

LAP is typically used at the beginning of each monthly block (approximately 40 hours of study). There is no reason, however, why LAP could not be used at other junctures, and this has in fact happened on occasion at the Centre.

An account of the LAP procedure

The example which follows is taken from a course at an elementary language level. The tutor's general aims for the block prior to using LAP were:

- to begin to involve the learners in the decision-making process of constructing the syllabus;
- to prompt an understanding of the value of learning co-operatively from each other;
- to identify activities which in the students' view promote learning;
- to identify areas of weakness (group and individual);
- to introduce the notion of the communicative purposes of grammar;
- to initiate the learners in recognising the importance of process during task work, as well as product;
- to introduce evaluation sessions and explain their purpose;
- to foster 'study competencies' (Waters and Waters, 1992) such as 'self-confidence' and 'the ability to think critically and creatively'.

The students in question were false beginners (at least band 3 on IELTS) who constituted a very heterogeneous group in terms of age and background. They had been studying at the Centre for 60 hours, and had been exposed to a wide variety of activity types. Given the students' level of English, all the planning discussion took place in the students' mother tongue, although this would normally be done in English with students on more advanced language courses. Procedurally, the students worked in groups through the five steps, as detailed in the following sections.

Step 1: Ranking for difficulty

They first ranked the set of four drawings illustrating the language skills in order of perceived difficulty, based on their experience with tasks in the classroom (see examples in Figure 10.2). They then compared their sequences with other groups, and attempted to come to a consensus through a plenary discussion with the class. (As is inevitably the case, this meant accepting the views of the majority.)

Step 2: Grouping 'communicative acts'

Next, the students grouped the cards illustrating 'communicative acts' according to each skill and, if appropriate, arranged them in order of perceived difficulty (see examples in Figure 10.3). These cards were a selection made by the tutor representing the work covered to date. They

Figure 10.2   Examples of language skill pictures

Figure 10.3   Examples of communicative act pictures

then compared these results with other groups and tried to find a class consensus, again through plenary discussion.

Step 3: Looking for correspondences

They then looked for correspondences between cards from the 'reasons for difficulty' set and each of the communicative acts chosen (see examples in Figure 10.4). The reasons included items like 'lack of vocabulary' or 'fear of making mistakes'. Some acknowledged reasons for difficulty were, as expected, repeated with more than one skill, and the set of cards allows for this. A secretary in each group kept notes.

Each group then told the teacher in plenary the results of the analysis from steps 1–3. These findings were written up on the whiteboard under the headings 'language skills', 'communicative acts' and 'reasons for difficulty'.

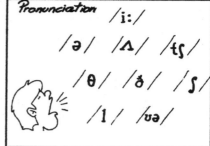

Figure 10.4   Examples of reason for difficulty pictures

Figure 10.5   Examples of learning preference pictures

Step 4: Selecting learning preferences

Groups next arranged, in order of preference, a choice of cards from the set of 'learning preferences' (activity types; see Figure 10.5 for examples) and, again, arrived at a class consensus through plenary discussion.

Step 5: Reflecting on the decision-making process

The final stage of the process involved reflection in plenary on the decision-making process and the recording of all the aims and objectives that had been agreed on by the group as a whole. At this stage, the tutor contributed to the discussion, and legitimately so, as a member of the group, to negotiate aspects of his own agenda.

Figure 10.6 shows the learning chart for the group which was written up on the first page of the retrospective account for the month. The immediate outcome of this activity, then, was a statement of learning

SKILLS (priorities)	COMMUNICATIVE ACTS	REASONS FOR DIFFICULTIES	LEARNING PREFERENCES
1. Speaking 2. Listening	expressing feelings	vocabulary, shyness, fear of making mistakes, pronunciation, translation	drama dictation
3. Writing 4. Reading	making questions	auxiliary verbs, prepositions, shyness, word order	games video
	giving instructions	modal verbs, prepositions, vocabulary, pronunciation	jigsaw reading
	narrating	prepositions, shyness, word order, pronunciation	music
	describing characteristics	vocabulary, prepositions, pronunciation	
	reading for enjoyment	guessing words	
	informal writing	word order, prepositions	

Figure 10.6   A learning chart

priorities based on perceived difficulties, typically for the following month. It also provided specific objectives that encompassed the learning difficulties to be tackled, and an agreement over the choice of materials and their treatment. The tutor pointed out that the chart was not to be seen as a statement of priorities to be followed strictly in sequence, but rather as a guide and a reference framework to emphasise in the following lessons. (The retrospective account for the first week is given in Appendix 10.1.)

The column headed 'reasons for difficulties' is usually very revealing. In this particular case, given the frequency of certain reasons cited as causing difficulties, the students were encouraged to reflect on the following areas, not only with regard to themselves as learners, but also thinking of their peers:

1. prepositions;
2. word order and vocabulary;
3. shyness and pronunciation;
4. fear of making mistakes, translation, auxiliary verbs;

My reflection chart				
Name of activity	What I did/what I practised	What I learned	Remaining difficulties	Feelings about the activity in general
1				
2				
3				

Figure 10.7   A reflection chart

5. modal verbs;
6. guessing words.

The usefulness of this data for tutors is that it can inform their observation of tasks in process in the classroom.

The lesson ended with the distribution to the learners of the reflection chart shown in Figure 10.7 – which is commonly used by tutors at the Centre – with the suggestion that this might help monitor individual progress, difficulties and feelings, and with the advice that they should attempt to record things that they found significant, not necessarily only on a day-by-day basis.

Comments made by learners in their reflection charts over the following two weeks included the following:

'I learned how to defend my ideas and opinions in English.'

'This activity called my attention to my difficulties.'

'It was difficult to choose priorities, and the results of the group's priorities did not always coincide with my priorities.'

Two weeks later (half way through the block) the group reviewed the learning chart that had been agreed. Groups were invited to discuss the following questions, with reference to the original chart and their own reflection notes (where these existed):

● What has been done?
● What hasn't been done?
● What changes to the chart should be made?

Plenary discussion revealed that insufficient attention had been given to expressing feelings, narration and giving instructions. The teacher acknowledged that this was indeed the case, and had resulted partly from his judgement that narration had been focused on to a great extent during the course of the previous month. This explanation was accepted. Discussion continued and, finally, it was agreed that the only change for the remainder of the block would be the priority order recorded for 'learning preferences'. The experience with drama, for example, had not matched expectations, and dropped to fourth place in the list.

The next step was to reach agreement with the learners on a timetable for 15-minute counselling sessions. Regular private discussion with the tutor has always been a feature of the approach at the Centre, but for those tutors who have adopted the LAP procedure, these sessions enable a focus on any discrepancies between the learning priorities of the group and the individual. The tutor can indicate how personal priorities and perceived difficulties can find expression in classroom activities or in the self-access centre (available in the British Council Centre) or through home study. The learner can find that, as self-awareness grows, he or she is better able to articulate deficiencies and needs. This discussion informs the drawing up jointly of a learner contract: a written statement kept by the tutor and the learner of action points agreed which is reviewed in the subsequent counselling interview.

Normally, after another month's intensive study, the LAP activity is given again. On this and subsequent occasions, greater sophistication can be expected of the learning chart, and the focus can move from perceived weaknesses to promoting self-diagnosis of deficiencies with regard to target needs. For this reason, all the 'training priority' cards are employed with the suggestion that unimportant or irrelevant items can be omitted.

Developing the LAP procedure

Figure 10.8 is the analysis, for comparison, that resulted from LAP with another group of learners, this time at a pre-intermediate level of English. Themes have been included in this chart as a natural development of the LAP process, because at this level we find that learners can cope better with the language demands of topic-based activities and have developed an awareness of the skills practice inherent in the treatment of the texts. It is interesting to see that some of the themes, such as 'education' and 'health care', seem to conform to more conventional EAP/EOP focuses, while other topics, such as 'current affairs', suggest an appreciation by the learners of the underlying skills work

TRAINING PRIORITIES	REASONS FOR DIFFICULTIES	LEARNING PREFERENCES	THEMES
listening	vocabulary, pronunciation, speed, expectations	groups/pairs questionnaires	culture
writing essays	fear of making mistakes, time, prepositions, word order, organising ideas/ sentences/ paragraphs	music jigsaw reading imaginative writing video	art current affairs behaviour famous people ecology
speaking	grammar, shyness, expectations, auxiliary verbs, feelings, making questions	presentations drama research dictation	tourism education people at work
reading for enjoyment	translation, dictionary dependency, guessing words from context		
writing informal letters	as with 'writing essays'		
reading for exams	exam expectations, time, vocabulary		

Figure 10.8   Analysis resulting from LAP at a pre-intermediate level of English

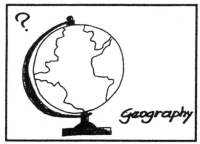 

Figure 10.9   Examples of theme pictures

involved in dealing with texts on subjects that interest them personally (see examples of theme pictures in Figure 10.9).

Our own experience of the LAP procedure suggests that it should not be seen as a straitjacket, but rather as a means of informing discussion and eliciting negotiation. LAP appears to be effective and useful, but much depends on the open-mindedness, flexibility and authenticity of everyone involved. Clearly, to go through the motions of the steps we have described but then to disregard the decisions reached through negotiation is much worse than not having carried out the activities at all.

We find that the elements of the LAP procedure are constantly evolving simply because any perceived shortcomings serve as input to discussion with the learners and prompt negotiation over whether improvements can be made. The procedure therefore evolves to become appropriate to the particular circumstances. Students contribute with suggestions such as 'Why didn't you include X?', 'You forgot Y', 'Why don't we make a cartoon for Z?'.

While we cannot claim any experience of transferring of LAP to other teaching–learning situations, we believe intuitively that (perhaps in a modified form) the methodology can be employed in a variety of different classrooms. LAP would be relevant to any situation where the teacher wishes to promote self/group diagnosis of learning difficulties or weaknesses. The procedure would be able to play a role in helping to determine target-situation wants/needs where these can be articulated. Above all, LAP would be a relevant option in any institution which pursues a policy of choice and negotiation, although there may be constraints on account of the availability of time, space and resources. We do not believe, however, that following a set coursebook, preparing students for internal or external tests, or the age of the learners automatically excludes the application of this approach.

Appendix 10.1

The retrospective account for the first week following the application of the LAP procedure with an elementary level group

Day	Theme/activity	Reasons for choice	Tasks	Specific objectives	Focus (language, function, skills, learner development)	Daily evaluation
1	'close friends' and questionnaire 'How well do you know the person?'	see chart: • dictation • pronunciation • speaking and fears • listening	• describe childhood friends • answer questionnaire (dictated by teacher)	• to reduce fears of making mistakes: • to use 'wh', 'did', 'do' and 'does' question • to listen to Q-forms	• language of stative description used for oral skills in general	• Students took longer than expected so questionnaire wasn't finished • Talking about themselves • Stimulated lengthy chats
2	'Recife' and prepositions	see chart: • writing (word order, prepositions of location) • cocktailing info (reduce fears)	• pass on information find matching phrases, discover appropriate prepositions to link them • brainstorm Recife sights, produce a leaflet	• prepositions of location • word order • giving instructions to support their ideas with new vocabulary	• language of stative description • giving instructions • modal verbs • listening/writing	Still some confusion with: • in a pub • at somewhere else • in England, but on an island • students wrote lots about Recife

3	'The grammar auction' see 'Daily evaluation' day 2 and chart: • games • dictation	• students buy sentences they can correct • correct written work • present reasons	• to correct students' written work • to work on word order • to build self and peer trust • to introduce proof-reading	• listening skills • writing skills • to develop awareness for self-monitoring mistakes	• Great! We had lots of fun. Students loved arguing about their correction work. • I'll correct errors tomorrow.
4	'Four stories into plays' Gave out corrected errors see chart: • drama • Q-forms • narrating • word order	• read a short story – mime it to the others • discuss others' stories, ask questions about them. • write the one you liked most	• to have some fun • to review verb + ed • to make questions	• reading skills (information transfer) • Q-forms • past tenses	• students use less Portuguese now, lots of English. • Shyness and fears have reduced. • Question forms still difficult.
5	'Another day in Paradise' – song see chart: • song/music • listening/ pronunciation • vocabulary • speaking	• discuss old woman picture • invent a character/ personality for her • cloze activity	• pronunciation practice • listening • input of new vocabulary • to point out process is important too	• listening and speaking	• Some parts of tape were too difficult, but mostly OK. • Students enjoyed the link picture–song

Weekly evaluation: Students said they wanted more activities like 'The Grammar Auction' with miming (or even with speech, i.e. role plays). Expressing feelings still a bit of a mystery. So, I'll do some more humanistic type activities like day 1.

11 Reality therapy: using negotiated work in a technical-writing class

Wendy Newstetter

By all accounts, today's workplace is changing. Some of the trends that are transforming the comfortable mega-corporations of earlier times to the leaner and more competitive organisations of the future include

1. the re-engineering of organisations;
2. the subsequent downsizing of companies, and contracting of work to outsiders;
3. the move to ensure quality measures that seek both client and worker input.

Naturally as these trends work to remould the very idea of what successful organisations look like, companies are redefining what the ideal employee brings to the workplace. This is particularly the case with engineers.

Certainly, the engineer of today must possess state-of-the-art technical skills. However, in contrast to the era of more commodious corporations, these skills are not in themselves sufficient. Increasingly, as shrinking organisations shed the buffers that historically existed between technical and non-technical employees, engineers are having to sharpen their oral and written communication skills. Working directly with non-engineering staff or with engineers from different specialities, they must be able to produce and talk about technical and non-technical documents in ways that are sensitive to and reflect downsized organisations. Engineers must also have the ability to work with uncertainty and ambiguity for, as quickly as the workplace is changing, so are expectations and demands. As a teacher of writing in a competitive engineering school in the south-eastern part of the United States, I have incorporated negotiated work into my technical-writing class for upper level engineering students. I like to think that in structuring the course this way is to give the engineers a preview of what they will experience in the changed workplace. You could say I am giving them a bit of reality therapy.

The context

To speak of negotiation involving students and faculty at the institution where I teach is to speak of something that rarely, if ever, goes on. Most technical institutions of higher education embrace the transmission model or what Paolo Freire (1972) refers to as the 'banking' model of education. Professors lecture to classes of 100 and upwards, depositing knowledge or information in students in the same way that the average account holder deposits money in a bank account. Underlying this model of education is the notion that the account or student is empty until the deposit has been made. This model of student emptiness or, if I may use the term, disenfranchisement, is further exacerbated by institutional cultures which embrace the bell curve in testing situations, that is student grades must fall within a range that conforms to a statistical bell-shaped curve which lowers some grades while increasing others. Such a system in effect pits student against student and ultimately student against teacher. The end product of this cultural orientation is students who are very competitive and determined but highly teacher dependent. Just getting students to understand how work might be negotiated in such a climate is a challenge.

Nevertheless, recent constructivist movements in education and cognitive science have directly challenged the transmission model as promoting shallow, non-transferable learning. Advocates of constructivism stress the need to encourage learners to engage in activities that push them to construct plausible interpretations of events based on their current knowledge and the scaffolding provided by the teacher (Papert, 1980; Brown, *et al.*, 1989). Perkins (1992) emphasises the need for 'active learners' who are not only processors of information but more importantly elaborators and interpreters as well. Such approaches to learning resonate with Freire's problem-posing methodology which actively encourages and engages the students' current skills and knowledge in acquiring new ones.

As an instructor, my movement towards a more constructivist or problem-posing approach occurred in the third term that I taught the technical-writing class. In the two previous terms, as I was new to this area of writing pedagogy, I followed a more traditional curriculum where students all wrote the same set number of teacher-determined assignments meant to represent the range of technical documents they might encounter as professionals. Trained as an applied linguist and ESL/EFL teacher, however, I was troubled by two things. The first was the glaring lack of authenticity in such a curriculum. The range of students populating these technical-writing classes is impressive. Any class might include the following majors: chemical, civil, systems, electrical, textile, aerospace, mechanical, computer or biogenetic engineering, architecture and management. To assume that professionals from such a wide variety of fields will write the same documents, even though the majority are in technical fields, is naive at best and bad pedagogic practice at worst. Some would justify having students all compose the same documents on the grounds that writing of any kind that causes students to consider differing audiences and rhetorical modes would improve their written use of the language. Something may be said for this. However I felt that I was participating in some kind of charade, and I wondered about the level of student motivation in what appeared to be a bogus situation. This point of view was heightened by my own lack of expertise in current workplace documents. I had no idea what kinds of reports, say, chemical engineers write, so to be making decisions about what such students should write was in some ways preposterous. When questioned by students about assignments, I was finding it hard to justify decisions I had taken.

Tied to this problem of authenticity was the troubling realisation that the traditional curriculum fostered teacher-dependent, non-reflective student behaviour. Students did not have to think about the kinds of writing they would need once they left the institution; I was doing that for them. Like a manufacturer, I was 'assembling' these students like cars on an assembly line. All they had to do was wait for the next part to be added, for the next fixed assignment to appear on the board. Since no input on assignments was solicited, even though many were qualified to provide it, no independent decision-making or reflection was required. I had constructed passive roles for them. I was playing banker along with others.

I found this problematic for, as a veteran ESL/EFL teacher, I had seen the value of involving students in classroom decision-making. When students have to determine what they will do and then negotiate it with others, they develop valuable skills. They must first reflect on current and future needs which calls for independent assessment and decision-making. Then they must develop a plan that addresses those needs, articulating it, justifying it and persuading others that their plan is sound. These steps require strong communication skills. Student participation in decision-making also requires students to invest in both the process and the outcomes of these negotiated assignments, for if they are not authentic or valuable the students can only blame themselves. Finally negotiation forces students to work with uncertainty, for they must project and hypothesise about what is best for them. I could see that by adding a negotiated component to this class, I could develop skills that would serve them well in the workplace. I could also address the two problems of authenticity and motivation if students were deciding what documents were best for them to produce. Consequently after two terms, I totally restructured the course. In the following section, I provide an account of negotiated work in my technical-writing class.

An account of the process

In the previous section, I explained the problems with the traditional approach: lack of authenticity and failure to encourage independence or reflection. Here I show how I have attempted to address both of these problems in what I refer to as the Workplace Writing Project. Students begin working on this in the fourth week of the term. Prior to this, we work on developing skills that allow them to understand the elements that make for successful technical documents in general: language use, structure and graphics. These are then deployed by the students throughout the project.

Workplace Writing Project

Step 1: The ethnographic interview

One way to ensure that students are working on documents that are authentic to their future careers is to have them conduct workplace interviews with practising professionals. In the Workplace Writing Project, students are individually responsible for setting up an appointment to conduct an ethnographic interview with an engineer in their speciality to determine the types and amount of writing that the engineer does. Before these interviews, I spend one class period training students for this type of interview which differs from what they associate with interviewing. I ask for a student volunteer who has workplace experience to come to the front to be interviewed by me. We sit down at the desk and I model for the class the ways in which ethnographers conduct interviews. When I have finished, I ask for observations of what I have done. From their comments, I draw out the main features of such interviewing: take nothing for granted, go deep not broad and assume an inferior position, heed insider terms and terminology and find out what they mean. I also explain the purpose of ethnographic interviewing for anthropologists and how good ethnographers have the ability to listen and gather data that allows them to comprehend the meanings and specialised understandings that reside in a culture. I point out that as novice engineers in unfamiliar workplaces, such skills can be extremely useful. I also clarify how this kind of interview differs from other types; for example: the interviewee is in charge of the topics, questions arise not from what is heard in advance, and specific answers to specific questions are not sought. Although one opportunity to use this kind of interviewing technique hardly guarantees facility, it does make the students aware of the value of asking particularised questions in unfamiliar environments.

Step 2: The group report

Using data gathered from the interviews, discipline-based student groups assemble a report on workplace writing practices found in a particular area of engineering. For example, the electrical engineers collaborate to produce a report that presents the types of documents that such an engineer might encounter on the job. The objective of this step is for the students to reflect on writing in their specialisation by developing analytic categories and commentary. They are to look for similarities and differences across workplace environments, and to think about and then write on what these might represent. They also begin to think about the kinds of documents they need to practise and would like to produce as part of the course.

Step 3: Proposal for reports 2 and 3

At this stage of the project, each student proposes two writing assignments that they would like to undertake as part of the course. The proposals are based on the students' perceptions of the writing demands they will encounter as practising engineers. These assignments may be individual or collaborative, long or short, highly technical or oriented more towards the organisational structure of the work. I ask students to:

1. indicate type of document;
2. justify the choices of proposed documents.

I expect the students to demonstrate that they have reflected on the data gathered from Steps 1 and 2, on previous workplace experiences and on future writing demands. It is possible for them to propose documents that do *not* appear in the group report, but that relate to other job or future-related activities. An example would be a former student who planned to go to law school the following year. We negotiated a proposal for two reports related to his future plans:

1. a report, generated by an interview with the Writing and Research

Instructor at the school he intended to enter, on the types of writing
first-year law students encounter; and
2. a law brief of the kind he could expect to write the following year.

What I look for in these proposals is thoughtful consideration of future
writing contexts and their concomitant demands.

Step 4: Negotiation

In the negotiation phase, I discuss the proposal for the two reports with
each student. Their job is to convince me that the documents they have
chosen are appropriate and authentic to current or future professional
needs. The criteria they use to argue for a particular document should
derive from the workplace data they have collected. They must also
demonstrate that they have given critical thought to choosing the
document types. I can veto proposed documents based on insufficient
evidence of authenticity to current or future endeavours. I can also ask
for refinement or changes of various sorts. I sometimes encourage
students to reflect more on why they have chosen one document type
over another. This process of arriving at a mutually agreeable set of
documents is carried out orally and I can request a resubmission of the
proposal if there are major problems. My overall aim is to help students
see how taking responsibility for identifying and practising documents
they will write in the future offers them an opportunity to refine skills in
a relatively benign setting. They will not lose their jobs or irrevocably
damage their reputations because they have produced an unsuccessful
document; rather they can learn from the experience and hopefully use
that knowledge in the future. Once I am satisfied that my criteria have
been met, I sign off.

Step 5: Reports 4 and 5

At this stage, depending on their proposals, students work either
independently or in groups to produce the final two reports. I use class
time to lecture on and discuss a variety of document types that have
arisen as a result of their proposals. To generate these document types, I
pass around a sheet which requests their input on what documents we
should cover in class. If I have expertise or knowledge in the requested
documents, I conduct the class. Otherwise I ask a student who has
experience with such documents to assume responsibility. So far we
have been able to accommodate all requests. It can be seen, then, that
the proposals for reports 4 and 5 not only give students the freedom to
determine their own assignment but they also determine what will be
studied in the remainder of the course.

Step 6: Feedback

The feedback students receive focuses primarily on whether the document achieves a kind of 'ecological validity'. In other words, does the document have linguistic, semantic, organisational and formatting features that are consistent not with school-based documents but workplace documents? Students are so used to writing for teachers in classrooms that many have developed a five paragraph essay style that seeps into anything they produce. The feedback I provide aims to identify locales of seepage. I also point out where formatting or organisation of the document either succeeds in bringing across the message or fails. Overall, as I use an information-processing approach in teaching writing, the feedback offers observations on how well the document delivers information. Given a longer term, individual conferences and discussions with the students about the reports would allow us to collaboratively negotiate a common understanding of the document as a potential artefact of the workplace. Unfortunately, the ten-week term does not afford this luxury.

Some observations

Getting them to hear

Although every term I feel somewhat anxious about students abusing the freedom to determine the documents they write, up to now nothing has justified that fear. The problem has not been with the quality of work or student investment, but in just getting them to 'hear'. During the first quarter, although the negotiated parts were in the syllabus and I had talked about them several times in class, the students behaved as though they could not understand me. Finally, as we neared the due date for the proposals, one student sheepishly asked in class 'You mean we can decide what we want to do for reports 4 and 5?' The way he asked the question indicated that he was sure he was asking an impossibly idiotic question. Clearly for this student, the idea that he could decide what to write for an assignment was bordering on lunacy. He was not alone, however, in his inability to comprehend this system. It was soon apparent from follow-on questions that term and in every one since that he was just the boldest. Nearly every student finds it difficult to grasp the concept of a negotiated syllabus. This is not hard to understand given the institutional culture of bell curves and knowledge deposits in student accounts. Years of disenfranchisement withers the sense for these students that they might know best what they need to learn. Getting them to hear, in my experience, is the hardest part of a negotiated curriculum.

Outcomes

In the three terms that I have used this revised approach to technical writing, the quality of the student work, the variety of documents and the student evaluations have convinced me that negotiation is an important component of this course.

Quality of the work

By the time of the first negotiated work, I have already seen samples of every student's work. When I compare these with the negotiated documents, by and large, the latter are more professional, more committed and more authentic to actual work contexts. Many students come for assistance which is generally not the case with the assigned documents. Generally the grades go up on these pieces and the overall quality is higher.

Variety of work

From a reader's perspective, I enjoy the negotiated phase because it means that I see a variety of documents from 50-page bid proposals, to instructions for a piece of technical equipment, to a letter complaining of sexual harassment. In evaluating such a wide range of document types, I become familiar with varied genres and literacy events making me more knowledgeable as a teacher of technical writing. I benefit as much from negotiation as they do.

teacher benefits
variety / more timely

Student response

On the computer-tabulated student evaluation form used at this institution, there is a space for anonymous student comments. In the terms that I have used negotiated work, students have commented very specifically on the negotiated parts of the course. Here are such comments from the most recent term:

> I thought it was great that we could select the writings we wanted to do in assignments 4 and 5.

> I also appreciated being able to choose the final reports. They hurt my grade, but better a grade in school than failure in the real world.

I particularly liked the freedom of choosing what to write at the end.

I liked that we could pick our documents types in reports 4 and 5.

I'm not sure I prefer having all five reports assigned or being able to choose the last two. Choosing gives more flexibility, but it can introduce problems if the student tries a style he [or she] is not familiar with.

The first four comments indicate favourable reactions to the negotiation, while the fifth shows ambivalence. I believe this ambivalence stems from the inevitable uncertainty that exists when a syllabus is negotiated. Many students although recognising the value of making decisions about their work, resist this uncertainty because they are used to residing in a world of teacher-determined rules. Naturally they feel discomfort when the rules are not spelled out clearly and this discomfort is exacerbated by experiences with teachers who, from their perspective, have been unfair. As the second student points out, however, it is better to deal with and get used to uncertainty in school than when a job is at stake.

If, as a teacher of technical writing, my job is to aid the students' transition from school-based writing to workplace writing, then I must, to the extent possible, create a classroom which replicates aspects of the real world. In having student engineers reflect on and negotiate what they will write in my class, in making them take responsibility for what they will learn, I like to think I am introducing them to, and facilitating their movement from, the confines and relative predictability of academia to the changing and uncertain workplace that faces them today.

12 Negotiation of outcome: evaluation and revision decisions in the writing curriculum

Margaret Sokolik

The current emphasis on process in composition courses represents a significant improvement over earlier models in writing pedagogy. However, even in this approach to writing instruction, instructors or programmes often leave students out of the final stage of the process, that of evaluation. The final outcome from the essay, whether a grade or an instruction to rewrite, traditionally, and sometimes programmatically, rests only in the instructor's hands. Indeed, there are scores of research articles describing ways that instructors and programmes can evaluate students (Chaudron, 1983; Brown and Bailey, 1984; Conner and Kaplan, 1987; Zamel, 1987), yet little on how students can participate in the evaluation process (for an alternative view, however, see Elbow 1993).

The following account describes a process of negotiation that fully involves students throughout the evolution of their essays, including evaluation. In this description, negotiation involves the co-operative development of a vocabulary for discussing and carrying out evaluation. It does not suggest a lock-step vision of what a 'good' or 'bad' paper is. In addition, in this model, negotiation occurs not only between student and instructor, but also among students. This underscores the importance of the fact that negotiation takes place not merely as an exercise of power, or a sort of 'bartering' for a grade, but as a shared effort that places the discussion of writing within a community context. Co-operative, student-centred learning in this way has been shown to be a successful curricular strategy (see, for example, Kagan, 1986; Johnson, 1989a).

Context

The process described here takes place within a first-year writing course in a four-year programme at the University of California, Berkeley. Most first-year students are required to take a writing examination upon entrance to the university. A score of '6' or above in this examination exempts students from the writing course, and satisfies one part of the university's reading and composition requirement. Students who score below '6' are required to take the course.

The required writing course is intensive, and meets for six hours a week for a 15-week semester. It carries six units of credit, as opposed to three or four for other reading and composition courses. In addition, it requires a minimum of 40 pages of written text, some of which is presented in a final portfolio.

Many of the enrolled students (approximately one-third) speak English as a second language (ESL). Some sections of the course are designated for ESL students, although students who are identified as exhibiting significant second-language competence in their entrance examinations are not required to enrol in those specially designated sections.

Rationale

Negotiation allows students who have been passive consumers of evaluation and grades to become key players in the assessment of their own work. This may be particularly effective with students whose interaction with English writing has been either as 'outsiders', that is, as speakers of English as a second language, or as 'failures', that is, students who are unable to satisfy university writing standards upon entrance. Such students often appear to have had minimal interaction with writing, either with discussing or critiquing it, either their own work or the writing of others. As a result, they appear to view the marking of their papers as a mysterious process; they surrender their work to an 'authority' or 'expert' and then hope for the best.

This attitude can be detrimental to students' confidence in their own writing abilities. When students have not fully involved themselves in understanding the features of good writing, or they misunderstand instructors' comments on their papers, the grading process can sometimes be seen as capricious. Similarly, it leads students to decide (rightly or wrongly), as one student informed me, that teachers do not take 'effort' into consideration when grading papers – that all we care about is 'nit-picking with red pens'.

In this context, then, negotiation performs two functions: it involves students directly in the evaluation process, and allows them to make decisions as to the quality and degree of completion of their work. Thus, they are in control of revision decisions as well. The following description explains further how these functions are implemented.

A procedure for negotiated evaluation and revision

The procedure described here can, of course, be tailored to fit different schedules and needs. However, it is important that all the steps be completed to prepare students fully for the task of self-evaluation. Without this preparation, students would most likely find the task of self-evaluation confusing, or even too difficult.

Step 1: Reading preparation

Many students upon entering the university have had little or no experience in discussing the qualities of good writing. Although they have read and written in high school, their experience in critiquing text often revolves around comprehension exercises or theme-based writing tasks. Thus, before engaging students in negotiation and self-evaluation, they must become comfortable with using a common vocabulary in evaluating writing.

In order to foster discussion of the writing process, all students are given a set of three papers written by former students. (These papers all respond to the same assignment and represent a range of strengths and weaknesses.) The students take the papers home with instructions to make remarks about all aspects of the writing: content, organisation, grammar, mechanics and so forth. They are instructed that they must make positive comments about the writing in addition to critical ones. They then fill out a chart, summarising their comments (see Figure 12.1). After commenting on the papers, they must also rank-order the papers, and be prepared to defend their rankings.

During the next class session, students form small groups of three or four. They compare their comments and charts, and combine and condense them onto a blank table. A general class discussion regarding their combined comments then takes place.

Step 2: Creating a rubric

After the class discussion, and in the same small groups, students now create a list of factors they believe important in the evaluation of an essay. They use their charts (from Step 1) as guidelines for this new list. Each small group presents its final list to the class as a whole. The class then narrows, focuses and finally negotiates a list of the most important elements of essay evaluation. If they feel it necessary, they may also weight each element for its relative importance.

At this point the instructor first supplies his or her opinion, and enters into the negotiation of the rubric/evaluation scheme. The instructor

Paper	Negative aspects	Positive aspects	Ranking
First paper title			
Second paper title			
Third paper title			

Figure 12.1   Chart for commenting on the sample papers

may find it necessary to introduce ideas that did not come out of the discussion, or to ask students to think more critically about some of their choices. For example, in one discussion, the students had decided that 'grammar shouldn't count'. This led to questions of what issues of grammar *were* important to them, and how meaning and grammar might be intertwined. After discussion, the students came to the conclusion that they did not mean that grammar 'didn't count', but that grammar alone should not decide the fate of a paper's evaluation. This was a negotiated outcome that both I, the instructor, and the students could live with. Above all, the instructor may need to arbitrate unresolved differences and to help students develop compromises that are satisfactory to the class.

Step 3: Norming sample papers

Once the final negotiated rubric is completed and printed, the students participate in a 'norming session'. The instructor supplies the rubric along with another set of (anonymous) sample essays, either copies of the entrance exam or papers from a previous semester. Then again in small groups the students read the sample papers (each group receives the same set of papers), rank-order them, and finally complete an evaluation for them, assigning them grades. The papers are then discussed by the entire group, and the rankings and evaluations negotiated. This session can be extended to two class sessions, or repeated later in the term to keep students focused on the standards they have established.

The norming session, combined with the previous reading and commenting on sample papers, allows students the opportunity to see clearly the different ways of reading and thinking about writing. Students rapidly recognise that there is not necessarily only one way to read or mark a paper. They also see the intermingling of factors in evaluation: how grammar affects meaning, how the introduction may guide the organisation, how vocabulary choice affects coherence and so on.

Step 4: Self-evaluation

After the students have finished writing an assigned composition, they submit it to the instructor. The instructor comments extensively on the papers, but does not put grades on them, nor does he or she make any grade decisions (either overtly or covertly). The instructor then returns the essays to the students, who then use the rubric (see Appendix 12.1 for a sample rubric/evaluation page and Appendix 12.2 for a completed one) developed by the class to review the comments by the instructor, reflect on their own assessment of their work and then complete the evaluation form.

The evaluation form is returned, with the paper, to the instructor. The instructor reads the students' comments and the grades they gave themselves. If the instructor feels a student has misunderstood his or her comments, or inappropriately assessed his or her paper in some way, the instructor schedules a conference with the student to discuss these discrepancies. If the instructor feels that the student has evaluated his or her own work fairly and has followed the standards established by the class, the grade is recorded.

In a case when a conference needs to be scheduled, it is important that the teacher does not simply 'take back' the reins of control by informing the student that he or she is 'wrong' in the assessment of the essay. In the spirit of true negotiation, the conference should present an opportunity for both the instructor and the student to discuss their understanding of the strengths and weaknesses of the paper, and to decipher comments and evaluation of the work. It is also important that the instructor go into the negotiation conference with an open mind and a willingness to listen to the student's concerns. One mistake in negotiating would be to go into the conference already convinced that a paper deserves a particular grade. Even trained readers evaluate pieces of writing differently (Elbow, 1993: 188), so it is critical that the instructor value the student's thoughts on his or her own work, and not be inflexible on the issue of a grade.

In addition, teachers should be attuned to the 'hidden messages' that are present in students' self-evaluations. I have found that students who 'overestimate' their own work often want some recognition for their 'effort', that is the time, research, reading and rewriting that may have gone into the final product. Conversely, students who 'underestimate' their own work (which, by the way, happens much more frequently than overestimation), seem often to be signalling that they did not put their full effort into the work, or that they had hoped to devote more time to the process. In each of these cases, however, this opens up the opportunity for a rich discussion about how time and effort expended can be evaluated in the context of evaluating a 'product' – that is a paper – and whether time and effort should be evaluated at all. These discussions should always be framed by referring to the rubric, which helps the students to ground their remarks in the negotiated decisions of the class.

Finally, during this evaluation process, the instructors must ask themselves how important the final grade on a writing assignment is. That is, if a student has given herself an A–, and the instructor believes the paper to be a B+ paper, how convinced is the instructor that his or her assessment is the 'right' one, and that there would be grave consequences if the A– were assigned, rather than the B+? Again, the student's opinion on this matter must receive consistent consideration and weight in order to fulfil the promise of true negotiation.

Step 5: Making revision decisions

Inevitably, after reading the instructor's comments or rereading their own papers, many students will want an opportunity to revise their work. One option in this case is for the instructor or student to deem the essay 'not ready for a grade'. If this decision is reached, the student and instructor negotiate a meaningful revision plan, in which specific strategies for improving the paper are created. After the revision is completed, the students and the instructor repeat the last two stages (Steps 4 and 5).

Outcomes

The positive outcomes have been outlined above, but they bear some repetition. First, through the process of discussing writing samples and negotiating a class rubric/evaluation scheme, students develop the ability to see strengths and weaknesses in their own writing. In addition, they can discuss their writing in a language common to the classroom community. Through self-assessment, students develop an 'investment' in the writing, revision and evaluation of their own work. They have not merely given up the final outcome from the paper to a higher authority; in turn, this helps to demystify the process of reading and evaluating.

However, there are potential difficulties with this system. Differences in cultural or educational background can present resistance to this method in certain students. These students may feel uncomfortable with taking on the role of evaluator. As one student informed me, 'That's your job'. Also, some students may feel it inappropriate to give themselves high marks, or to write positive comments about their own work. In these cases, one-to-one conferences with those students can help to clarify the difference between accurate, honest assessment and 'bragging'.

Another potential problem with this system is that it is more time-consuming than a simple one- or even two-step evaluation process. Teachers may need to find ways to lessen the burden of reading not only essays, but now evaluations and revision plans as well. It may help to limit self-evaluation to certain assignments (especially ones that present especially thorny evaluation issues, such as personal essays), or to limit the number of times a paper can be submitted and revised. Although in an ideal world, revision would be allowed until 'perfection' was attained, in the real world, all writers work under deadlines and must finish their work. However, it is equally important that instructors do not become 'composition slaves' (Hairston, 1986).

Conclusion

Negotiation – between students and instructor, or among students – is a powerful tool in assessment of writing. For the teacher committed to a process approach, it offers an alternative to the somewhat incongruent practice of giving students control over their writing up until the moment of truth, that is the moment when grades are assigned. Thus, it also removes the 'grade *ex machina*' stage of the writing process. Instead, evaluation and revision become integral parts of the student's repertoire, not merely decisions left to the instructor's greater wisdom and expertise.

Appendix 12.1
A student-developed rubric

The following rubric was developed by students in the spring of 1994.

ESSAY EVALUATION

<u>Instructions</u>: Read the instructor's comments carefully and reflect on your own thoughts about your essay. Then answer the following questions fully and honestly. Return this page and your paper to the instructor by the next class meeting. You may write on another sheet of paper if you need more space.

1. Evaluate the content of your paper. Did it satisfy the assignment? Was it focused and interesting? Was it long enough? Did it argue effectively?
2. Evaluate the organization of your paper. Does it have an effective introduction and conclusion? Did you use appropriate transitions? Does the order of paragraphs make sense? Are there problems (such as run-together paragraphs, undeveloped paragraphs, etc.)?
3. Evaluate the diction and expression in your paper. Did you use the appropriate tone for the type of writing this is? Did you have many difficulties with idioms or word choice? Was it repetitive or wordy?
4. Evaluate the grammar of your paper. How many different grammar problems are you able to identify, and what type are they? Explain fully. Are they, in your opinion, minor problems, or do they interfere with understanding?
5. Evaluate the mechanics of your paper. Were there many spelling or punctuation errors? Did you indent properly and leave adequate margins? Were quotations appropriately formatted and cited?

Based on your assessment, give yourself a grade. Explain your choice of a grade.

GRADE:

Explanation:

Appendix 12.2
A student evaluation

This is an example evaluation, written by a Vietnamese immigrant student. It concerns his essay, an analysis of *Life and Death in Shanghai*, by Nien Cheng.

ESSAY EVALUATION

<u>Instructions</u>: Read the instructor's comments carefully and reflect on your own thoughts about your essay. Then answer the following questions fully and honestly. Return this page and your paper to the instructor by the next class meeting. You may write on another sheet of paper if you need more space.

1. Evaluate the content of your paper. Did it satisfy the assignment? Was it focused and interesting? Was it long enough? Did it argue effectively?
   The paper, I believe, is quite good. It satisfied the requirements for an analytical paper. The topic was interesting for me to write about because it contradicts what I believe Nien Cheng really is. While writing, I often have to put my personal feelings aside and just stick with my arguments. I am surprised at how well it turned out.

2. Evaluate the organization of your paper. Does it have an effective introduction and conclusion? Did you use appropriate transitions? Does the order of paragraphs make sense? Are there problems (such as run-together paragraphs, undeveloped paragraphs, etc.)?
   My introduction and conclusion are good. The body is a little bit unorganized and the transitions are rough. However, compared to the overall structure of the paper, the problems are only minor and unnoticeable, like a small speck of dust on a table.

3. Evaluate the diction and expression in your paper. Did you use the appropriate tone for the type of writing this is? Did you have many difficulties with idioms or word choice? Was it repetitive or wordy?
   I feel that I did use the right tone for this paper. There is some wordiness, but overall good.

4. Evaluate the grammar of your paper. How many different grammar problems are you able to identify, and what type are they? Explain fully. Are they, in your opinion, minor problems, or do they interfere with the understanding of the paper?
   There are a few grammatical errors. I have trouble shifting the verb tenses from the present for analysis and past for quotations and past actions.

5. Evaluate the mechanics of your paper. Were there many spelling or punctuation errors? Did you indent properly and leave adequate margins? Were quotations appropriately formatted and cited?
   There are only one or two mechanical errors in my paper. One of those two problems is that I didn't leave a space between the letter 'p.' and the page number in the citation of the quotation.

Based on your assessment above, give yourself a grade on this paper. Explain your choice of a grade.

GRADE: *A*

Explanation: *I feel that this paper is an A because like you said, 'nicely argued.' I believe I have put a lot of effort and time into writing this piece. There are a few problems, but overall a good paper.*

13 Learners, practitioners and teachers: diamond spotting and negotiating role boundaries

Lucy Norris and Susan Spencer

This paper examines an English-language course for vocational and technical teachers and managers from colleges throughout Indonesia. We examine the course participants' reactions to the initial plans for the course, the consequent tensions faced by the course organisers and how negotiation became the preferred and only option for the participants, who had very diverse backgrounds, disciplines and language levels. The account shows how a process syllabus became possible, and how the course participants and the course organisers gradually searched for common ground, respecting the different skills and learning styles of individuals.

The account also explains how different strands of the course were developed: how the whole class produced 'learning festivals' during weekly tasks, and how 'study buddy' groups worked during 'activity days' to devise activities focusing on skill areas for their peers. We explain how the idea of 'hot spots' was introduced in which individual participants, in consultation with a course organiser, drew up learning action plans, established learning journals (a diary recording comments and progress of the course) and wrote personal letters reflecting on the week's work. Finally, we suggest some ways in which the overall framework of the course could be improved in the future.

Background

The course took place at the Indonesia–Australia Language Foundation (IALF) in Jakarta. The IALF was established by the governments of both countries, and provides English-language training for study, business and work-related purposes. It operates in Jakarta and Bali with a total of 60 teachers.

The course was entitled 'Pre-departure English for Training Abroad', and lasted for eight weeks. There were two classes with 16 participants in each, taught over five days a week, with four daily contact hours and four self-study hours. The participants, who were funded by an aid project (Indonesia–Australia Technical, Vocational and Educational Project), were preparing to attend Masters courses in teaching and educational management at universities in Australia. They were all technical and vocational teachers and trainers from a wide range of disciplines and included engineers, Balinese dancers, silversmiths, hairdressers, and education administrators from institutes throughout Indonesia.

A significant proportion of the course participants had undergone some prior form of training abroad, mostly in Canada, America, Australia or Britain. The group consisted of individuals from diverse educational, social, ethnic and cultural backgrounds, with wide-ranging levels of English-language proficiency, sophistication and familiarity with Western culture, learning and teaching styles. All the course participants were living in temporary accommodation with severe budgetary restrictions in the harsh environment of inner-city Jakarta. The majority of them were Muslim, and half of the course was conducted during the month of Ramadan, which entailed strict fasting between the hours of sunrise and sunset.

An account of the course

The principal aim of the course was to enable each participant to become proficient in English in order to survive and study in Australia on a variety of academic courses. To support our work, files of materials existed from previous, successful courses, and we did not, in fact, believe that a great deal of negotiation would be essential. The existing materials had, however, been developed for relatively homogeneous groups of course participants with similar language levels. The course that we were to run was for a quite different cohort, with varying language levels, backgrounds and personal aims, and this clearly created a difficult task in training terms.

At the beginning of the course, after an orientation week, our first reaction had been to panic, and provide what we thought the course participants needed most: survival English. In order to stem a rising feeling of tension, this was done in a playful way through games and role plays. However, after the first week, it became clear that the course was fundamentally amiss. The narrow focus of the course materials treated learners as 'language-item deficient units' and aimed to top these units up with a hotchpotch of functional, structural and notional language 'bites' within the context of a traditional task-based syllabus. The classes had not gelled, and a general air of disaffection and passive resignation characterised the attitudes of both course organisers and course participants.

The initial skills-swap activity

Our immediate solution was to discard the central tenets of the planned course and to begin to consider the course participants as individuals ('diamond spotting'). All the participants were highly practical, competent teacher-practitioners. There was a dazzling variety of skills within the group, and this prompted us to redesign our plans for an end-of-week task at the end of the second week. We chose a skills-sharing task, for which each student chose, prepared and taught a skill or set of skills to a partner. Thus, a mechanical engineer demonstrated how to clean an air filter, a Balinese dancer showed steps from the lion dance and an architect explained how to distinguish different types of arches. This task succeeded in raising high levels of motivation, achieved by the excitement of bringing the external 'otherness' of the course participants' lives into the inner sanctums of the classroom.

The participants' eagerness to acquire the right language for their teaching led to workshops on specific and general structures, vocabulary and collocations, as well as identifying steps in the process of information transfer, that is, getting the teacher-practitioner course participants to focus on their teaching as well as on the language they needed. Throughout the morning of the end-of-week task there was a degree of engagement previously unseen in which participants used classroom space in a variety of ways with a splendid collection of props, realia and aids, the others in their groups asking for clarification, further explanation and repetition in order to be able to identify skin type, to sex a fish correctly or to perform a segment of a dance. Evaluation involved participants re-pairing and passing on the skills they had just learned and acquiring a further set. The 'original' trainers assessed the success of their teaching by getting their partners to teach them back. Assessment in many cases involved isolating the steps and procedures followed by trainers and identifying areas of weakness, such as insufficient information or unclear instructions.

The success of the second week, compared to the first, led us to decide upon a negotiated approach to the syllabus for the remaining weeks of the course as the only feasible basis for meeting the variety of needs of the course participants. We had created a very clear basis for uniting the course participants from our skills-swap activity: that the teacher-practitioner course participants were all involved in the process of both teaching and learning. The 'leap of faith' made by the participants in undertaking the skills-swap activity firmly logged them into a view of themselves as professionals with competencies, rather than language students with problems. The resulting shift in the direction of the course prompted by the skills-swap activity was a turning point for all involved as the psychological contract between 'helper' and 'helped' was established during the activity. Our roles and role boundaries were renegotiated and the course organisers and course participants felt united in a common, practical profession, whereby each individual had specific talents and skills.

After this point, it is difficult to separate the various threads of the course since it evolved in many different directions, feedback and discussion generating further negotiation and adaptations to the programme, often unaided by our intervention. Role boundaries at both an interpersonal level and 'working mode' level (working individually, in pairs, in small groups or altogether) became more fluid, and it was, in fact, only after the course had ended that we realised that a process syllabus had been attempted. It is worth, however, outlining some major aspects of the course as it developed: weekly evaluation meetings, whole-class weekly tasks, 'study buddy' group activity days, and learning to learn sessions.

Weekly evaluation meetings

Building on the success of the initial skills-swap activity, we introduced the idea of weekly evaluation meetings. These focused on the work done during that week and allowed brainstorming of the tasks for the coming week, thereby providing a realistic basis for expectations of the course participants' own progress. At these evaluation sessions the groups also engaged in self-congratulation for their achievements and in soul searching to define the work to be done. In addition to these meetings, participants also wrote personal letters to the course organisers, who answered them and 'posted' them back. The letters reflected on the week's work, a culturally acceptable means of expressing oneself without causing loss of face.

Whole-class tasks

The whole-class tasks were designed and chosen by the course participants during evaluation discussions at the end of each week. These tasks were authentic, publishable and involved an information exchange between groups of course participants. For example, one task designed by the participants was to set up an educational exhibition focusing on the Australian universities where they intended to study. Each group focused on a different institution. When the exhibition was held, they were interested in finding out the information they needed from the other groups. They presented the facts using a wide variety of audio-visual, visual and verbal communication. Their interaction was video-taped, was later watched by themselves and eventually was used by another class as a resource. This type of 'learning festival' mode (as opposed to 'teaching spectacle'; see Coleman, 1987) was extremely popular with the course participants. The wide range of media and modes which they employed reinforced their sense of self-esteem as teachers, with competencies of skilled communicators.

'Study buddy' group activity days

As the course progressed, a list was built up of skills and language areas which the course participants felt they needed. Dividing into smaller 'study buddy' groups, participants researched and designed materials focusing on a particular area, negotiating the selection of an area from the common list. Having selected an area of difficulty, study groups then divided into subgroups and drew on all the resources of the IALF – from published sources to *ad hoc* chats with librarians and teachers – to devise relevant activities for their peers. The course organisers were available to help with the design and evaluation of activities and the selection of resource material, but the production of the activities was the ultimate responsibility of the 'study buddy' groups. Not only was this activity an attempt to improve skills, but it was also a highly practical exercise designed to enhance group processes between course participants.

Learning to learn sessions: strategies, journals and 'hot spots'

We introduced a variety of learning to learn sessions into the course, with the aim of supporting the course participants' own development. These included ideas for learning strategies, such as the small notebook which we gave to each participant so that they could create a personalised survival English phrase book, and work on dictionary skills and vocabulary learning.

Some of the learning to learn areas we investigated with the participants were different learning styles and how to adapt strategies suggested by others to meet individual learning needs. We analysed aspects of the learning process by demonstration, with activities and taped class discussions. Early in the course, for example, it became clear that team building was needed in order to establish a harmonious working environment. We used a variety of teacher-led activities to focus on group processes, so that participants could analyse their own individual contributions when negotiating and working together. One activity, for example, involved designing, building and testing a container capable of catching an egg from a drop of 12 metres without breaking it. After focusing in this way on group processes, participants started to make connections with other areas of the course. Some of the participants discovered that perhaps sessions plodded along due to dominating or inflexible participants, and it was a group responsibility to ensure that turn-taking in conversations was more equally divided.

We also introduced reflective learning journals in order to provide an ongoing dialogue between ourselves, as course organisers, and the course participants. These journals allowed the participants to express their thoughts and provided an individual, direct syllabus for us to jointly negotiate and then fulfil. Increasingly, this led to participants asking for further input via their journals. For example:

> I want more conversation about the party.

> [W]hat I still want to learn is more about the language of Western Social interaction and its culture, for example, friendships and appropriate language/behaviour between men and women.

Another idea that we initiated were five minute 'hot spots', or individual consultations. During these sessions, where mutual feedback was given and received, action plans for self-study time were negotiated and journals were reviewed. A participant profiling-system was adopted for record keeping, enabling participants to see their strengths and weaknesses, and what action they were taking to enhance their learning. Each participant kept a folder of documents to build up a rounded picture of their own progress. These included marked final drafts with the relevant feedback and evaluation. The charting of objectives achieved in the profiles covered social and cultural issues as well as language and personal growth. Some examples of written feedback from course participants are:

> Befor [sic] I'm ashamed to speak in public but now I could.

> I want more help in this aspect: grammar of explaining. . .

> I think that this activity lasted too long and some of us got borin. Better next time, maybe to limit the time. . .

In retrospect: the nature of the negotiation

As the account has made clear, the nature of the course participants, with their varying needs and experiences, necessitated a complete change in focus for the planned course; towards a process syllabus. This required a shift of perceptions on many levels:

- to view the programme as education rather than training;
- to regard the participants as competent teachers in their right, rather than examinees with grades;
- to view ourselves as skilled, confident and experienced educators rather than founts of language knowledge; and
- to see both course organisers and course participants as creators of materials, rather than recipients of published material.

Underlying the desire to change focus were deeply seated ideological attitudes central to the belief systems of both ourselves – British course organisers – and the Indonesian course participants. In general, Indonesian philosophy is based on creating a sense of unity from diversity, harmony, co-operation, self-reliance and national esteem. Indonesian teachers and public civil servants are required to follow courses in this prescribed national ideology. We, the course organisers, had been trained and educated in the British primary-school philosophy of the 1970s – that of small group activities, learner choice of activity, freedom of movement throughout the class, individual help and class project work which was displayed, published or recorded in some way. Although the Indonesian teachers and ourselves thus came from different ideological and pedagogic backgrounds, underlying both sets of value systems were strong similarities. These were the importance of creating self-esteem and self-reliance, co-operation, freedom of choice and mutual respect of the individual.

Once this value base had been established through the skills-swap activity, negotiation began to take place. Underpinning the negotiation was a desire on the part of the both course participants and the course organisers to find a common topic or theme for discussion; there was a desire to attempt to create understanding not just between the helpers and the helped but also between peers. As the course participants were all teachers, we all felt that the themes of culture, training and education would be appropriate topics. The following are some examples of the weekly tasks:

- a trainer/course participant teaching another participant one of her or his technical skills;
- small groups comparing aspects of culture in Indonesia and Australia; and
- large groups organising exhibitions for disseminating information on institutes and colleges in Australia.

One area of negotiation, which prompted the learning to learn sessions, was how the participants wanted to learn. During discussions on learning styles, it became apparent, for example, that the technical and vocational teachers learned best experientially and reflectively: this was their general preferred style, with tasks and activities tending to be practical and aesthetically pleasing, rather than conceptual and logical. During the study groups and 'hot spot' consultations, the participants were able to reflect on what they had learned and enjoyed, and use this information to feed into the design of the following week's tasks.

Once we had agreed on a common theme and learning methodology, during which an atmosphere of equality was created, free and open discussion could take place. Joint goals were set, decisions made, work implemented and evaluated, and plans redesigned. Within class time, participants chose the task they wished to complete the following week, and how and with whom they wished to carry it out. Study groups decided which skill area they would like to focus on during the activity days, and designed materials which other participants could use. Individual participants discussed with the organisers their action plans and what materials they would need from the library. The negotiation was therefore evolving, overlapping and multi-directional amongst course participants, course organisers and materials.

Participant reactions and revisions to the course

Undoubtedly, one of the biggest difficulties of the course was the struggle towards transferring the responsibility for learning from ourselves, as the course organisers, to the course participants. As the participants were simultaneously teachers and learners, many of them slowly and guardedly realised that if they were to survive in a Western academic environment then they would have to make deep-rooted attitudinal changes. Their journals illustrated a range of responses to this rather threatening concept:

> If I learn alone and have difficulties I can't ask other people. In groups I am shy. If the teacher gives me all her information, I'll be very happy . . .

> [I] seem to be very weak at reading and writing, therefore I am going to concentrate on these two skills more than the rest. I shall do this by using the self-access materials provided and double-checking with my study-buddies . . .

> I want to be what my office hopes and more. I can only do this by myself, it is up to me now I have better ideas on learning strategies and a proper action plan to help me. . .

Retrospectively, and for many of the reasons previously outlined, there are a number of changes that could hone the course framework that finally emerged. One of these would be to make clear the overall aims of the course, learning strategies and possible working modes, and to make these a clear focus for negotiation. The success of the activity days, for example, was obvious, and it was highly stimulating for teachers to observe how students would adapt classroom activities they had particularly enjoyed or found useful. Yet, there was a sense of overkill after the third session, perhaps a lingering suspicion that the course organisers were not overtly in control of proceedings. For example, having given students instructions on timing and an expected number of activities they should aim for, and aiming to encourage initiative, we left students alone. Feedback suggested that we 'should have rung a bell'; a perception of logistics gone astray. We tried to focus the participants on how they would have changed this themselves. A number of participants were not happy, however, without the presence of a course organiser in the near vicinity for a greater proportion of the time, although this was clearly an impossibility since seven or eight classrooms were set up with the various activities at any one time.

Clearly, one of the main reasons for the overall success of the course was our initial decision to take the plunge and abandon the existing materials and course design. Fortunately, we were working in an institution where it was possible for the management to tolerate this degree of flexibility and, indeed, to welcome and support the change with enthusiasm. Central to our successful response, however, was our attempt to discover a values system common to both course organisers and course participants, and to appeal to this system throughout the course. Once we had a mutual sense of professionalism, the structure of the course could be successfully negotiated in the public arena of the classroom and the private learning goals of the course participants.

Part 3   Accounts of practice in teacher education

Overview

A common discovery in the chapters that follow is the impact teachers feel when they participate in negotiation about a course which they are attending. All the writers agree that teacher education should provide access to alternatives in classroom pedagogy. Whilst many language teacher-education courses offer participants readings or lectures and discussions about such alternatives, it seems that few provide actual experience of them. Recurring feedback which the authors of the following chapters received once they had initiated negotiation with teachers was that reading or hearing about process work in the classroom was a pale reflection of the challenges, tensions and realisations that emerged from direct engagement in it. As the writers reveal, participants' reactions to the experience are very diverse and range from positive adoption and trialling of negotiation with their own students, through dismissal because it was seen as impractical in a situation outside the particular teacher education context, to one or two teachers even wondering whether they could continue teaching as a career! One aspect of the experience remained consistent, however. It directly engaged participants' values and attitudes about language education and generated serious reflection on the relative roles of teachers and students and what it means to teach and to learn.

The following chapters also confirm that, once we have been trained and socialised in the role of 'the teacher', we constantly struggle with the distinction between being the authority and being authoritative in our classroom work and relationships. The writers themselves directly experienced this tension in being positioned by certain institutional demands, student expectations and their own self-imperatives as teacher educators, so that they were constantly obliged to juxtapose these with their beliefs and practices in working through negotiation. The teacher participants in the writers' courses most certainly transferred their assumptions about the teacher's role onto the teacher educators themselves, and such moments often became a focus of dissent and/or a significant opportunity for reassessment of themselves as teachers. Despite accepting the current rhetoric of 'learner-centredness', 'collaborative learning' or 'autonomy', for example, several of the teacher participants strongly resisted the challenge that they themselves become less teacher dependent and take greater responsibility for their own learning. The chapters that follow describe such tensions and their resolution in a range of different teacher education situations. They describe different ways and the different extents in which negotiation was initiated and, in particular, the various reasons why teachers questioned or valued their participation in it.

Confronted by a mixed group of pre-service and experienced teachers in her language-teaching methodology course at Boston University, USA, Suzanne Irujo, in Chapter 14, realised that the very heterogeneity of the experiences, needs and interests of such a group could only be resolved through negotiating the syllabus for their semester together. Irujo describes her unplanned discovery of the positive impact upon her students' involvement through shared decision-making on course content, procedures and assignments. From this discovery, she adopted negotiation as a key element within her course in subsequent years. She traces an interesting evolution over four years from this initial discovery to 'negotiation by choice' through 'negotiation as challenge' and thence to 'negotiation through change'. She adapted her course at each phase and concludes why she has come to see negotiation with teachers as providing them with experientially-based access to some of the current developments in applied linguistics. She also concludes by emphasising some of the key deductions she has gleaned from developing a process syllabus.

Almost all of the authors in Part 3 reveal that negotiation in teacher education is not a straightforward and easy undertaking and that one of the reasons for this appears to be that teachers find it particularly challenging because of their seeming lack of practice in doing it. In Chapter 15, Michael McCarthy and Michael Makosch raise the interesting possibility that greater explicit awareness of the conventions and workings of discourse is likely to enable and refine the capacity to negotiate. In endeavouring to facilitate change in perspectives upon language as subject matter, and in the classroom practices of experienced teachers of languages to children and adults in a very wide range of teaching contexts across Europe, McCarthy and Makosch have organised a series of two-week residential courses in Britain over a period of ten years. The inevitable diversity of priorities, interests and experiences of the participants combined with the intensity of a residential course appear to the writers to provide an ideal opportunity for some negotiation of course contents and working procedures. A key aspect of the course in which negotiation appears unavoidable is the requirement that participants collaborate in small groups in order to undertake a project which most often entails data gathering in the local community. Past experience of the tensions that arose within groups and between course tutors and participants during this major piece of work has led the writers to provide initial intensive work through a range of tasks upon discourse such as, for example, the discourse of teacher–student exchanges in the classroom, or discourse that typifies student interaction during language-learning tasks. In this way, McCarthy and Makosch see the content of such work as enabling participants to become discourse analysts and, thereby, attain sharper awareness of how they themselves participate in discourse. The writers believe that such initial work not only provides the teachers with an informative knowledge base for teaching languages but also a refined capacity to undertake negotiation during the latter part of the course in more effective ways.

The final two chapters in Part 3 provide accounts in which the teacher endeavoured to negotiate virtually all aspects of the curriculum in which she and the students were engaged. In Chapter 16, echoing Irujo's longer term experience, Roz Ivanič describes the unfolding of a course devoted to professional issues in language teaching which sought to engage experienced teachers in the negotiation of the content, working procedures and assessment. The 20-week course is part of an MA at Lancaster University, Britain, for English language teachers from a very wide range of countries. Ivanič bases her account on eight years' experience as one of the team of tutors on the course. She describes the rationale for the course and its essential characteristics. Ivanič identifies four key elements of the experience relating to the role of negotiation, the explicit emphasis upon process, the issue of content selection and the centrality of the prior work experience which participants bring to the course. Finally, Ivanič provides a revealing account of the tensions and difficulties which the course provokes.

In Chapter 17, Kate Wolfe-Quintero identifies her experience of negotiation during a course for ELT professionals as a 'participatory dialogue'. Her account of initiating negotiation on the content, working procedures and assessment with participants on a teaching of writing course at the University of Hawaii, USA, is particularly informative because it is based upon detailed data collected during the life of the course. These sources of evaluative reflections include her own journal, student journals, and observational and interview data collected by a researcher colleague. Although the main focus of negotiation with the participants was initially upon course content, as in other writers' experiences, the sharing of decisions and its wider implications began to reverberate through all aspects of the course. Her account echoes that of Ivanič, particularly on the issue of the roles of teacher/teacher educator in relation to student/teacher participant. Wolfe-Quintero identifies the crucial issue of recurring conflict between providing a supportive context for learning and the seemingly naturalised asymmetry in the social relationship between teacher and student. Through the challenge of negotiation, most of her students became particularly alert to this conflict in their feelings of relative comfort and commitment when participating in classroom decision-making. A major discovery of Wolfe-Quintero was the impact of the particular experience she offered on the teachers' perceptions of their prior pedagogical experiences. Although the course was about the teaching of writing, the negotiative process enabled an ongoing dialogue about broader pedagogical practice. For some of the participants, this proved to be a frustrating distraction while, for others, it was an unanticipated revelation.

14   A process syllabus in a methodology course: experiences, beliefs, challenges

Suzanne Irujo

As education has moved from a traditional transmission model of learning to a more collaborative, learner-centred model, the roles played by students, teachers and teacher educators have changed. For teacher educators, these roles are often contradictory. We must encourage students to rely on their own expertise, allowing them to discover and construct their knowledge and practice, supporting them as they learn for themselves how to be teachers. At the same time, we are the 'experts', possessors of specific knowledge and skills that students must acquire, and the 'gatekeepers' who judge their readiness to become teachers. The tensions created by these contradictory roles have been a major factor in my development as a teacher educator. I want my students to be able to explore areas of interest to them, engage in activities that they feel will be useful, and participate in evaluating how well they are doing. My institution states that I have to include certain material in my courses, ensure that my students meet certain competencies and pass judgement on their teaching abilities.

This chapter is the story of one of the means I have used to ease the tensions created by these contradictory roles. For several years, I have been experimenting with different ways of negotiating the content, procedures and requirements for a language teaching methodology course. What began as a means to ensure that the course met the needs of a particular group of students has become an ongoing cycle of action and reflection. It has enabled me to give students more autonomy, and allowed them to take more responsibility for their own learning. It helps me provide a model of learner-centred teaching, and allows me to operate within all of my contradictory roles.

Past experiences

Year 1: Negotiation by chance

I did not deliberately plan to implement a negotiated syllabus in my methodology course. I teach in a college of education in a large university in the USA, and for many years I did not question the requirement that I prepare a syllabus for the first day of class, listing course objectives, textbooks, reading assignments, written assignments and grading criteria. The students in my methodology class were extremely diverse (ESL, modern foreign language, bilingual education; kindergarten through to twelfth grade; graduates and undergraduates), but most of them were pre-service teachers. I felt that I was meeting their needs by covering basic techniques for presenting and developing language and content area skills, with a heavy emphasis on lesson planning, curriculum and objectives. At the start of one academic year, however, I found out that the majority of the students were experienced teachers, and it quickly became apparent that my syllabus was not going to meet their needs. We talked about why they were taking the course, what they hoped to achieve and how they thought this would be best achieved. They were forthright in expressing their belief that lesson plans and objectives were not what they needed and made some suggestions for the kinds of assignments that they felt they did need. These suggestions became a list of assignments that could be chosen as alternatives to those on the syllabus. I gave them suggestions for journals and books they could consult for information beyond what was included in our basic textbook. By the end of the first class period we had revised the course readings and requirements. Our new jointly-constructed syllabus provided for options based on what individual students felt they needed the most. The inexperienced teachers in the class could still do classroom observations and lesson plans; the experienced teachers could explore topics of their choice in term papers or curriculum projects. Those who felt that they needed a basic text could use the ones recommended on my syllabus; others were free to explore journals or more specialised texts to expand their knowledge beyond basic levels. I would meet individually with each student to decide how the final grade would be determined.

During the rest of that semester, it seemed that these students were more involved in their learning than had previously been the case. With freedom to choose their readings, they read from a wide variety of sources. With freedom to choose their written assignments, they chose those that would be most useful to them. There was one exception, and this was a student who was very reserved for most of the semester. She later said that her first reaction to the class had been extremely negative. She expected teachers to tell students what to do; because I had not done that, I must not be a good teacher. This was the first of what was to become a series of conflicts between students' expectations of what teachers' and students' roles should be, and my desire to change those roles.

The differences I saw in my students' performance that year compared to other years could very well have been due to their greater maturity. However, I wanted to find out whether it was also possible that having a voice in course requirements had led them to take more responsibility for their learning. The course evaluations contained positive comments:

> [I] appreciated Dr. Irujo's allowing the class to state preferences as to what to cover.

> I like the way that Suzanne put the students' performance into the hands of the students.

I decided to continue using a jointly-constructed syllabus, and hoped that in future classes, by explaining my purposes in doing so, I could avoid negative reactions from students with differing expectations.

Year 2: Negotiation by choice

The following year I began the semester with no syllabus, explaining to the students why I wanted them to join me in developing one together. I began the first class by asking them to brainstorm around the phrase 'language learning'. We then did the same thing with the phrase 'language teaching'. The discussion that followed helped students become aware of differences between what they had experienced in language teaching and what they believed about language learning so that they could begin to focus on how they themselves might want to teach. They were then asked to answer the following questions:

1. What would you like to learn in this course?
   Please list topics you would like to cover.
   Please list objectives you would like to attain.
2. What are the best ways to learn what you want to learn?
   Please list activities which can be done in class.
   Please list assignments to be done outside of class.
3. How would you like to be evaluated on your learning?

We synthesised the various suggestions, decided what topics to cover, made a list of written assignments for students to choose from and agreed that they would give themselves final grades at the end of the

semester. I was pleased with how the syllabus negotiation had progressed thus far.

It soon became apparent, however, that many of my international
students were uncomfortable with the results of the negotiation process.
Several of them wanted me to tell them what to read and which
assignments to do. One wanted a list of readings for all the topics that
would have been on the syllabus if we had not negotiated the content.
They all resisted having to give themselves grades. One of them said:

> It has never occurred to me that students can have a say in their
> own gradings. My culture prohibits me to take the liberty of
> evaluating the performance of myself.

I worried that semester, too. I worried that students were choosing
the easiest assignments rather than the ones that would be most
beneficial for them. I worried that they might give themselves grades
that weren't justified. I worried that I was supposed to be covering
certification competencies that weren't included on the syllabus. I
worried that my belief in the syllabus negotiation process was going to
be eroded by these concerns, by the resistance of some of my students
and by the institutional demands of my university.

Year 3: Negotiation as challenge

In order to address some of my own concerns, as well as those of my
international students, I decided to take a more active role in decision-
making during the next year's negotiation process. A teaching unit
would be strongly recommended for the final project, although individuals could get permission to do other projects. Peer teaching and
dialogue journals would be strongly suggested as procedures, although
the specific methods that we chose to carry these out would be open to
negotiation. Grades would be a combination of teacher-evaluation and
self-evaluation. I hoped that these adjustments would make the process
acceptable to students whose expectations differed from mine, and
would also enable me to fulfil the roles of 'expert' and 'judge' that my
institution demanded of me. The negotiation process itself, however,
became much more difficult that year. In the past, my classes had
consisted of eight to 15 students, so it was possible to ask everyone to
make suggestions, to then discuss these, and finally to come to a
consensus. That year, however, I had almost 30 students, and negotiation by consensus would have been far too cumbersome. I therefore
prepared a list of possible topics, plus my suggestions and other options
for written assignments, in-class activities and out-of-class activities (see
Figure 14.1). Students were asked to mark those that they were most

Topics

___ Methods and approaches   XXX = MUST INCLUDE
    ___ In general   XX   = WOULD LIKE
    ___ Specific   X   = DON'T CARE
        ___ Natural Approach   = DON'T WANT
        ___ Total Physical Response
        ___ Communicative Approach
        ___ Other _____
___ Language acquisition theory
___ Listening
___ Speaking
    ___ Pronunciation
___ Reading
___ Writing
    ___ Dialogue journals
    ___ Process writing
___ Grammar
___ Vocabulary
___ Error correction
___ Content-based language teaching
    ___ Mathematics
    ___ Science
    ___ Social studies
    ___ Literature
    ___ Music
    ___ Art
    ___ Drama
___ Games
___ Problem-solving activities
___ Information gap activities
___ Culture
    ___ Acculturation
___ Programme models
___ Use of the native language
___ Cooperative learning
___ Individualization of instruction
___ Use of aides, tutors, volunteers
___ Lesson planning
    ___ Writing objectives
    ___ Sequencing instruction
    ___ Unit planning
___ Curriculum development
___ Testing and evaluation
    ___ Standardized tests
    ___ Teacher-made tests
    ___ Portfolio assessment
___ Materials
    ___ Evaluating materials
    ___ Adapting materials
    ___ Developing materials

___ Technology
    ___ Language labs
    ___ Computers
    ___ Other _____
Please add your own topics:

Written Assignments
My suggestion: I would like everybody to do a teaching unit as their final project. If you feel that some other kind of final project is more appropriate in your particular case, please talk to me about it.

Comments:

Options for short written assignments:
___ Lesson plans
___ Materials evaluation
___ Materials adaptation
___ Materials development
___ Classroom observations
___ Interviews with teachers
___ Journals of teaching/tutoring experiences
___ Critiques of journal articles
___ Short research papers
___ Resource lists
___ Very short assignments on each topic in which you apply what you have learned about the topic.
___ Other:

In-Class Activities
My suggestion: I think some kind of peer teaching is very useful. How you want to do it can be negotiated.

Some suggestions:
Individual presentations to the whole class: one presentation, about 15 min.

Group presentations to the whole class: one/two presentations, about 45 min.

Individual presentations to small groups: many presentations, 5–10 min. each
• Groups can be homogeneous by field and level
• Groups can be homogeneous by language
• Groups can be heterogeneous, but the same each time
• Groups can be heterogeneous, different each time

Comments:

Other Activities
___ Lectures by the professor
___ Discuss readings
    ___ Homogeneous groups
    ___ Heterogeneous groups
    ___ Whole class
___ Discuss issues related to readings, but not specific readings per se
    ___ Homogeneous groups
    ___ Heterogeneous groups
    ___ Whole class
___ Participate in activities related to topic (problem-solving, cooperative learnings, etc.)
___ Participate in demonstrations of teaching techniques
___ Discuss/evaluate videotapes and/or transcripts of real classes
___ Other

Out-of-Class Activities
My suggestion: I have always found dialogue journals to be extremely useful. They take a lot of my time, but I'm willing to do them. I would especially like to try electronic dialogue journals, and I can set it up so that everyone in the class has an account on the mainframe computer, and we can all communicate by e-mail. You would have to be able to access the mainframe computer, either with a modem or by going to the main computer room.

Comments:

Other Ideas:
___ Dialogue journals between students in the class
___ Response journals in which you write your reactions to the readings, then react to your responses.
___ Other

Figure 14.1   Questionnaire used in Year 3 negotiating process

interested in learning about and doing, add other topics and activities, and make comments.

This procedure did not work well. Almost everybody wanted to cover everything, they all agreed with my suggestions for assignments and activities, and they wanted to do all of the options that were listed. Tabulating all of this took a great deal of time, and we still had to try to negotiate by consensus during the second class meeting. The syllabus that emerged was almost exactly the same as one I would have developed myself, and there were complaints that the negotiation process took too long and was a waste of time. These comments, from the final course evaluations, were typical:

> Although it is her strategy to keep the structure of the class open and flexible, I think the class is managed too loosely.

> Disappointed with amount of time wasted on planning the course, 'negotiated syllabus', etc.

Another concern I had was that once the syllabus was negotiated and put into place, it functioned in exactly the same way as more traditional syllabuses do. Typing it up and handing it out was like etching it in stone. It became the 'road map' for what we were supposed to do for the rest of the semester, and there was never any thought of going back and renegotiating it.

Year 4: Negotiation through change

Another year came, and with it another chance to try to find a better way to negotiate my methodology syllabus. As in the previous year, the class was large, and it was more diverse than ever. Consensus-building discussions were out of the question, and the questionnaire procedure from the previous year hadn't worked well. Feeling a little discouraged, I developed the syllabus myself, listing the topics and procedures that I felt were most important (see Figure 14.2). I also listed a variety of textbooks that students could choose from according to their own interests and a variety of written assignments from which to choose, but in all other respects it was a very traditional syllabus.

I was not sure what I was going to do with this syllabus on the first day of class. In order to keep it from being used in a traditional way, I wanted to find some way to overcome my students' inclination, and my own, to treat the printed word as unchangeable. It was at this point that I read the initial proposal for this volume, and I began to think of what I had been doing as 'process' rather than 'negotiation'. Perhaps making an analogy between 'process writing' and a 'process syllabus' might help all of us, since we were all familiar with the concept of a first draft in process writing as something that is meant to be revised. So I presented the syllabus as a 'first draft'; subsequent drafts could be changed based on suggestions from students or on changes I might decide to make as the course progressed. Certain things would be non-negotiable. For example, unless they were experienced teachers, students would have to show somehow that they could write acceptable lesson plans. In addition, some kind of peer teaching or teaching demonstration would be required.

Methods of Bilingual Education and TESOL
Methods of Teaching Modern Foreign Languages

Texts:

Bilingual and ESL Classrooms. C. J. Ovando & V. P. Collier. Mc-Graw Hill, 1985.

Language and Children – Making the Match. H. Anderson Curtain & C. A. Pesola. Addison-Wesley, 1988.

Making It Happen: Interaction in the Second Language Classroom. P. A. Richard-Amato. Longman, 1988.

Teaching English as a Second or Foreign Language. M. Celce-Murcia. Newbury House, 1991.

Teaching Language in Context: Proficiency-Oriented Instruction. A. C. Omaggio. Heinle & Heinle, 1986.

Topics:

1. Introduction to methods of teaching languages	7. Teaching language through content
2. Theories and methods of language teaching	8. Language and culture
	9. Language teaching programme models
3. Teaching oral skills	10. Curriculum and lesson planning
4. Teaching written skills	11. Classroom organization and management
5. Teaching grammar and vocabulary	12. Evaluation
6. Games and activities, music, drama, stories	13. Commercial materials
	14. Adaptation and supplementation of materials
	15. Technology in the classroom

Requirements:

A. Preparation of readings, attendance, participation in class discussions, peer teaching, dialogue journals

B. Three short papers to be chosen from the following:

A series of three sequential lesson plans	Critiques of two journal articles
Evaluation of a textbook or other materials	List of community resources for language teaching
Adaptation of a lesson from a textbook	Interview with language teachers and students
Development of original teaching materials	Administration and critique of a language test
Critical observations of two language teachers	Other assignments as approved by the instructor

C. Final project to be chosen from the following:

– A teaching unit consisting of a rationale, an overall plan for 2–4 weeks of materials, specific plans for one week of lessons, and a resource list. Resources should consist of adaptations of commercial material as well as original material.

– A case study of your on-going efforts to teach a language to somebody. The instruction should continue for most of the semester, and the study should document what you did, how well it work, and why you believe it worked or didn't work.

– A research paper on a topic relevant to bilingual education, ESL or foreign language teaching, with application of the research findings to practice, either through observations or through your first-hand experience.

– Other projects with approval of instructor.

Figure 14.2   Draft syllabus used in Year 4 negotiating process

The negotiation process that year was easier than it had ever been. Students understood immediately the concept of the syllabus as a draft that could be changed as we worked with it. At first they suggested no changes, so I decided to model the process. At the end of the third class it was obvious to me that we needed more time to discuss the teaching of oral skills, and the students agreed. I asked them to decide what other topic to take the time from, and a short negotiation produced a decision to eliminate the 'games and activities' topic, incorporating part of that into a second class on teaching oral skills. As the course progressed, the students began to take ownership of the course content. For example, a suggestion to spend more time on teaching language through content and to eliminate programme models came from them. They suggested turning in lesson plans for their peer teaching demonstrations, thus giving them more flexibility in choosing other written assignments. Decisions about how the written assignments would be evaluated were made jointly.

This procedure now seems to satisfy most of my concerns. More traditional students can use my draft as a guide and not be upset with a perceived lack of direction. I can recommend particular textbooks or written assignments to individual students without feeling that I am imposing my preferences on the whole class. In order to satisfy myself that certification competencies are being met, I can stipulate that certain topics and requirements are non-negotiable and must remain as they are on the draft. I am able to fulfil my multiple roles of facilitator, expert and gatekeeper with less tension and fewer contradictions.

Present beliefs

Underlying my desire to find a way for learners to participate in the development of their own course are three overlapping areas of beliefs about learning and teaching. The first has to do with 'practising what we preach' in teacher education, the second with the value of learner-centred teaching and the third with models of how learning occurs.

'Practise what you preach'

Many writers have pointed out that the process of teacher education often does not correspond to the methods students are expected to use in their own classrooms (Stern and Strevens, 1983; Milk, 1990; Porter *et al.*, 1990; Wright, 1990; Kroll and La Boskey, 1996). Most teacher educators are aware of the contradiction inherent in lecturing about co-operative learning, but it is less obvious that there is a contradiction in including Nunan's (1988b) work on learner-centred curriculum as required reading on a teacher-mandated syllabus. If we believe that negotiating a syllabus is an approach that has many benefits for students in language classes, we need to allow our students, as future teachers, to experience that approach. Teacher educators must remember that we have very little time in which to help our students think about teaching in new ways, and we cannot hope to do so by talking about things we do not practise ourselves.

There is another way in which the use of a process syllabus in a methodology class represents 'practising what we preach'. The benefits of collaborative learning have been documented by Wells and Chang-Wells (1992), who describe how collaborative talk about content to be learned helps learners acquire the kind of literate language that is required for academic success. Future teachers may have never experienced collaborative procedures, making it difficult for them to implement this kind of classroom structure. Negotiating a syllabus can provide that experience because it requires that students work together, share ideas and come to a consensus on what will be included in the syllabus.

Reflective teaching is a third way in which a process approach to syllabus design allows us to 'practise what we preach'. Reflective teaching is seen as a major way of helping teachers continually improve their teaching (Peck and Westgate, 1994; Richards and Lockhart, 1994; Stanley, 1998), and is something that we try to foster in various ways in our students. A process syllabus requires that both teacher and students periodically review goals, content, procedures and evaluation. This allows students to observe the teacher engaged in a process of reflective teaching and to participate in that process.

Learner-centred teaching

On a more general level, the process syllabus is one of several techniques that contribute to a learner-centred approach in my methodology class. The advantages of learner-centred approaches over transmission approaches have been well articulated (Altman, 1983; Kreidler, 1987; Cummins, 1988; Tudor, 1996), but transmission teaching continues to be prevalent in many teacher education programmes. Freeman (1992: 16) has called the dependence on knowledge transmission the 'Achilles heel of second language teacher education'. Language teacher educators, who are often the very people advocating a learner-centred approach, must give up their own transmission approaches if their classes and programmes are to be effective in implementing change.

A process approach to syllabus design exemplifies a learner-centred approach in several ways. First, it transfers part of the responsibility for the design of the course onto the learner. This prevents students from passively following the instructor's syllabus and assuming that, by doing so, they will learn everything they need to know. Instead it forces them to take more responsibility for their learning. Second, it provides a mechanism for meeting differing needs of diverse students within the same overall class structure. Nobody comes into teacher education with exactly the same background as anybody else. Nobody, therefore, needs to learn exactly the same things as anybody else in order to become a teacher. A process syllabus is a workable way to individualise instruction in a methodology class. Third, it helps students develop the skills they need to continue learning on their own after the course is finished. Learners who are dependent on a teacher to tell them what to do in order to learn find it difficult to learn on their own. Learners who have thought about how they can best learn will be independent life-long learners.

How people learn

The theoretical basis for learner-centred teaching is provided by constructivism, a view of learning that suggests that learners create their own knowledge based on their previous experience and their social interactions. The three principles of constructivism outlined by Poplin (1993) are all instantiated through the use of a process syllabus. The first principle is that learners acquire knowledge by constructing new meanings through social interaction, not by receiving knowledge from an outside source. When the content of a course is pre-determined by the teacher, learners view the content as coming from the teacher and/or the textbooks. They do not view either themselves or their fellow students as sources of knowledge, which limits the amount of interaction that they engage in. If we share the belief that social interaction facilitates the construction of new knowledge, we should be fostering interaction among our students and helping them see each other as resources. A process syllabus helps to do this.

Poplin's second principle is that learners transform new experiences through what they already know. No knowledge becomes truly our own until it is filtered through our own prior knowledge and experience. Students are much more likely to make connections between new knowledge and previous knowledge when they have a say in deciding what and how they are going to learn. A process syllabus makes the content and procedures of the course more meaningful to students so they better understand what they are learning.

Poplin's third principle is that learning is self-regulated and self-preserving. True learning only occurs when one wants to learn; nobody can be 'forced' to learn what somebody else wants them to learn. With a process syllabus, students are learning what they want to learn. They will be much more likely to continue learning on their own because they have taken responsibility for, and ownership of, their learning.

Future challenges

I continue to refine the ways in which I implement a process syllabus, acting on my beliefs and reflecting on how my actions move my students towards greater responsibility, ownership and autonomy in their learning. As I do so, I will keep in mind some of the things I have learned from the different approaches I have taken in negotiating my syllabus:

- Class characteristics affect the negotiation process. The size of the class, the ethnic background of the students, their teaching experience or lack thereof, and their expectations concerning teacher and student roles influence the ways in which negotiation can be done.
- When possible, the specific techniques used to negotiate the syllabus should come from the students themselves. Spontaneous negotiation procedures have been more effective than those that are pre-planned.
- Not every item on a syllabus must be negotiated. Certain items can be non-negotiable without sacrificing the benefits of the process.
- It does not matter if the result of the negotiation process resembles a more traditional syllabus. The sense of ownership that the process conveys to students is beneficial in itself.
- How students are evaluated needs to be part of the negotiation process. The teacher cannot attempt to retain total responsibility for evaluating students and still expect students to take responsibility for other aspects of the class.
- It is important that the negotiation process be ongoing. As Nunan (1988b) says, 'No decision is binding.'
- The name that is given to the negotiation process can influence how it unravels. In my case, the 'negotiated' syllabus became a traditional syllabus as soon as it was developed, but the 'process' syllabus remained negotiable throughout the semester.
- For a process syllabus to work, teachers must give up the idea that they are responsible for students' learning.

The use of a process syllabus can help to reconcile the teacher educator's conflicting roles of facilitator and expert, of supporter and evaluator. A process syllabus makes it possible to facilitate students' social construction of their own knowledge while still guiding them towards specific areas of knowledge. It makes it possible to support students' self-directed learning while still exercising the authority that society and its institutions demand. Finding a workable way to do this is not easy, and some students always resist the process. If, in the end, there is a decrease in the number of students who say things like 'There needs to be much more direction set by the instructor,' and an increase in the number who say things like '[she] exemplified in her own teaching of this course everything she was teaching us how to teach,' then I will be satisfied.

15 Discourse, process and reflection in teacher education

Michael McCarthy and Michael Makosch

This chapter reports on problems and prospects in a process-based approach to teacher and teacher-trainer development seminars conducted under the aegis of the International Certificate Conference (ICC) in Europe. The members of the ICC organise language courses and examinations for adult learners in 14 countries across Europe in a wide range of languages in general and vocational language learning. The ICC has recently introduced new language-learning syllabuses at an advanced level and has changed certain aspects of assessment to bring them more in line with task-based approaches to language learning and discourse-based descriptions of the languages involved (for the principles of a discourse-based description see, McCarthy and Carter, 1994). These changes affecting teachers implementing ICC programmes have created a need for in-service education and professional development programmes at all levels, including that of teacher trainers. The subject of this chapter is an annual two-week ICC residential teacher and teacher trainer development seminar held at Lancashire College, Chorley, UK, which the authors have helped develop and run for the last 10 years. Each year, the seminar involves approximately 30 participants who are expert non-native and native speakers of English working as language teachers/teacher-trainers in the ICC member countries. Meeting and working with each other for the first time in a residential centre away from home for a limited but extremely concentrated period of two weeks means that participants are exposed to intense personal, social and professional pressures. Their expectations and goals differ as widely as the contexts from which they come. Examples of the type of participants are: Catalonian secondary-school teachers, part-time German evening-school teachers, Hungarian teacher-trainers and Norwegian directors of studies in adult-education institutes.

A central aim of the seminar is to raise awareness in trainers and teachers of the approach that has informed changes in the syllabuses and examinations and their methodological implications. The philosophy of the seminar is that knowledge about intended change without awareness of its rationale is unproductive and likely to lead to rejection. Equally important is the conviction that such awareness cannot be merely transmitted; it can only be achieved through experience, and therefore it has to become shared. Just as the ICC philosophy of language learning rejects the 'conduit' metaphor for language acquisition, where the learner is the 'empty vessel' that has to be filled with rules, so too the teacher and trainer are respected as complex social beings who bring their own experience and cultural identities to the seminar. Thus, change is conceived as two-way traffic, implying a process approach to teacher education in which new systems and constraints are flexible and responsive to a bottom-up push of evaluation which, it is hoped, accompanies the pull from the top.

One of the difficulties – which, in our opinion, originates in an overemphasis on methodology at the expense of pedagogic content that has tended to dominate our profession in the 1980s – is that seminar participants sometimes fail to make a distinction between language descriptions, syllabuses and methodology, and they expect any descriptive innovation to be synonymous with new methodology. (A common recurring phase during the seminar is when individuals and/or groups of participants start talking about discourse-based descriptions of language as a new teaching method.) This lack of a bridge between paradigm shifts in language description and what happens in syllabus design and classroom practices is, in our experience, the single most significant challenge that those who advocate language-as-discourse as the descriptive base for language teaching continue to face (for further discussion, see McCarthy and Carter, 1994: chapter 5). It is an attempt to confront and resolve this dilemma which therefore informs the process-orientation at the heart of the Chorley trainer seminar, and which we describe in this chapter.

The structure of the Chorley seminar

The ICC annual seminar is organised so as to focus attention in its first week on the roles of teachers and learners, through a programme of tasks planned and managed by two tutors chosen from the previous year's participants. This last point is by no means otiose: there is no one better than a previous course participant who can empathise with the insecurities and tensions experienced by the next year's intake and, it is hoped, remember well what it felt like to be thrown in at the deep end and be required to work with strangers from unfamiliar cultures.

In its second week, the seminar considers discourse-based views of language and task-based learning. At this point two new tutors (the present authors) arrive in Chorley and the approach of the seminar shifts from the carefully planned tasks of Week 1 to a more open, negotiated process for Week 2. The first week is thus crucial in establishing the context in which the second week's activities are to be evaluated. By the end of Week 1 participants' expectations have already been challenged by working through a series of exploratory, self-directed and auto-evaluating tasks. They have been working on given tasks accompanied not by 'tutor experts', as many participants would have expected, but by two tutors who one year previously were in the same position as they are now in. This challenging of the novice–expert paradigm for teacher education is deliberate. Despite this foregrounding of the participants and course leaders as peers in the first week, the expectations for Week 2 are great: two new tutors (fresh blood!) are taking over (authority at last!) to deal with innovations in approaches to language-description and language-teaching methodology; (there is a perception that new knowledge, and therefore something concrete to take home at the end of the seminar, will be forthcoming). A hiatus occurs between Weeks 1 and 2 as participants evaluate their first week, look forward to Week 2 and collect ideas for their own project work which they undertake as part of their work during Week 2. It is with the implementation of this second week, and our cumulative experience over 10 years, that the remainder of this chapter is now concerned, for it is in this second week that a process orientation offers the best way to negotiate a path among the diverging perceptions of roles, status and procedures described above and thus presents a major challenge to both the tutors and the participants.

Week 2 of the seminar: balancing constraints and processes

As seminar leaders, the authors have seen their responsibilities and goals as encompassing the following principles, some of which, on the face of it, may seem mutually irreconcilable:

1. to introduce participants in an efficient and economical way to current developments in discourse and genre analysis and applications of these in language description and pedagogy (see Carter and McCarthy, 1995; McCarthy, 1998);
2. to raise awareness among the participants of the notion of language-as-discourse;
3. to investigate the potential of task-based learning as an appropriate methodology for the new ICC syllabuses and examinations (see Long and Crookes, 1992; Skehan, 1996; Forster, 1998);

4. to negotiate with participants a framework in which they may pursue (1) and (2) above, working as individuals or in groups to do project-based work that has a positive outcome in their own teaching and/or training context on return to their jobs after the seminar.
5. to encourage trainers to become researchers, both in the sense of language researchers and action researchers in their own professional contexts (see Allwright and Bailey, 1991: 13).

Aims 1 and 2 above would seem to imply some responsibility for directed input on the part of the seminar leaders and this is exactly what the participants often eagerly await. Aim 3 suggests a more exploratory and programmatic context. Aim 4 takes us more squarely into a process-based orientation, while Aim 5 is the most open ended of all. As the seminar has developed over the last 10 years, Aims 3, 4 and 5 do indeed result in a maximum degree of process-based organisation of the seminar. There are still challenges and difficulties in the attempt to wed the external and collectivising constraints of Aims 1 and 2 to the individualising and customising trends inherent in Aims 3, 4 and 5. The resolution of these problems necessitates continuous negotiation between the tutors and the participants, attempting to reconcile these five areas with the participants' own concerns.

The discourse-oriented input of the seminar takes place during a series of interactive workshops or modules offered by the tutors during the second week of the seminar. The week begins with all participants attending workshops, but as the week proceeds and their own project work becomes more clearly defined, the attendance becomes more selective, and the contents and thrust of the workshops become more tailored to the participants' needs. The workshops consist of a series of modules designed to raise awareness of the following discourse features in spoken and written language:

1. the differences between concocted and spontaneous dialogues;
2. the centrality of the exchange as a discourse structure (Sinclair and Coulthard, 1975);
3. the differences between traditional teacher–pupil exchanges and exchanges outside the classroom;
4. the turn-taking and topic-management strategies which occur in task-centred activities in contrast with those in the traditional teacher-fronted classroom (Forster, 1998);
5. the rhetorical patterning of coherent texts, following a clause-relational approach (see, for example, Hoey, 1983). This centres mainly around the 'problem–solution' rhetoric as a fundamental everyday discourse which becomes simultaneously a structuring metaphor for the whole of the second week of the seminar.

The experience and metalanguage of the language-as-discourse work-shops and of the project work (described in the following section) together create a framework within which task-based learning can be investigated as a link between the seminar and the participants' own teaching context. With this in mind, the discourse-awareness modules are themselves activity based and task based. (Activities are conceived of as a broad spectrum of operations which have a language-awareness outcome as their main aim, whereas a task is essentially defined as operation(s) plus non-linguistic outcome; in other words, it is defined as an outcome in real-world terms, even if simulated.) The gain in knowledge of the discipline of discourse-based descriptions of language (discourse analysis) may be small when based on activities and tasks, rather than cramming a reading list of well-known papers and books by the 'experts' and 'the great and the good' of applied linguistics; however, the use of tasks in the first stage of the second week of the seminar is crucial in terms of experiential learning. When, as usual later in the week, task-based learning is discussed, the participants have already been involved in working that way and can critically reflect on it as a shared experience; they do not have to conceive of it in the abstract. Also, the vital link will, it is hoped, have already been forged between classroom methodology and different outcomes in terms of the discourse generated by different classroom environments (for example, teacher-fronted, group problem-solving, teacher-in-the-background group tasks, etc., and the different types of talk they typically result in). Here a twin-level of reflection is also crucial:

1. reflecting on the different discourses which are the object of the tasks and activities; and
2. reflecting on the discourse milieu in which the tasks and activities on reflective approaches to teacher education in general activities have themselves been conducted (see Wallace, 1991).

Reflective aspects of the seminar thus become central, and the plenary discussion forums are a time to 'stop and take stock', something the participants frequently praise in the course feedback. This link between action and reflection is further strengthened in the central, process-based element when participants negotiate their project-based research, as we describe below.

In performing activities upon texts, participants, it is hoped, learn about the place of textual rhetoric in the analysis of discourse (for example, how common 'problem–solution' texts are in everyday life), but they are also acquiring explicit consciousness of a template for the negotiation process of their own situation as course participants. Process (as it is conceived here, the decision-making that shapes the seminar) is a 'problem–solution' discourse. Furthermore, process can only become a reality if the other key discourse features that are focused on in the tasks are ably managed by the participants themselves in interaction with one another: exchange, topic-strategies, turn-taking, convergence, co-operation, effective discourse marking, etc. The consciousness raised in the first stage of the second week becomes the frame for the process of negotiating the rest of the week's work and for analysing language learning and teaching methodology.

Process orientation and project work

The project component of the seminar is negotiated. Participants find co-workers, plan a project whose usefulness they feel the whole group can share and devote Week 2 to its development. Constraints are few since the aim is to foreground the process of negotiation and exploration rather than 'doing what the experts tell us to'; however, participants are offered the following suggestions:

1. data collection: reflecting the emphasis on real data in the discourse analysis sessions;
2. problem-solving: reflecting the 'problem–solution' discourses explored in the discourse sessions and the over-arching 'problem–solution' structure of the negotiation process leading to the project;
3. interaction with local resources: for example, street interviews, recordings of service transactions, etc., reflecting the spoken discourse features focused on in the discourse sessions;
4. qualitative analysis of their data: using their new awareness to create plausible interpretations of their material.
5. identification of the tasks associated with assembling and completing the project and negotiation of responsibilities for each task: reflecting the focus on tasks in the discourse sessions;
6. ongoing evaluation of the process of doing the project: reflecting the evaluation of responses in the 'problem–solution' paradigm and raising awareness of the nature of process-based learning.

Within these parameters, participants work on a project focused on any area that interests them. Being based in a small English town, participants have ample opportunity to make contacts with local people and often conduct interviews as a way of eliciting answers to specific questions or problems generated by their project. Not all projects are, however, related to collecting data and analysing it. Outcomes of the seminar also include collections of information, realia and opinions on specific areas of life in and around Chorley. For example, sets of materials or poster displays on the town market versus out-of-town superstores or on cultural institutions such as pubs and fish-and-chips are just two of the many cases in which participants explicitly divorce the discourse-analysis thrust of Week 2 from the object of their project, but adopt it to reflect on the project process. Almost every year at least one group goes about using the tutors and other participants to produce materials illustrating certain discourse features which they find pertinent to their teaching situation back home. One year even saw a project on projects which threatened to implode under the pressure of multiple layers of reflection and negotiation on the process of reflection and negotiation; this became a veritable hall of mirrors that produced disorientation and vertigo even amongst its own creators. Participants' evaluations of the seminar consistently record an awareness of and reflection on the discourse of the process of the week and, despite the diverse outcomes of the projects, this runs as a common denominator throughout.

The parameter in terms of time which is set for the project is that it must be ready for presentation at a plenary session on the last day of the seminar. Participants set interim deadlines for ongoing evaluation sessions and work on the projects is frequently interrupted and complemented by attending workshop sessions offered by or requested of the tutors. Experience over the 10 years has shown that the negotiation process prior to deciding on the shape of the project, and especially during the week, can be intensive and fierce among participants, with personality tensions emerging, competing needs and interests pulling in different directions, loose cannons moving off to do their individual thing, tears of rage and frustration bubbling to the surface, and lengthy and utterly exhausting planning sessions. These phases are, as described above, central to the experience of the process of negotiating for the participants. When they come to evaluate the two weeks in Chorley, these experiences give participants and tutors alike great pause for thought as to the viability of negotiated syllabuses and methodologies (Clarke, 1991), whether in their own language classrooms or in a teacher-training context.

In order to illustrate the inner-workings of the process approach in Chorley, to show the type of experience the participants can refer to in evaluating the seminar as a whole, and to explain in part the variety of outcomes at the end of the week, we present here a taste of the conflicts during the week. A key source of conflict is the insecurity provoked by the amount of public reflection on and verbalisation about many differing but overlapping levels of analysis, such as:

• personality factors in communicative processes;

- the status and role of cultural values;
- presentation of self during the seminar;
- one's own status and behaviour in group negotiation;
- long-held views on language, learning and teaching;
- the authority or otherwise of the native speaker, etc.

Some of the participants, for example, have degrees in formal linguistics and feel threatened by having to confront new linguistic paradigms that were not current when they were studying. Others feel that, as experienced and successful teachers (with perhaps 20 or 30 years in the classroom), such new and troublesome complexity as is presented by a discourse-based approach to language is an unnecessary rocking of the boat: this is the 'if it ain't broke, don't fix it' response, which is natural and understandable. Some participants therefore attempt to reduce the degree of complexity of the seminar as they experience it and reserve the right not to participate in certain aspects of the week, an obvious source of conflict in such an intense setting. Back-biting and faction-fighting is not uncommon as a result of individuals expressing their own firm convictions about the situation.

Tensions arising from insecurity, affective tensions, fatigue and doubt as to the value of the seminar are more often than not solved within the peer group. The workshops, on the one hand, and the project, on the other, give participants the chance to shine or fade when and where they feel fit. One particular feature which encourages a collaborative and mutually supportive atmosphere amongst the participants is the aim of the project to create a 'product' by the end of the week. This also often leads to a collective sense of panic. Group membership shifts, even up to the last day of the week, as interests develop and a collective 'mucking-in' takes place in order to make sure everyone is involved and satisfied by the end. After having lived together for almost two weeks, this final spurt reveals hidden talents but also hidden (often bitter) rivalries. However, the 'threat' of resolving these rivalries in the group is lessened by the framework of discourse paradigms with which 'problem–solution' have been analysed and, of course, by the promise of 'release' from the close-knit community as the end of the seminar nears.

At the end of Week 2, participants and tutors often return to their homes emotionally and intellectually drained and exhausted. To the dismay of certain participants, roles change, as the tutors' image as 'seminar leaders' – which they had projected through to Week 2 after the experience of Week 1 – emerges as that of facilitators, informants and advisors. The progress of the projects and the changing role of the tutors means that differences of opinion between the participants and the tutors also intensify; examples are:

- Input relevant to specific teaching situations or individual projects is asked for and has to be diverted or planned into late-night sessions.
- Reassurance about project methods and aims is required from the tutors who would prefer groups to set their own standards.
- Adjudication is needed to solve issues about fair use of limited resources.

These are but a few types of conflict which are probably not unique to this seminar, but for the participants they result in constant and explicit revision of their perception of the tutors' status within the seminar and what they expect of them, their goals for the week, the relevance of the input workshops in general and to their particular project and, fundamentally, to their self-image.

Conclusion: process-oriented language awareness in teacher education

The account of the Chorley seminars and detailed description of what takes place each year both at an emotional and affective level is a useful basis for the formulation of the model that has underpinned our activities for the last 10 years. We now conclude by presenting that model in the abstract, fully aware that much of what we have described only fits together in a retrospective view, the live experience being more disjointed: the snags and hassles, the personality clashes, the set-backs to plans for projects, the time constraints, the tears and perspiration, the sheer cussedness of day-to-day reality when confronted with idealism and ambition. However, underlying our narrative has always been the model or template shown in Table 15.1, which we offer for replication in teacher-education contexts.

The linear nature of the stages implicit in the summary does not, of course, reflect the development of the seminar in real time: all stages inevitably overlap. The entire seminar design model is itself a 'problem–solution' discourse, as conceived by Hoey (1983). The situation was carefully laid out in the first week – referred to at the start of this chapter – when the roles of teachers and learners are explored in depth. The problems are of two kinds:

- those inherent in the discipline to be confronted, that is discourse analysis; and
- those raised by its challenge to traditional teaching modes and the participants' identities.

The response to this challenge (tasks and projects) and its evaluation as

Table 15.1   *Model of course structure*

Stage	Actions	Aims
1	Producing and collecting data; working on texts through activities and tasks	Learning about, experiencing and reflecting on discourse and task-based activity
2	Planning and negotiating of projects	Planning tasks, deciding roles and responsibilities and experiencing the negotiation process
3	Completion of projects	Implementing the 'problem–solution' cycle; engaging in discourse in real-world situations both within the projects themselves and about the projects
4	Evaluation	Evaluating discourse awareness, task-based learning, process-based programme approach and the negotiation process

a solution to the overall problem is, at its heart, process-driven and negotiated among tutors and participants. This process has recorded modest but highly rewarding achievements for all involved and, we hope, will continue to do so. What the ICC seminars have tried to achieve is a raised awareness of discourse-based linguistic description and of task-based learning and process-based syllabuses, along with an induction of participants into a new metalanguage that is increasingly influential in their discourse community. If we hold that discourse analysis has a useful role to play in teacher and trainer-education programmes (useful in the sense that it goes beyond mere language description, as we have tried to show, and is an ideal bridge towards task-based and process-based learning) then we must acknowledge that we need a lot more experience and experimentation in designing teacher-training modules and more basic knowledge of learners' language needs at the discourse level. Our work has been but a very modest beginning. What we hope to have shown is that discourse analysis can be a door-opening on to a keener understanding of innovative and challenging methodologies both for the language class-room and for a teacher-education seminar.

16 Negotiation, process, content and participants' experience in a process syllabus for ELT professionals

Roz Ivanič

In this chapter I first describe how we operate a process syllabus on a course which is part of an MA programme for experienced ELT professionals. I then identify four elements in a process syllabus, and comment on their role in the course. I discuss the way in which negotiation interacts with the other elements, and the effects of prioritising one focus over another. I then identify tensions and difficulties which we have experienced with the course and suggest some ways of dealing with them.

The Professional Issues in Language Teaching course

The process syllabus I am writing about is part of an MA programme in Linguistics for English Language Teaching (MAELT) at Lancaster University, UK. The programme is for ELT professionals with at least three years full-time equivalent professional experience. Most participants have been ELT professionals for a period of between 5 and 20 years. The programme itself is becoming increasingly 'negotiated' in that there are no compulsory courses and students have to make up a personal programme of courses to take for credit and courses to 'audit' (that is, courses to attend without being assessed) from a wide selection. The Professional Issues in Language Teaching course (known affectionately or otherwise as 'PILT') constitutes approximately one tenth of the programme, and it is the main opportunity for participants to develop their knowledge and understanding of practical and professional issues. Other ELT-related courses in the programme focus on theory and research in second-language acquisition, testing and other more specific and theoretical topics. PILT has been run with a 'process syllabus' for over 10 years, and I have been part of the course team during eight of those years, from 1986 to 1994.

The course is timetabled for a three-hour session once a week during the first term of the MA programme. There are usually between 20 and

30 students on the course, divided into three small working groups of 8 to 10 according to a list prepared in advance by the course co-ordinator to ensure a mix of age, gender, professional, linguistic, cultural and ethnic backgrounds. We usually work with three tutors, each of whom takes responsibility for one sub-group. While reading this chapter, it is important to bear in mind the small group size and favourable student–tutor ratio.

There are many variations in the course, and I explain some of these as I proceed. Conversely, there are also some basic principles and procedures which remain more or less stable from year to year. Of course, the whole idea of anything remaining stable when a course is *negotiated* may be considered as something of a contradiction. Doesn't negotiation mean 'let the students decide?' In practice, there are several principles and procedures which are decided in advance, but this is very different from having the content, method and assessment format set in stone: these latter elements are those which are negotiated.

Aims

First, we are more or less unwavering in what we see as the aims of the course. These are to provide a working context in which participants can:

1. learn from each of the participants' professional experience (that is, not just the tutor's) and contribute to each other's learning;
2. choose areas of content and ways of working;
3. directly experience and reflect upon the process of shared curriculum planning, implementation and evaluation;
4. make connections between their own professional concerns and the rest of their MA studies.

Students receive a statement containing these 4 aims as part of a two-page description of the course during the introductory week of the MA programme, along with descriptions of other courses from which they select their programme.

Of these aims, (3) is perhaps particularly important and particularly relevant to this volume. Being ELT professionals, many MAELT students have heard of 'the process syllabus'; some have already worked in this way in their own settings. We think the best way for our students to learn about this important topic is to feel what it is like for themselves, and then to think about how they can adapt their experience to language-learning classrooms. Of course there is one big difference: on PILT the outcome is not language learning, but learning about pedagogical issues related to language teaching. The added dimension of using a process syllabus as the opportunity for communicative language learning cannot be experienced, but it can be discussed as a separate issue.

Content

In preparation for the first activity of the course, students are asked to think carefully about their personal agenda for the MA programme as a whole, and particularly about aspects of it which do not seem to be catered for in other courses. Figure 16.1 shows an example of wording for the instructions for this preparation. Almost all students follow these instructions assiduously and come to the first session with three cards, each containing a focused question which represents one professional issue that is of interest to them. Some have said that they were at first rather taken aback by this task and were not instantly able to identify anything which was of burning interest to them. However, the requirement to bring those three completed cards led them to think about their own interests and either identify latent ones or, at worst, invent something to which they were willing to put their name.

For the first session the participants work within their sub-groups. They already know each other by this time, having met during introductory week activities. The three-hour session is based entirely around the questions the participants have brought with them on their cards. It is important for the sub-group size to be small at this point in order to ensure that each individual's agenda is given adequate attention. A tutor joins each sub-group to promote and facilitate the personal and possibly face-threatening discussion which is engendered by this activity, to ask the questions which will bring out into the open tensions and contradictions between topics which are mentioned on the cards, and to ensure the discussion is brought to a productive conclusion.

In the first two hours or so the participants literally 'put their cards on the table' and informal discussion about them ensues:

> That's really interesting because in Ecuador it's completely the opposite.
>
> That wouldn't apply to younger children because . . .
>
> How does this question relate to the job you have come from?
>
> Oh yes, I'm really interested in that too, but I didn't think of it.
>
> What do *you* mean by self-access?
>
> Why are you interested in the relationship between communicative language teaching and EAP [English for academic purposes]?

Session 1: Developing a group syllabus
Aim

The session will be spent sharing and discussing the professional issues which are of most urgent interest to group members with a view to establishing a group syllabus for Term 1 of the course. The idea is to foreground those things which are usually hidden in a classroom: the silent thoughts in participants' minds along the lines of:

> 'I hope this will help me with . . .' 'I really wish this course would be relevant to . . .'

A list of people's immediate concerns are often quite different from what any of us might have imagined as a 'syllabus'. But the attempt to respond to them inevitably raises most if not all the key professional issues, helps us to look at them from new perspectives, and helps us to make novel connections among them.

Preparation

In order to contribute to this you need to have identified your own 'personal syllabus' of professional issues, questions and topics which are important to you. Please do this before the first PILT session of Tuesday 5 October. Allow yourself about an hour for it.

1. Check your list of questions/topics/interests on your '*Personal Syllabus*' sheet. Is there anything you wish to add? Can you refine your questions/interests/topics further? Be as specific as you can.
   Rewrite this list in your own format if you prefer.
2. Check your list against the descriptions of the courses you are taking. Do you expect any of your topics/questions to be covered in those courses? If so, tick them on your list.
3. Now focus on your topics/questions/interests which do NOT seem to be covered by existing courses. Read through these and select the three which seem to you to be of most immediate importance to you. Don't lose sight of the others, but we will only have time to consider three from each group member to start with.
4. Now rewrite each of your chosen topics/questions/interests so that they are in the form of *focused questions* (if you have not already done so). For example, rather than 'Reading' a more focused question might be 'How can one encourage adult students to read outside class time?' or 'How far might reading problems be language problems?'
5. Once you are happy with your three questions, copy each of them on to its own separate card supplied to you.
   Please write in large black writing: it needs to be legible from two metres.
   Bring these cards to your first PILT session. Be ready to talk more about why they are important to you, how they relate to your professional concerns, *etc.*
   P.S. *Please bring your 200 word self-description to your PILT session.*

Figure 16.1   Sample instructions for preparing for the first session

These are the sorts of comments that are made and additional questions that are asked. When this activity is more than half-way through, the tutor suggests that, as more cards are added to the ones laid on the table, we start identifying overlaps and groupings.

> That connects with what Maria was saying about . . .

> I don't really think that goes with that because . . .

Figure 16.2 gives an impression of the outcome of this activity. It was copied from the cards on the table at the end of the activity by one group in a recent year of the course.

Towards the end of this session the students receive a course outline: Figure 16.3 is a recent example. The most important aspect to notice about this course outline is that it consists by and large of blank spaces. In addition to the blank spaces, it is important to notice that there are certain non-negotiable events in the programme and that the right-hand side sets out a detailed timetable for assessment procedures. Some details of this document vary from year to year, as I explain in the next section, but in essence it is a standard feature of the course.

The tutor explains that the programme for the first term is be based on the topics which have emerged as priorities for the group from the first activity of the course. Exactly how this is done, and exactly what gets written in the blank spaces on the course outline, vary from tutor to tutor and from year to year, but the unchanging feature of the course is that its content *is* generated by this initial activity. There are then approximately seven weeks in which the sub-group follows a programme which is based around the participants' interests. Exactly how far the programme corresponds to each individual's interests is an important and crucial question; I say a little more about this in the second half of the chapter.

A working practice which is a regular feature of the course is the production of retrospective accounts. Two members of each group are delegated to keep notes of what took place in a given session. These provide input for a review at the beginning of the following week's session. Those tutors who believe that the real agenda for this course is somewhat different from the list of topics on the week-by-week schedule set particular store by this practice, treating these accounts as a kind of 'retrospective syllabus' for the group. The ideal of having two of these accounts is based on a belief in the subjectivity of knowledge: each person interprets the same learning experience differently and, consequently, have a different focus or perspective to bring back to the group for discussion. By seeing at least two of these, participants can become aware of the range and richness of learning opportunities in the group

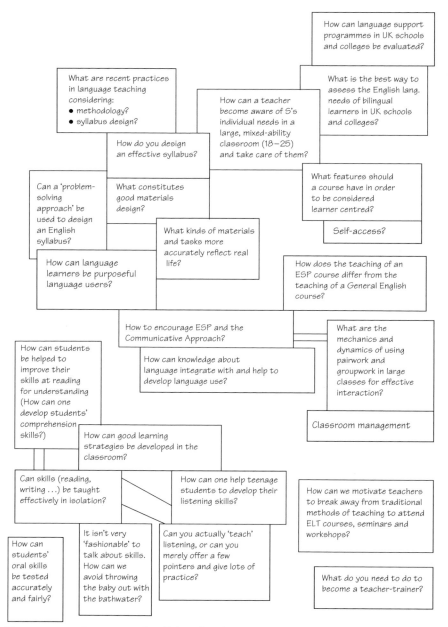

Figure 16.2   A negotiated syllabus for the content of the Professional Issues in Language Teaching course for one sub-group

MA in Linguistics for ELT

> # Professional Issues in Language Teaching Course 1:
> ## *People, Process and Content*

PROPOSED STRUCTURE FOR TERM 1

Week	Group meeting timetable	Course business	Assignment timetable
1	Creating a group syllabus	Arrange group reps. Read 'Abdication and responsibility'	
2			
3		Introduce assignment	Form groups to design possible assignments
4	Academic supervision meetings		Circulate assignment proposals by end of week
5		Standardise assignments and discuss criteria	Choose topic and start work on assignment
6			
7			Circulate draft assignment by end of week; read each other's over the weekend
8	Feedback on drafts		Work on final draft
9	Academic supervision meetings	Discuss evaluation procedures	Hand in final version by end of week. Read each each other's over the weekend
10	Collaborative assessment Review and planning ahead		

Figure 16.3   A course outline for the Professional Issues in Teaching course

sessions and have an opportunity to see how subjective interpretations can be.

Method

So far I have written about how the content is generated for the course. The *method* of working on this content is also negotiated. At the end of the first, and every subsequent, session the group decides how to proceed for the following week. They usually make a few suggestions and then two or three members of the group volunteer, or are encouraged, to prepare and run the activities for the next session. The session leaders make their preliminary plans, then meet with the group tutor who advises them on resources and ways of working which might complement their ideas so far. In this way method is not fully negotiated by the whole group, but mainly by two or three delegates of the group. There is a potential contradiction in this approach. Students often feel that they have chosen topics to pursue because they want to know more about them and that they are therefore not in a position to lead a session on them. This is a problem for those who see the real aim of the course to be the transmission of content, and it is hard for them to be satisfied by discussion which draws on experience and critical thinking to focus and reframe a question, without necessarily coming up with definitive answers. This issue is at the heart of the underlying philosophy and focus of the course, as I discuss in the second half of the chapter (see pp. 242 ff; 'Four key elements in the course').

Assessment

Another non-negotiable element of the course is an assignment which is assessed as part of the requirements for the MA programme as a whole. The nature of the assignment is, however, negotiated.

The assignment is sometimes called a 'practicum' to emphasise the intention that it should focus on a practical professional problem and the issues involved in finding a solution to it. Students form small 'task design' groups, and each of these produces draft specifications for a task. These may sometimes run to several pages, since they are often based around a real-life document, such as a syllabus or a code of practice. The typical format of a practicum is as follows:

1. to provide some information about a particular institutional setting;
2. to explain the particular circumstances, such as the introduction of a communicative language-teaching syllabus, which give rise to the task; and then

3. to outline the task itself, which might be to design some activities for the teaching of writing to a particular age group.

Following this, we run a session in which all participants 'moderate' these tasks (see Week 5 on the Course Outline in Figure 16.3) to ensure that they all pose comparable demands. For example, the format described above would be approved, but two modifications might be suggested. First, it might need to be modified so that it allows students to bring in experience from their own professional settings, perhaps requiring a section which compares and contrasts the effect of a communicative language-teaching syllabus on the teaching of writing in different settings. Second, the practicum would not be fulfilled simply by designing the activities: it would have to include a justification for the proposed activities, drawing both on the discussion of issues which are so central to the course and on related reading of theory and research.

At this session we also discuss the characteristics of a good response; these provide the criteria for assessment. In some years we insist that these assignments be undertaken collaboratively; in some years we make collaborative work optional. We arrange for the draft responses to the tasks to be circulated and devote Week 8 of the course to providing feedback on these drafts in groups. In recent years we have added the idea of collaborative assessment to our standard procedures. This means that, by the last session of the first term (see Week 10 on the Course Outline in Figure 16.3), tutors must have read and responded to all the final versions of the assignments, and students must have read one or two others in addition to their own. The students exchange summative feedback – sometimes in writing and sometimes in group discussion – and the responsibility for arriving at a grade is either left to the authors themselves in discussion with a tutor or negotiated in the group.

Communication among sub-groups

Every year, course participants feel uneasy during the first term of PILT about the fact that they are probably missing something good which is taking place in one of the other sub-groups.

> Two groups are addressing the same topic: why don't we get together?

> Group tutor C knows more about this topic than our tutor, so can't she lead our session on it?

> Another group is giving more attention to the topic which interests me most: could I change groups?

In teacher education

There are various responses in order to deal with this uneasiness. We sometimes appoint group representatives to keep each other informed. We devote a part of a notice-board to this course, so that groups can exchange their retrospective accounts and other notes. We organise occasional whole-course meetings so that groups can exchange information, as well as discussing structural issues and, of course, airing grievances. The structure is flexible enough to accommodate changes in response to such requests, and on the whole we do. However, the last request to change groups can cause problems. One year we tried grouping according to shared interests from the start of the course, and we found participants lost more than they gained. We therefore encourage participants to stay in the pre-planned mixed groupings during the first term, but those who attend the PILT course in the second term are able to re-organise themselves into 'special interest groups', which are topic-based and determined by the students' interests at the end of the first term.

Four key elements in the course

Our commitment to negotiating the work on this course has led us to reconsider all aspects of running a course for ELT professionals. Prioritising different aspects of what is involved in a process syllabus has different outcomes both in terms of the precise characteristics of the course and in terms of student response. In this section I describe each of the elements mentioned in the title; I then turn to the effects they have on each other and on the overall nature of the course.

Negotiation

On the PILT course, 'negotiation' is intended to mean that all participants collectively make the decisions about as many aspects of the course as possible. While staff provide the structures and act as consultants, students have the major say in this decision-making process. Inevitably, some students have a greater say in these negotiations than others: some people are culturally and personally more disposed to arguing their point of view than others, and to persuading others to follow. One of the tasks of the tutor is to make all participants aware of this issue, and another is to intervene in order to encourage balanced negotiation if necessary.

Negotiation is always a central element in PILT. In fact, the invariable features of the course described in the previous section amount to the fact that the content, working procedures, assignment tasks, assessment criteria, assessment procedures and grade are, in different ways, negotiated as far as we think is practical without the students becoming frustrated by the inevitable investment of time entailed. The only aspects which are not negotiable are the course aims and the structuring of the first term's activities: in other words, the process of negotiation itself.

We have many reasons for prioritising negotiation which I can but summarise here. First, we believe in putting students at the centre of their own learning. Ideologically, this puts the power in the hands of those whose interests are to be served by a course, and redresses the balance found in traditional pedagogic settings. Pedagogically, we believe that students learn better when they recognise that the course is designed around their own needs and interests. Any course which does not have an element of negotiation in it is paying only lip-service to these principles.

Second, negotiation redistributes not only the rights but also the responsibilities for productive learning: students have to become active in making their learning opportunities serve their own needs, rather than being passive consumers of teaching.

Third, no syllabus can serve the needs of all individual students all the time. Negotiating the syllabus means that we can ensure at least that we are not completely by-passing many of the needs of most of the learners, and that the reality of differences in individual learning agendas is brought out in the open. It then becomes the responsibility of all participants in the learning situation to find ways of serving as many of these different needs as possible; in essence, acting within a learning community. In addition, we believe that the ability to negotiate is of value to the course participants when they leave the MA course, possibly moving into more responsible positions in the ELT profession. Building negotiation into the course might contribute to developing this practical ability for some students.

Process

'Process' is an important element in PILT in that the students are expected to learn as much from experiencing the process of negotiation as they are from the content of the course. The remainder of the MA programme is also constantly emphasising the importance of 'process', focusing on process as opposed to product – that is classroom processes, the reading process, the writing process and the research process – so that attention to process on PILT has applications beyond the course itself. Some years we foreground this aspect of the course more than others. For example, one year recently we subtitled the course 'Process and Content', and in the proposed structure for Term 1 (see Figure 16.3) we headed the middle column 'Process', in order to make explicit that the students were supposed to be learning about the process of negotiation by engaging in the activities listed there. We find we need to continually repeat the point that the participants are supposed to be learning as much from the process of the course as from its content, and it pays dividends if we set aside time to discuss explicitly what participants have been learning from this process.

Content

I think that 'content' is the most controversial element in the course. Many students take it for granted that this is the only point of the course, and everything else is a time-consuming diversion from what really matters. Some students never move from this position and, on the whole, they are the ones who derive least satisfaction from the course. At the other extreme is the view of some tutors and some students that the content is really irrelevant to the course: the only thing which really matters is experiencing the process of negotiation itself, and the content is just a vehicle for that experience. For them, the process *is* the content.

While I share the view that the process is the most important content of the course, I think this view is self-defeating if carried to the extreme. In order to focus on the process, it is essential for the content in the more traditional sense to have some substance. It seems to me that there are at least three types of content on a course like this. First, the 'content' of the course might be specified in terms of the sorts of topics which emerge from the introductory activity. Examples of topics are recognised ELT topics such as syllabus design, the teaching of reading, English for special purposes, materials design and communicative methodology. Related to this is a second, extremely practical approach to content which focuses on such topics as 'how to run a simulation' and 'ideas for using video in the ELT classroom'. Many students are very eager for this sort of content, especially since it may be their only chance to find out how colleagues in other countries do the same job. This is perhaps more suitable to a pre-service or in-service teacher development course than an MA; however, I do not think that this sort of content should be dismissed – certainly as a starting point for PILT – since it is often the chosen starting-point for the participants themselves. A third way of conceptualising the 'content' of such a course is that it consists of the more theoretical underlying issues of ELT, such as the role of purpose in language learning, the importance of social context, gender issues and critical perspectives on ELT. These issues tend to arise in relation to any or all of the sorts of topics mentioned first, and feature significantly in the 'retrospective syllabus' rather than the 'prospective syllabus' as defined by the weekly topics. In my experience, these issues gradually become the *real* or central content of the course. Another way to express this is perhaps to state that my own agenda for the course is that it should ultimately be about these things. The fact that one is reluctant to be explicit about this agenda from the start of the course throws up a fundamental contradiction in the principle of a 'negotiated syllabus', which I discuss on p. 246 ('Tensions and difficulties on the course').

Participants' experience

This element is, in a way, an aspect of 'content'; it is, however, worth singling it out because it represents an important underlying principle of the PILT course. We believe that ELT professionals learn about key issues in ELT best by reflecting on their own experience. This parallels our belief that students learn about a process syllabus best by experiencing it.

In practice, focusing on participants' experience means spending a lot of time describing our own working situations and our own professional practices, comparing and contrasting them, reflecting on them, identifying puzzles and problems within them, and hypothesising and theorising on the basis of them. In contrast to the conventional academic embargo on anecdote, we prize it, believing that stories are a source of rich understanding of such a complex phenomenon as language learning. (For a detailed elaboration of the view that 'experience' and 'anecdote' provide the material for critical reflection and hence can be turned into useful knowledge, see K. Carter, 1993; for the idea of making personal experience central to learning in a wide range of educational contexts, see Boud *et al.*, 1993.) Published authorities are given a second place, and what they write is assessed according to how useful it is to us in addressing the puzzles and issues raised by our experience. This approach defines academic achievement in terms of wisdom, understanding, and the ability to analyse and critically reflect on evidence, rather than defining it in terms of knowledge of existing theory and research.

Students often react negatively to this approach at first. They feel that they have come on an MA to learn, that learning involves a lot of new input, and that if it isn't 'above their head' it isn't real learning. For some students this attitude persists, but others relish the opportunity to focus on their practical experience and to learn how to reflect on it critically and productively. At best they finish the course feeling fully equipped to grapple with and make well-informed and principled decisions about the whole gamut of professional issues.

Those tutors who prioritise this element in PILT may even resist the temptation to set an agenda of weekly topics, suggesting that participants take turns in talking about their experience in relation to some of the issues raised during the introductory activity. This turns the group's attention to the interrelatedness of issues and, in my view, leads more quickly to identifying the underlying issues I mentioned under 'content'. Those tutors who do not make participants' experience central to the sessions do, nevertheless, allow time for them by, for example, recommending that everyone should bring samples of their own to a session on materials design.

Tensions and difficulties on the course

There is a tension between our overarching aim of giving the students the experience of negotiating the curriculum and the fact that they are not always very good at negotiating. We are perhaps rather too reliant on a 'sink or swim' policy, expecting students to 'learn by doing', when they may, in fact, need some expertise in negotiating in order to benefit from the opportunity to practise it. One of the roles of the tutor in each sub-group is to support the group members through this experience, to intervene where necessary to ensure that everyone's voice is heard, and to bring discussion about the negotiation process itself out into the open. This may not, however, be enough. The fact that students do not always seem to benefit fully from the experience of negotiation on this course has led us to consider introducing an extra component on the course – possibly as a course within the MA programme as a whole – on how to work in small group situations, and how to learn from such situations. This is an issue to be explored further in the future.

Another tension within the course is between recognising the value of learning through experience of the negotiation process and wanting some tangible evidence of making progress and of learning something. The course typically suffers a crisis of confidence around Week 5: having given us the benefit of the doubt to start with, several students become disillusioned with and resistant to the process. Participants often complain at this stage that they do not see the point of working in the way we do, and that they feel they are not progressing on the course. They want to revert to teacher dependency and to relinquish the responsibility for what they are deriving from the course. We respond to this by calling a course meeting, an event which appears to be spontaneous, although it is such a regular feature of the course that we could probably timetable it in advance! At this meeting the central topic of discussion is process: we discuss the fundamental issue of control over learning in an attempt to revitalise everyone's commitment to joint responsibility for making the course meaningful and productive. I do not wish to suggest that the struggle involved at this point is minimal: when other courses on the same programme are 'delivering the goods' in the conventional way, and participants are feeling threatened by the start of work on assignments for assessment, it is not surprising that it is difficult to maintain their faith in what for many is a very radical and demanding learning experience.

Conclusion

The PILT course is a rich and complex undertaking for both students and tutors. Every year working on it forces me to rethink what learning is about, and I become interested in some new aspect of it. Perhaps it captures the spirit of the course to say that I am explicit about my own current pre-occupations with the students: I believe that they should know about these, engage with them and be considerate of what *I* am learning from our joint endeavours as much as vice versa. One point is certain: the course is never the same two years running. How could it be when the participants who are negotiating the curriculum are different, and the regular tutors have developed their thinking from one year to the next. This unpredictability is, in my view, a tribute to the underlying principles of the course (which do not change), and this is part of the challenge and excitement of negotiated classroom work.

17   Negotiation as a participatory dialogue

Kate Wolfe-Quintero

In a graduate course for ELT professionals on the teaching of writing that I taught in the ESL department at the University of Hawaii, USA, I negotiated both the content and the format of the course with graduate students based on the concept of 'process syllabus' as discussed in Breen (1987). I had never negotiated a course with students in this way before. In this chapter, I analyse what took place from the point of view of 'participatory' pedagogy as proposed by Auerbach (1990; 1993; 1995). With representative quotes from data that was collected during the course, I will show how the experience of negotiation challenged expected power relationships in the classroom, how it encouraged responsibility for learning, and how it transformed our later pedagogical practice.

Participatory pedagogy

Classroom negotiation is neither learner-centred nor teacher-centred, but 'participatory' (Auerbach, 1990; 1993; 1995). The teacher, who cannot abdicate his or her authority in the classroom (Freire and Macedo, 1995), opens up the class to dialogue between all participants. Content is shaped by the teacher's knowledge and by the students' lives (in this case, their lives as teachers and their conceptions of education). According to Kutz et al. (1993), the role of the teacher is to support and challenge the students, 'to shape a route and then reshape it with those who enter' the classroom environment (p. 84). Based on Freire's (1970) problem-posing, dialogic model of education, Kutz et al. go on to state that 'the object of knowledge is ... something that students and teachers think about and construct together in public dialogue' (p. 84). When this dialogue takes place, there is a fundamental 'reconceptualization of who has knowledge in the classroom' (Auerbach, 1990: 88). As Auerbach (1993) notes, this approach to pedagogy is political because the teacher is leading a critique of the social situation, whether it involves the lives of immigrants or, in this case, the role of a teacher in the classroom.

A participatory pedagogy is experiential, dialogic and learning-centred. It is consistent with a Vygotskyan (1978) view of the social nature of teaching and learning. Vygotsky described learning as socially-mediated interaction between a student and an expert in a particular domain, with a dynamic relationship between the student's experiences and the subject matter to be learned. In Vygotsky's theory (D. Russell, 1993), the role of the teacher is to begin 'where the students are' and to bring them to a curricular goal that has been socially-determined, that meets their needs and which can be transformed through their participation. Setting up a dichotomy between learner-centred and teacher-centred pedagogy, or between individual and content, is false. The goal of the dialogue between teacher and students is learning, or integration of the individual and the content within the social situation. The goals I had for the writing methodology class were consistent with this approach to pedagogy, and I explained this to the students while I was teaching the course:

> I firmly believe that we all learn by doing, that the things we do should be real and meaningful things that we can see the purpose for within our social context, that how we carry out the doing should be as much under our control as possible, and that there should be knowledgeable people around to help us with our questions or provoke us to deeper thought about what we are doing. I don't think this is just theory, I am struggling to make it a reality within my courses.

The participatory approach can be contrasted with the 'learner-centred curriculum' that Nunan (1990b; 1995) advocates, in which curriculum decisions regarding content and tasks are made in advance by teachers on the basis of data 'about' typical learners. The teacher explains and justifies the curriculum to the students, follows up any difficulties that students are having with the tasks and encourages student self-assessment. Because the tasks are determined by the teacher, negotiation is limited to asking students for feedback once they have completed a task, asking students to choose which task they'd like to do first, or asking students to examine the pedagogical goals of a particular task. This conceptualisation of negotiation does not involve the creation or modification of a syllabus by participants.

The participatory approach can also be contrasted with another view of a learner centred classroom, what Clarke (1991) calls the 'strong version' of the process syllabus, in which students are expected to determine wholly the course of their learning, and to arrive at a consensus about the content and goals of the course. In this version, the role of the teacher is facilitator, a role that on the surface undervalues the knowledge and institutional status of the teacher (Holliday, 1994), and may be seen as an attempt to disguise the inherent control of the teacher (Freire and Macedo, 1995). Furthermore, when a teacher asks students to determine the course of their learning, it can lead to maintenance of the status quo, as illustrated in Budd and Wright (1992). In their study, when the students were asked how they would like to learn in the class, they decided that they preferred a traditional pedagogy with the teacher taking responsibility for determining class activities. This suggests that students who have not experienced pedagogical alternatives may not be in a position to change the circumstances of their learning.

In a participatory pedagogy, a challenge to the traditional classroom must generally be introduced by the teacher, and the challenge includes both dialogue and critique. Dialogue is part of the process syllabus, as illustrated in Littlejohn (1983) with ESL students and in Parkinson and O'Sullivan (1990) with graduate students. In both cases, the teacher led the students through the process of negotiation as a co-participant, with the issues to be negotiated introduced by the teacher. However, a participatory pedagogy is a development of the dialogue towards a process syllabus. The process syllabus is an antidote to the traditional conceptualisation of learning and teaching, while a participatory pedagogy is a challenge both to traditional teaching *and* to the institutional implications of such teaching. A participatory, process pedagogy provides a way for students to critique their pedagogical experiences at a time when they are developing an informed pedagogical philosophy of their own as teachers. A participatory, process pedagogy also challenges the institutionalised power relationships that students and teachers have come to expect in the classroom, by providing them with a lived, alternative conceptualisation.

The context

This chapter is based on the teaching of a post-graduate-level writing course that lasted 15 weeks within an MA degree in ESL. In the course, there were 12 graduate students majoring in ESL and one graduate student majoring in English. They included one Caribbean, one Eastern European, one Chinese, one Malaysian, three Japanese and six American students. Two of these students were not doing the course for credit, and they participated by coming to class and keeping a journal. One other student dropped the course when he found out that it would be negotiated. Throughout this chapter, I refer to the students by means of pseudonyms when recounting what they said or wrote.

One of the auditors (Scott Todd) proposed early on that he do a qualitative study of the course for an ethnographic research methods course he was taking during the same period. I agreed, and he began to take observation notes and conduct interviews with me and the students. The students also wrote a dialogue journal as part of their interaction with me and, after obtaining permission from them, I photocopied all of the journals as part of the data record. At the end of the course, Todd and I interviewed all of the students and transcribed the interview data. We thus had triangulated data from four sources: interviews, journals, observations and course-related documents. Todd analysed the data for his final scholarly paper in the department where he found that the personal nature of the class, the issue of control, the evolution of expectations and the relationship between process and content were salient themes (Todd, 1995).

Analysis

When I began to analyse the data myself for this paper, my rather open-ended research question was: What are the roles of the teacher and students in a negotiated class? I discovered that during the course the participants (including myself) were preoccupied with three issues related to this question:

1. the power relationships in the classroom;
2. taking responsibility for learning; and
3. thinking through our approaches to pedagogy.

I discuss each of these themes in the sections that follow.

Negotiation and power

> [W]e were all trying to find out what our role was, not just the teacher.
> (Gwen)

The negotiation process in this writing course involved chaos, choice, control, responsibility, trust and reflection. The negotiation process challenged what we all believed about classrooms. The students entered this experience expecting the teacher to be authoritarian, to control the class dialogue, to make all major decisions, and expecting to follow the teacher-determined path. I entered this experience wanting to change the balance of power, but not knowing quite how to achieve this. I thought at first that negotiation meant giving up control of the classroom to become a facilitator. As we struggled together with what our roles should be, I gradually came to an understanding that negotiation should be conceived not as an abdication of teacher control, but as a participatory dialogue.

Initially, I provided a tentative syllabus for the students that listed two required textbooks, a journal, a presentation, a project and various topics in the field of writing methodology. The previous year I had provided an eight-page syllabus with all of the topics, readings, requirements and dates specified, along with additional references. Since I was new to negotiation, I began with the syllabus I had originally developed and started cutting from there. I changed the requirements to allow more student control, took out the percentage allocated to each requirement, and listed potential topics rather than required readings. I chose the two texts because they represented very different views on teaching writing, and I wanted to stimulate a critique of ESL methodology. The resulting syllabus was one page in length, and invited students to consider what topics mattered to them (see the initial syllabus in Appendix 17.1). For me, this represented the crucial first step in allowing students to control their own learning.

The students did not have a choice whether the course would be negotiated or not, because I didn't want them to choose the status quo. I determined that we would all take the risk of negotiating the syllabus in order to experience what that meant, whether or not it was comfortable. During the first half of the course, I negotiated with the students how the requirements would be met, what we would read, how we would handle the readings and how the work would be graded. We negotiated and discussed the topics of the course primarily by means of smaller group interaction (for this the students worked in one initially self-selected group of about 4–5 members). I would listen to the students, and then decide what we would do on that basis. The pervasiveness of the negotiation process was acknowledged by all of the students, as this quote from John illustrates:

> Gosh, [there were] all kinds of negotiating: negotiation of topics covered, negotiation of what she expects, negotiation of who goes when, all kinds of negotiation, but stuff where she says like, 'OK, you guys tell me what you want to do.' That kind of thing, and then we all reply or whatever [laughs].

Early in the class, many of the students expressed the view that the negotiation process was changing the balance of power in the class, which they had not expected:

> I'm not used to a teacher negotiating a syllabus, so I was waiting for her to take charge. She, maybe wringing her hands, let us decide what was going to happen. I thought when she was doing that she gave us too much authority, which is kind of ironic because we're not used to giving any input regarding how we should even have class. So she really did more relinquishing of her power than I expected her to.   (Gwen)

> I don't think that the teacher is just an equal that we're just supposed to equally discuss something. She wanted to just be an equal with us. And I thought, 'Why is she even trying? She knows she's not an equal. I know she's not an equal.'   (Matt)

Some of the students wanted me to control the structure of the class so that they could feel more comfortable in their traditional role as students:

> Almost all the classes I've attended so far are passive. I listen to the teacher very carefully and memorize everything he says. At first I thought I wouldn't learn much in this class.   (Emiko)

> I feel uncomfortable and nervous when I don't know what is going on in class. Without knowing how many articles I have to read and what we are going to do for next week, I feel overwhelmed.   (Jenny)

> I think my view has strengthened as to the fact that the teacher has to take some control in class, because I just see this class as really chaotic.   (John)

Marilyn observed this conflict between what the students felt they needed and what was happening:

> I've seen you [Kate Wolfe-Quintero] teach before and I've experienced your class before and this was different and I didn't know what was going on. My initial expectation was that even if this were going to be a negotiated class, the teacher would impose a preliminary structure. It was possible to see real struggles going on in the class in general as each person worked out their need for externally provided structure.

If students are given the choice, they would not choose this. The negotiation was participatory rather than learner-centred because it challenged what students thought they wanted and needed on the basis of a critique of traditional learning and teaching, while simultaneously involving them in determining the direction of the course. Although there was initial discomfort and resistance (as in Willett and Jeannot,

1993), the students gradually discovered that the lack of a teacher's structure allowed them to examine their own learning and teaching in a fundamentally different way.

Two classroom observations illustrate how both I and the students struggled with our roles during this initial process of negotiation. In the first excerpt, I revealed my uncertainty about what I should be doing as the teacher in this situation. And Emiko expressed her desire for me to tell the students what they should do, which I resisted:

KATE: Now for the hard part for me: that's what are we going to do today? I have lots of ideas. I do have things for you to do, but I'm trying to resist a teacherly instinct to give them to you. I want you to choose from them. I don't want you to think I'm not prepared. I feel weird coming in and saying, 'This is what we're going to do,' but it's also weird to come in and say, 'OK, what do you want to do?' [Offers: work in groups or in whole class to discuss parts of the textbook or presentation formats]

EMIKO: Are we still working in groups today? [Kate smiles] If it's group work, the groups could do different things.

KATE: Well, one question is: what do you want your groups to produce?   (Todd, 1995:18–19)

In the second excerpt I more clearly presented the options, while some of the students (including Emiko) voiced confident opinions about what they would like to do, rather than asking me to decide on their behalf:

KATHLEEN: What's the choice?
KATE: Talking all together about course design, or getting together in groups and working on discussing the mid-term evaluations or filling them out or finishing responding.
KATHLEEN: I'd like to finish responding about course design.
KATE: And, who else?
EMIKO: Yeah, I'd like to set the time at five minutes or something like that for correspondence on course design.
MATT: We should start with course design. Otherwise we won't have time for it.
JULIE: We will if we set a time limit for our group discussion.
KATHLEEN: Group work first.
KATE: OK, um, Go to it: 20 minutes, 15 minutes?
JULIE: 15 minutes.
KATE: 15 minutes. [Group discussion starts]   (Todd, 1995: 12)

Toshi described this classroom negotiation process, concluding that I did, in fact, have 'the final say' about what we would do, although my decisions were based on the negotiation process:

> [Something is] proposed by Kate, and there are discussions about her proposal by several students. I don't think all students participated in it. I think there was a lot of intervention from Kate's side, so it's not that students and instructor negotiated the syllabus on an equal basis. And I don't think we were capable of reaching agreement on everything, within a limited amount of time. So, there was always compromise. We discuss several things, and then Kate decided. But what Kate decided was based on our discussion, you know? So, Kate has the final say, but I think we could have challenged that. As Keiko pointed out, this type of negotiation meant that what happened in the class was largely determined by who was vocal in the classroom: [Kate would say] 'Do you want to do it?' And some people would say, 'Yes!' and that was the answer and we did it. Like, if somebody vocal said, 'Yes,' and Kate heard that, or said, 'No' that was the answer. It was like the majority, or not even the majority, like one or two people who were vocal made the decision. However, that was acceptable to quieter students like John: I found it really interesting that Scott mentioned that there are always two or three dominant students in class always ready to voice their opinions and Toshi remarking calmly that our class was no different. I was thinking the exact same thing at the same time. But I don't feel bitter in any way about those students – I think it makes for a very balanced class. I always get what I want out of a class my own way.

On the initial syllabus I had proposed reading the two textbooks one after the other, although we negotiated a different order of subparts of the texts, as shown on the final version of the syllabus (shown in Appendix 17.2). Early on, we decided to pursue the issue of responding to ESL students in depth, since one of the participants brought in examples of students' writing because she wanted feedback from the class on how to respond to it. This stimulated a discussion that revealed that responding was the single most critical issue the students were preoccupied with as teachers. Because of their interest, I brought in additional articles on responding (those listed on the negotiated syllabus under 'Responding to Writing I'). Like those on responding, I did not select any of the supplementary articles in advance, but provided them as the class unfolded, based on my knowledge of the field. Occasionally, the students brought in articles for the whole class to discuss. Although we concluded that even in a negotiated class it was impossible to escape the teacher having the final authority, we did find that the balance of power could shift so that students could have much more control over their learning than they normally would.

In addition to the classroom negotiation, there was ongoing negotiation between me and the students in the journals, which were dialogue journals rather than private journals because I was the audience and responder. At the beginning of the course we decided that the journals would be shown to me but not to other students except for some public parts that I would solicit. We also decided that the journals would include reflection and free writing, that there would be no specific amount of writing required, and that there would be no imposed topics except for occasional public pieces on a particular topic. I would remind students periodically to turn in their journals for feedback, but they turned them in on their own timetable. Occasionally I would write to the class as a whole, challenging the students on various issues that I had been thinking about. At times I asked them to reflect on their experiences in classrooms as learners, as writers and as teachers and, at other times, I asked them to describe their approach to a particular area of teaching in a public piece, such as how they approached responding to students' writing. The students would show their group members their piece, and later I would extract related excerpts from all the pieces, respond to the ideas, and then distribute the excerpts and responses to everyone for discussion. Some students would then continue the dialogue even further by responding in their journals.

The journals proved to be the place where honest, challenging dialogue took place, as several students acknowledged:

> I thought that [Kate] writing to us with the degree of honesty that she did, did a lot to break down student–teacher role relationships and barriers between real communication, like that first one where she really opened up and said, 'Oh, I'm feeling frustrated with this,' and whatever, I just remember that gave me the freedom to talk to her on a different level, with less formality and more real personal communication.   (Kathleen)

I sought to respond honestly and openly to students about my own life as a teacher, while challenging them to think more deeply about their opinions and experiences in relation to what we were reading. This allowed the students the freedom to respond in kind, in a shared dialogue. They acknowledged that this was based on trust:

> Sometimes I write negative things about Kate too, because I trust Kate. It took some time, but now I can trust Kate. It makes a lot of difference to me.   (Toshi)

> When I write something and I know that it's this particular person who is going to read and comment on my writing, I feel secure.   (Katia)

> The journal was a profound experience for me. And I didn't know that I was willing to commit myself to that kind of honesty. It was very scary. What helped a lot is that I know how you [Kate] operate and I can trust you. With your comments you were doing the same kind of in-the-gut soul-searching stuff that I was doing. It wouldn't have worked if the teacher had patted me on the head and said 'Nice journal. Nice journal.' It had to be a mutual, honest thing here.   (Marilyn)

These entries demonstrate that meaningful communication in the journal grew as a result of increasing honesty and trust on both sides.

Because the process of negotiation initially felt uncomfortable, the only way we could experience a negotiated syllabus was for me to lead the class through this process. A participatory pedagogy requires the teacher to introduce the students to an alternative way of conceptualising power in the classroom, to open up the class to dialogue, both verbal and written. As Kathleen wrote:

> I think that until students have been socialized into or at least experienced non-traditional models of education, the teacher will have to take a strong role in shaping the classroom. Maybe it's possible for the whole class to create something new from scratch, but I don't think it would come naturally.

A teacher's control of the class is not in opposition to a student's control over learning; rather, I discovered that although I controlled the basic premises of the course, the students could explore and communicate the ideas that mattered to them. I had to be willing to wait through some of the uncomfortable periods until students began to take control of their learning.

Responsibility for learning

> We ourselves create our own class.   (Keiko)

In the context of the negotiation and the change in classroom power, students gradually came to the realisation that they had to take responsibility for how they were going to learn:

> In the beginning I was really frustrated with what I thought was a lack of control; in the end I appreciated it because it basically made me take responsibility for whatever I was going to get out

257

> of the class. I had to take control of my learning, not the teacher. (Gwen)

> I had to take charge of my own learning 'cause it was obvious that you [Kate] weren't going to hand it to me on a silver platter. (Marilyn)

They had absorbed the reality that I was not going to control the learning process, and began to figure out what relevance the readings had to them. For some it meant preparing questions and issues for class discussion:

> I realized that I do have to participate and investigate on my own and bring interesting topics and questions to class. There is always a teacher to ask, too. It's just me who has to start and get going. (Emiko)

> I've been thinking about what I can do to get the most out of the class for the day. Instead of going to class, expecting to get information from the instructor, I have to prepare myself with questions and issues to discuss before going to class, to become an active learner. (Toshi)

For others it meant reflecting on their teaching and learning experiences:

> We were pretty much responsible for ourselves from the beginning, I think. Nobody told me to do certain things, like to reflect on my own students' writing, or my previous teaching or whatever, but all the thinking I did made me do more than was asked in the course. (Keiko)

> I really find the journal to be a good place to consolidate my thoughts about my teaching theories and practices. I have really found that I *do* actually have opinions about all kinds of things whereas I used to think of myself as a very neutral and rather passive receptor of information. (John)

As the class progressed, the students moved from being uncomfortable with the perceived lack of structure to the realisation that they had the power to determine the course of their learning. This is illustrated in a third classroom observation, which chronicles a class dialogue that Kathleen initiated several weeks into the course. In this excerpt, the students not only voiced their opinions about what they would like to do, but critiqued the way we went about doing it:

KATHLEEN: You know it seems like it goes on and on and it's all organization and not as much content as I would like.

MARILYN: [Says that she disagrees, sees the class as process, and likes it this way.]

KATHLEEN: I think that there needs to be a little more balance for me. I mean I like a little of both but I think it's way . . .

KATE: And so the conversation continues. [Students laugh.]

GWEN: One of the things that is important – choosing options, etc. – isn't that part of what we should be studying? So aren't we actually doing research as we participate in the process?

KATHLEEN: Yeah, I think that's part of it. I just don't want it to be all of it.   (Todd, 1995:28–29)

Some of the students continued this dialogue with me in their journals:

> Kathleen also brought up that interesting point about setting up time limits so that we can concentrate more on content than on organizational matters. While I do agree that we often get carried away and end up not really discussing the topics at hand, I cringe at the idea of timing our discussions or abandoning some interesting line of thought because it was time to move on. Marilyn's point that the whole process of organization was worth investigating was also well taken. I can see both points of view.   (John)

> In today's class we again spent a lot of time negotiating what we should do how we should do, instead of content itself. I agree with Kathleen's comment that although we benefit from negotiating syllabus, we also need to spend time on content; a balance is necessary.   (Toshi)

Toshi went on to examine his own interaction style in the context of this dialogue. His questions revealed the deeper reflection that the negotiation process had triggered:

> One thing that struck me during the exchange today is that I couldn't think well, I couldn't decide what I wanted to do. Some people can quickly react to problems raised in class. I can't. I just listen and let other people discuss and shape a decision. Today, this passiveness of my own bothered me. Why can't I participate? Why can't I react? I want to be more expressive.   (Toshi)

The overt disagreement about how much negotiation the students wanted in the class is an example of negotiation at work. The students openly discussed and wrote about negotiation; they had opinions that they felt compelled to express, and disagreements about whether the negotiation process was useful or not. These classroom and written dialogues show that the students were not merely going along with a negotiation process that I had set up; they gradually owned it for themselves, caring more about analysing their own learning than about my approval or authority.

In fact, it was the dialogue journals that opened up the negotiation process to a greater depth than was possible in class discussions alone. I believe that the journals were the crucial factor that allowed the more overt classroom negotiation to develop as it did. The journals allowed all students to have a voice, whether quiet or not in the classroom. The development of the students' voice and control can be seen in the following journal excerpts directed towards me. Kathleen didn't like it when I questioned the students' ability to critique what their teachers feed them:

> I need time to integrate and evaluate new perspectives before I'm ready to take a strong stance on them one way or another. Until that time, I don't want to be just a straw-figure to be knocked down by someone with more experience and knowledge to draw on.

Marilyn didn't like it when she thought I had asked her to answer specific questions about the textbooks:

> I felt rebellious when asked to write about the texts used for this class.

Matt didn't like my teaching style:

> I like a teacher-centered class better. I would learn a lot from lectures which you could give about the papers we read. After all, you are the teacher.

During one particularly memorable class, we discussed the issue of talkative versus quiet students, and John felt that Gwen and I had gone too far by pushing Jenny to talk in front of the whole group:

> I felt really bad for Jenny because today's class must truly have seemed like a nightmare for her. Today, both you and Gwen totally put her on the spot and she was really in a no-win situation.

And Jenny had her own question for me about this situation:

> Do I make you mad at me because I rarely talk in class? I always feel uncomfortable, nervous and empty in my head when I am forced to say something. I felt terrible after the writing class on Wednesday.

And finally, Gwen responded when I told her I was disappointed with her for editing a student's dialect right out of his writing:

> Boy, I got goose bumps when I read your note that said you were disappointed with me 'modifying' Thomas' story. It hit me like a ton of bricks, and I felt like I had made the worst mistake with Thomas' writing in my own obsessions to 'correct' the obvious. Maybe that is the reason why he is not participating with me anymore. (Gwen)

These are just snippets from much longer exchanges about these issues. The journals evolved into dialogues about pedagogy; they were not conversations between friends, nor written in a 'vacuous, feel-good comfort zone' (Macedo and Freire, 1995). Rather, they were gritty and honest and, for me, often gripping.

In the second half of the course, the students did two-day presentations on topics that they chose, selecting the readings for the rest of us. For example, one student explored the use of computers in writing courses because she was using *Daedalus* for peer interaction at her practicum (or placement) site. Another student spoke a Caribbean English Creole; she examined how local high-school students used Hawaii Creole English in their creative writing. (The topics that they chose to investigate can be found on the syllabus in Appendix 17.2.) I would not have thought to include many of these topics if the syllabus had been wholly determined by me, but they are topics that were relevant to their lives as teachers. I encouraged them not to follow the usual 'lecture' format of presentations but to involve the rest of us in a dialogue. The presenter generally provided some general comments on the topic, asked us to write about the readings in the interval between the two parts of the presentation, and asked us to discuss the readings and our reactions in small groups.

By the time the presentations approached, students had become much more comfortable with negotiation and had begun to realise that we had not negotiated the requirements themselves (journal, presentation, project), but merely their procedure and content. As we were preparing for the presentations, Jenny wondered out loud in class whether students had to do presentations at all, which sparked yet another class meta-discussion on negotiation. Toshi revealed in his journal how this discussion revised his thinking about what was negotiable:

> For example the presentation thing, we didn't really negotiate properly. Kate brought up the activity that we should do the investigation and we should present, but [later] somebody said it should be individual responsibility or freedom whether to present or not, and then I realize, 'Oh, OK I have to do it.'

The questioning of the presentation requirement indicates how the balance of power had changed. At the beginning, students felt that they had to do whatever I asked of them, but now everything became open for debate.

There was also an initial requirement for students to complete a final project, but I left it completely up to students to define the project for themselves. Some students wrote a more formal version of their presentation, other students summarised their philosophy of teaching writing, and a few investigated a whole new topic. I viewed the projects as an extension of the writing they had done in the course, and felt that it was up to the students to assess what role it played in their learning. Although there was no specific journal or project length requirement, the journals and projects together contained an average of 80 pages per person, with a range from 42 pages to 124 pages (either handwritten or typed). I found this remarkable. They wrote far more than the students in the same course the previous year when I had determined the journal topics, collected them at pre-determined points and controlled their evaluation. At the end of the course, Kathleen commented on how the experiences with negotiation and participatory dialogue had caused the course to be more in the students' control, and consequently more relevant to them:

> I felt that I had more potential for control than in other classes, that the class was there for the students, and not the other way around that the students were there for this pre-determined class. There was more freedom to think about what would really be useful for me.

This leads to the question of assessment. At the beginning of the course, I had decided that the students should determine their own grades. This requirement originally meant that the journals could only be self-assessed, so I asked the students to go ahead and assess themselves for the whole course. At that time I didn't feel that I could grade them. If I did not want to control the students' learning, I felt that I could not control the evaluation of that learning either. Along the way, I provided responses to what they did, including challenges to work more deeply, but never a grade-related evaluation. I felt comfortable with self-evaluation because this was a graduate-level course, although I have known teachers who used self-evaluation with undergraduates as well.

This self-evaluation process caused a problem for Gwen, who wanted an A, but felt that she actually deserved a B in the course:

> I didn't appreciate the fact that I have to grade myself. I knew I wasn't going to get an A if I graded myself. I have to be honest

and say 'now based on everything I wanted to do in class that I didn't do, then I would give myself a B.' Now, ironically, when Kate said in class, 'Well, students are generally harsher on themselves than I am,' I thought in the back of my mind, 'Well, yeah, you expect us to be, anyway.' I don't think that it's easier for students to grade themselves, especially if you establish a relationship with the teacher where the teacher knows if you're bullshitting or not, that it's not easy for you to give yourself an A if you don't deserve it legitimately.

Gwen told me she wanted the A, so I asked her what she should do, and she decided that she would write a paper to make up for what she hadn't done in her journal. She told the interviewer how surprised she was that I negotiated the grade with her:

> I know I want the A, but I gave myself a B. But then Kate negotiated with me and gave me an A. Negotiated with me. 'If you do this, then let's do that instead.'

I wanted to encourage her to go further in her learning rather than settle for a B that she didn't want. Gwen got the A, and three weeks after the course ended she turned in the paper.

Pedagogical practice

> I can't go back to the old way again.   (Jenny)

The negotiation in this class allowed us to envision the reality of a different type of pedagogy, a participatory, process pedagogy that seeks a balance between the teacher's voice and the students' input and control over learning. The process of negotiation provided a chance to experience first hand something that we had only read about, discovering as we went along how to interact in a new way. As the students became participants in the process, they also became increasingly confident of their ability to negotiate in other situations:

> You know at the beginning of the semester the instructor can say, 'We can negotiate it, everything, so if something's bothering you then bring it up.' Then, no negotiation [laughs]. Yeah, but we know that because we've experienced it, we can do that.
>   (Toshi)

> I was glad to experience this kind of thing, which you know I had done readings about, but not really experienced.
>   (Kathleen)

> I learned what people mean when they say 'negotiate the syllabus'. (Matt)

> Now that I've experienced it as a student, I have more confidence about using it in my future class. (Emiko)

> I can't say I learned what people mean when they say 'negotiate the syllabus' 'cause I think I already had a good idea. But I think I saw it in action. (Julie)

Both Toshi and I commented on the need for teachers to have direct experience with alternative pedagogies:

> I think one of the things missing in a lot of graduate training is the chance to experience something from the other end, to not just talk about it theoretically, but to experience it as though you were the student. (Kate)

> I've heard of this kind of thing, usually mentioned in the book, or briefly discussed in the class, but not so intensively. So this is a totally new experience to me. And I think the one major difference is we're actually doing it as students. (Toshi)

Almost all of the students felt that the experience transformed their perception of teaching, some in positive ways and some in more negative ways. One student who had initially disliked negotiation began to see it as a real possibility for his own teaching:

> Before I always thought that the syllabus was not to be negotiated with the students because – I don't know why – I was just brought up that way, but I think it's good to negotiate the syllabus with the students. (Matt)

Some students felt that they became more open to their students:

> I think [the course] really affected the way I teach. I tried to be a lot more open to what my students were trying to tell me.
> (John)

Other students felt that they grew as teachers:

> I feel that I have thought more deeply about teaching writing and what it means to be a writer and a writing teacher than if we had been assigned to read X and discuss Y. (Julie)

> That class made me feel more like I wanted to be a teacher. [There was] less artificial activity that was of no interest to anyone in particular involved in the class, but just kind of self-perpetuated by the system. (Kathleen)

Gwen felt that this experience caused her to question herself as a teacher. She felt less competent and less knowledgeable, but more interested in her students. Her self-questioning led her to have a genuine desire to know her students' agendas:

> I came in with a definite idea of what teaching writing was about. I came in with my own set of beliefs of how students and teachers should interact. And I basically came in with the idea that I have an agenda or a programme, and the students fall into my agenda. By the end of the class, I'm torn up into 12 pieces by the time, you know, I don't have an agenda anymore. I'm more interested in figuring out where the student is at, and find out what their agenda is so I can incorporate it into the learning process. And to be honest with you, I feel less competent now as a teacher than I did before the class. I realize that, hey, I need to learn a whole lot more about students and what works.

Gwen wasn't sure she should continue as a teacher, but another side of her wanted to quit graduate school and go back to teaching right away in order to find out what kind of teacher she could be.

Jenny wanted to give up teaching altogether. She felt that she would have to challenge the state system in her own Asian country too much. Experiencing negotiation had infiltrated her pedagogical philosophy to such an extent that she either had to be able to incorporate it into her teaching or she would have to quit:

> The more I learn from this class, the more I want to give up to be a teacher. Because what I've learned from this class is quite different from my learning or teaching experience. Though I love some ideas about negotiated syllabus and assessment, portfolio-based evaluation programmes and sequenced writing assignments, I couldn't think of any possibility to adopt their ways of teaching in the situation where the class consists of more than 50 students and where teachers must use the standard textbooks and are evaluated according to the scores students get from the monthly standardized test. I can't go back to the old way again, and that's why I want to give up.

Jenny subsequently wrote her MA final research paper on the possibility of pedagogical reform, based on classroom observations and interviews with teachers in her country.

In the process of this course, I began to find my own voice as a teacher. When I had first made the commitment to negotiate the class, I tried to abdicate my voice along with my power in the classroom, and this made everyone uncomfortable, including me. At first, I had no idea what my role should be in this situation:

> The struggle that I had from the beginning was what is the role of my voice if I did give up power in the classroom? I didn't know. And one of the possible conclusions is that I give up my voice entirely which is a false one but one that I played with. It's like the first thing that we think of when we think we have to let other people discover stuff for themselves is that we are now out of it.

The process of negotiation challenged me to rethink everything I had previously thought about myself as a teacher. The course was too chaotic at first, because I mistakenly thought I should try to give up all control. Later, I began to realise that the struggle was how to maintain authority as the teacher while giving up being authoritarian, how to foster dialogue rather than control it and how to encourage but not control the learning process.

I began to adopt new roles: responder, challenger and knowledgeable participant. Because of experiencing this class, I learned that I am not *outside* the dialogue. I now think that I have more of a real voice in the classroom when it is negotiated because I can stop pretending that I'm somehow an objective presenter and evaluator. I can be a subjective participant in the class, free to say and do whatever is meaningful for me in interaction with others. I found that I can pursue issues that I think are crucial with greater honesty and emotion, less 'academese' and false objectivity. I found that I can personally grow as a participant in ongoing dialogue.

During the class I spent time working out my own philosophy of teaching writing, which I presented to the class as my personal contribution to the dialogue. Toshi documented this change in my understanding of my role and his reaction to it:

> Monday's class was a little bit different from usual. Kate gave us a lecture first, then we went to small group discussion. It was more organized, more teacher-directed. I was a little taken aback because of its teacher-directedness at first, but it's nice to hear Kate's personal beliefs on writing in an organized way once in a while.

I was beginning to take responsibility for my own growth in the course. I didn't have to rely on comfortably presenting pre-determined articles in a pre-determined order; I could also explore for myself the topic that I was most interested in as a co-participant with the students.

I now see my role as the teacher as one of raising key issues, negotiating content, facilitating students' choices, co-ordinating the class time so that it isn't chaotic, and providing any relevant materials and expertise that I have. I can provide a place where dialogue can take place about the issues of the course. When certain issues emerge as central to the students' lives, we can pursue those further. I cannot escape the fact that I am given the final authority, but within that frame the students can have the freedom to contribute and choose in ways that are meaningful for them.

Through this experience, my eyes were irrevocably opened to new possibilities, new ways of conceptualising the classroom. This experience changed how I have approached every class since, although I have not repeated this experience in any of them. This happened to be the second time I taught this particular writing methodology course. The first time I had taught it, I controlled the content, the timing, the requirements and the dialogue. By the time I taught this course a third time, a year later, I was a different teacher. I neither completely controlled the class nor abdicated control, but I used my inherent control to foster a dialogue. Rather than obligatorily covering 27 areas of writing pedagogy as I had the first time, rather than leaving the syllabus completely wide open to negotiation as I had the second time, I decided to include within the syllabus those topics and readings that were personally meaningful to me. I decided to exploit the subjective qualities of my participation by providing readings and talking about issues that I felt passionately about, areas in which I could challenge students' thinking. At the same time, in addition to two required textbooks, I asked the students to choose from among 16 optional books several that they would most like to read. The students formed reading groups based on their choices, and I asked them to respond honestly in a journal to the ideas of the course that mattered to them, whether the ideas that I presented or those that they discovered in their reading. The syllabus changed several times as we negotiated our way between the ideas I wanted to bring into the class and the ideas they were sharing with each other and me. I gained the ability and understanding to allow the course to develop in this way only because the earlier process of negotiation had deconstructed my traditional views and new possibilities had risen in their place.

Conclusion

> You know you're chipping away at 30 years of hardened 'give the teacher what the teacher wants' type of thing.　　　(John)

Auerbach (1995: 10), drawing on Freire, has said that 'education inevitably either serves to perpetuate existing social relations or to challenge them.' I found that engaging in a participatory dialogue with students allowed them to critically examine their previous experiences, to investigate topics that mattered to them, and to transform their views of themselves as learners and teachers. And I know that this experience caused me to do the same.

I would argue that for students who are in the process of becoming professionals in the ESL field, the opportunity to experience this type of challenge to their beliefs is a crucial part of their pedagogical development. If they cannot experience and thus envision alternative pedagogies, their only option is to maintain a traditional stance to the students in their classrooms, perhaps spending an entire career without questioning what they are doing or ever really knowing what deeply matters to their students. To see this, we can look at the transformation of John as both a student and a teacher as the course progressed. He had always been a student who gave the teacher what she wanted:

> In most classes when I go in I'm kind of almost like a blank slate, you know. I always try to please my teacher. It's just the way I was brought up. You know you're chipping away at 30 years of hardened 'give the teacher what the teacher wants' type of thing.

But his experience in this class was different:

> I think that's the first time I actually thought about something, actually thought about it as opposed to just read it and process it and spit it back out. To get your [Kate's] feedback especially was good because I don't have that kind of relationship with teachers. To know how you felt and even try to put into words how I felt was very useful for me. I did think a lot about my own personal teaching philosophy and my teaching style which basically wasn't very well formed.

John had always believed that the teacher had the knowledge, a belief that he carried to his own teaching:

> I've always clung to this thing that I as a teacher should know more, has to know more, has to be right.

But he began to realise that he was missing something with his students:

> You know they were coming up to me mostly 'cause they had a problem with the homework as opposed to having a real dialogue about things, so I started talking to them a lot more. So, I guess for me the big thing was about how to deal with

getting a dialogue going with students, how to get them more involved in the whole process.

When John did open up his class to a dialogue, he was able to uncover what mattered to his students:

> I actually had a discussion with them, like about three-quarters of the way through the semester, when I just said 'How do you feel about what we're doing?' It was really eye opening for me 'cause here I was thinking that things were working, and there they were thinking 'Why are we doing this?' And even this whole issue of why are they even there and they felt insulted to be there.

John began a more participatory dialogue with his students, which had an effect on how open they felt with him:

> They saw me less as like this authoritarian type figure and more someone kind of feeling his way around and doesn't know everything and wants to know what they're thinking, wants to know their feelings. And then I think I saw a lot more of them coming to my office during my office hours after that.

This change in his experience as a teacher became the primary thing that he learned in the class:

> I think [the course] really affected the way I teach. I learned something about teaching writing but I learned a whole lot more which I hadn't expected. I think that redefining my role was definitely the key concept of the class for me.

What happened to John is what Auerbach (1995: 15–16) has described as a participatory dialogue that 'starts with collaborative investigation of what is important to students, ... not to fit learners into the existing order, but to enable them critically to examine it and become active in shaping their own roles in it.' What began as a simple goal to negotiate a graduate class became a transforming experience for those who participated.

Acknowledgements

I couldn't have written this chapter without the contribution of Scott Todd, who collected and transcribed many of the interviews, conducted the classroom observations and worked with me on a collaborative paper presented at the TESOL conference in 1995. I am also grateful to Kathy Davis, Pamela Minet-Lucid and Sara Rabie for their insightful comments at various stages of working on this chapter.

Appendix 17.1
Initial syllabus

ESL 614: ESL WRITING

COURSE OBJECTIVES
This course covers the teaching of writing to second language students. The goals are to familiarize you with the theoretical and practical issues involved in teaching writing, and to train you in thinking critically about writing pedagogy.

READING MATERIALS
Mayher, J. S. (1990).   *Uncommon sense: Theoretical practice in language education*. Heinemann.
Reid, J. M. (1993).   *Teaching ESL writing*. Regents/Prentice Hall.
Course packet to be determined by course participants.

COURSE REQUIREMENTS
Writing journal; assignments throughout semester
Due May 13, 4:00pm (to 478 Moore)

Writing pedagogy presentation
Investigation and presentation of literature relevant to topic

Writing pedagogy project
Investigation of writing process, classroom, materials
Due May 13, 4:00pm (leave at office, 478 Moore)

COURSE PLAN

Pedagogical Theory
  Mayher book

Issues in ESL Writing Pedagogy
  Reid book

Potential Additional Topics (To be negotiated)
  Ideology and history of writing pedagogy
  Approaches: process, whole language, literacy, . . .
  Writing feedback: peer feedback, teacher responses, conferencing
  Writing classrooms: syllabi, textbooks, instructional routines,
    collaboration, topic choice
  Writing: journals, freewriting, essays, portfolios, computer-assisted writing
  Academic writing: content-based, reading-writing connection, writing
    across the curriculum
  Language analysis: contrastive rhetoric, coherence and topical structure
  Writing assessment: analytic, holistic, and trait scoring, placement, grading

---

Appendix 17.2
Negotiated syllabus

ESL 614: COURSE TOPICS	
PHILOSOPHY OF TEACHING	
teachers & learners	Rose, Mayher 1–4
CURRENT TRENDS	
	Reid 1–3
RESPONDING TO WRITING I	
meaning & form, discourse communities	Reid 8, Sommers, Hendrickson, Zamel, Bullock, Schwegler
COURSE DESIGN	
syllabi, negotiation, activities	Reid 4–6, 10, Mayher 7–9, Cummins
ASSESSMENT & GRADING	
portfolios, measures	Reid 9, Johns, Flower Hamp-Lyons, Belanoff & Dickson
WRITING CONNECTIONS	
Student 1 global issues and writing	Reid 7, McGowan-Gilhooly, Leki Brinton, Snow & Wesche, Fisher & Hicks
Student 2 reading and writing	Carson *et al.*, Leki
APPROACHES TO TEACHING WRITING	
Student 3 social-process approach	Delpit, Branscombe & Heath
Student 4 creative writing, voice	Yamanaka, Lum, student writing
Student 5 computer-assisted writing	Sullivan, Sirc & Reynolds
Student 6 immigrant literacy	Huebner, Auerbach
Student 7 writing strategies	Gaustad & Messenheimer-Young, Laturnau, Dolly, Staton & Tyler
Student 8 awareness of audience	Rafoth, Roen & Willey, Four Voices
RESPONDING TO WRITING II	
Student 9 peer and teacher responses	Slavin, Kagan, Mittan
Student 10 error correction	Bley-Vroman, Brock, *et al.*
Student 11 contrastive rhetoric	Leki, Kaplan, Takano

18 The practicalities of negotiation

Michael P. Breen and Andrew Littlejohn

As we detailed in Chapter 1, the rationale for introducing what we have termed 'procedural negotiation' into classroom work has come from many quarters. These have included influences from humanistic conceptions of society, a role for education in fostering the development of democratic citizenship and a view of human psychology that emphasises the socially constructed nature of learning and the learner as an active participant, not merely a recipient of transmitted knowledge. Specifically within the field of language education, the purposes of classroom work which aim to develop the communicative capacities of the learners have given further impetus for incorporating communication about learning as a beneficial part of classroom interaction.

In addition to these philosophical and theoretical views, many of the writers in this volume have revealed immediate, practical considerations which suggest negotiation as the logical, indeed at times, the only viable, way forward in decisions about course design and in their implementation. Among the imperatives for negotiated work, we can list the following familiar situations:

- when the teacher does not share the background of the students and, of necessity, must therefore share decisions about course contents (Nikolov, Martyn, Newstetter);
- when a limited number of teaching hours on short courses make teacher-determined choices of contents arbitrary (Slembrouck);
- when there is a heterogeneous student body and there is a need to find a common ground (Norris and Spencer);
- when it is difficult to identify the varied nature of learner achievements (MacKay *et al.*);
- when there is an absence of published course materials (Edmundson and Fitzpatrick);
- when there is an explicit need to take into account the experiences of students (Irujo, Ivanič);

- when the course itself is open-ended and exploratory in nature (Ribé, McCarthy and Makosch).

While the rationale for negotiation is strong at both a theoretical and practical level, each of the previous chapters has also stressed the need to consider factors which can directly affect the success or otherwise of efforts at introducing negotiation directly into classroom work. Negotiation is clearly not a straightforward undertaking. The extent and the focus of negotiation are influenced by the context in which teachers and students work and they may require abilities and sensitivities not conventionally expected of teachers and learners in their work together. The purpose of the present chapter is, therefore, to draw together aspects of practice and to set out some of the lessons which can be learned from the accounts provided in this volume. With the intention of supporting teachers in experimenting with the development of process syllabuses in their own classrooms, the chapter also provides a practical framework for negotiation.

Some practical considerations

The variety of contexts described in the preceding chapters affords us a detailed examination of the numerous factors which need to be borne in mind when developing classroom work involving negotiation. These range from external factors such as the existence of pre-specified curriculum plans, time constraints and class size to the personal responses of teachers and students, the background of the students and the wider cultural context in which negotiation is to take place.

An externally determined curriculum

A number of chapters in this volume (Smith, Linder and Serrano-Sampedro) discuss the implications that an externally determined curriculum – required, for example, by a Ministry of Education – may have on the possibilities of negotiation. Whilst it is obviously the case that a detailed external curriculum places limitations on what can be negotiated, each of those chapters also argues that the existence of an external curriculum may help to frame or delineate the boundaries for negotiation. As Serrano-Sampedro (p. 126) explains:

> All the apparently limiting factors – such as the existence of an official syllabus, or the need for final-year students to prepare for a university-entry exam – have had a positive influence upon

the negotiation process. Apart from providing the learners with a sense of guidance, a map in which they could draw their own learning route and a checklist for self-evaluation, they have contributed valuable learning opportunities for both the learners and myself. These were derived, for example, from the attempt to solve conflicts between the aims and content of the curriculum and the needs and interests of particular learners at a given time.

In these situations, whilst the aims or content may be prescribed, it is less frequently the case that aspects of methodology are equally detailed. Teachers with their classes can, in fact, determine their classroom procedures, such as the pace of the work, the selection of types of tasks or when to evaluate ongoing learning. Additionally, teachers can, for example, suggest varied approaches to prescribed materials and add supplementary materials of their own choice (see p. 281, 'Guidelines for practice').

Time

Some writers in this collection make the point that negotiation can be a time-consuming process (for example, Smith and Sokolik). On the surface, this may suggest that it is far easier and quicker for the teacher or some other external authority to make decisions about course contents, the way of working and evaluation. While considerations of time do need to be borne in mind as a factor which may constrain the scope of negotiation which it is feasible to undertake and which may limit the stages through which negotiation is taken, there are, however, at least two further important points to be brought out with regard to this.

The first is that we cannot equate like with like in this context. The rationale and purposes of introducing negotiation extend beyond the rationale and aims of 'conventional' transmission-based course decisions. We cannot, therefore, claim that one mode of working is more or less 'efficient' than another. Indeed, without exception, all of the teachers' accounts in this book indicate that negotiated modes of working achieve a wider range of learning outcomes, including confidence, motivation, quality and richness of learning, quality of students' work, abilities to work independently and with responsibility, and so on. Linder (p. 102) for example, commented on:

> the positive impact in terms of increased participation, increased use of the target language and the generally more satisfactory assignments submitted (these were higher in both quantity and quality).

Serrano-Sampedro (p. 125) similarly, found a positive impact on the students' initiative and effort:

> The learners' self-confidence increases. They show more initiative in communication and in organising their work . . . They learn to learn a foreign language. They solve problems, foresee them, identify advantages and disadvantages of alternatives, take into account contextual limitations (for example, suitability of available recorded material) and act to overcome them. They work harder and more effectively (which usually results in better learning).

The second point about time as a constraint, as we argued in Chapter 1, is that, in a context where the teacher makes most of the decisions regarding classroom work, learners' ongoing understandings and misunderstandings may for the most part be hidden and, because of this, may inhibit, disrupt or delay the learning process for individual members of the group. Misunderstandings may actually slow down the process of learning for many students and, therefore, work against the time we may have available with them. MacKay *et al.* for example, found that when students are encouraged to set their own goals, these are 'sometimes more realistic than those of the teacher' (p. 52) and that students become highly motivated to achieve those goals. One immediate result of this is that students therefore approach learning tasks knowing what to expect and what is expected of them and that, since teachers' expectations are negotiated, they become better understood by the students. In this regard Smith (p. 60) provides a revealing comment from a student who had been involved in negotiating her grade. She had become more aware of her strengths and weaknesses:

> I know that I was okay in English, but I never really knew where I had to put in more work in order to improve my grade. After knowing how the grade is formed and being asked to give myself a grade, I realised that much more work had to be put into my compositions. I have to structure them more and see too that my spelling improves.

Class size and diversity of student abilities

It is perhaps an irony that larger class sizes may appear to make negotiation more difficult whilst, at the same time, making more urgent the need for negotiation to take place. The phenomena of students 'learning alone in a crowd' is frequent and very real. Larger class sizes inevitably give individual students reduced possibilities of personally contributing to their lessons, and encourage the taking on of the role of a spectator of teaching. Similarly, wide variations in student abilities may imply that more time needs to be devoted to support specific students and to relate classroom work more directly to their needs. In both these respects, therefore, there is a strong argument in favour of incorporating negotiated work. As Serrano-Sampedro (p. 125) argues:

> The advantages of working within the framework of negotiation are acknowledged by the clear majority of the learners and by fellow teachers who have tried to apply it. Those that have been identified include the following:
>
> • It allows learners to work in different ways and at different rhythms in accordance with their needs and interests. As a consequence, their sense of progress and achievement increases and so does their motivation.
> • While learners work in groups the teacher can give more individual attention. This facilitates the attention to learner diversity: learning styles, rhythms, needs, interests, etc.

Yet, wide variations in student abilities and large class sizes may make it difficult to seek a class-based consensus in the work to be done or to provide feedback and opportunities to support individual students or groups of students working simultaneously on different contents and in different ways. To this end, Serrano-Sampedro (p. 124) provides a number of practical strategies which she has developed in response to the problem of class size and student variation in ability. Her aim is to maximise the use of class time so that it is still possible, if not easy, to keep a balance between self-direction, support and control:

> One such way is involving learners in the development of class norms aimed at a more effective use of time and resources. For example, solutions can take the form of peer correction or not calling the teacher every time they have a doubt, but trying to solve the problem by consulting reference books or asking other learners; if it is still unresolved, to take a note of it and carry on working till they have accumulated several doubts or have finished their work. Another way is to develop more effective and economic follow-up techniques on the part of the teacher, such as group analysis of work or carrying around the class all the original group plans and writing quick notes on the process and performance of each group and its members on the back of those plans.

Serrano-Sampedro, therefore, provides a good example of how the initiative to include negotiated work can lead teachers to identify ways to achieve what is practically possible in the given circumstances.

Teacher response

A number of the contributors to this collection report on the anxiety for the teacher which can result from introducing negotiation. Smith (p. 61), for example, points out that:

> Teachers often feel the need to use the authority they have been given, and if they give up on it, they feel they are in danger of losing control.

Clearly, any redistribution of power and decision-making within the classroom brings with it a redefinition of both teacher and learner roles. For teachers who are most used to attempting to exercise full control over classroom events, or who believe they can actually achieve this, a move towards involving learners in decision-making may make new demands for flexibility, tolerance and risk-taking, and require a strong faith in the capacity of learners. Such teachers may need to come to see their own plans for classroom work as simply proposals – as did the contributors to this book – which learners have the right to reformulate, elaborate upon or even reject. At the same time, such teachers need to be willing to suspend their own judgement over the suitability or value of suggestions for classroom work made by learners, in the spirit of drawing out and building upon the learners' own capacity to review and evaluate the work they have done. As Serrano-Sampedro, Irujo, Wolfe-Quintero and others report, the ability to work successfully through negotiation is one which gradually develops with practice over time. Wolfe-Quintero (p. 267), for example, speaking of how her teaching approach has changed, reports:

> Through this experience, my eyes were irrevocably opened to new possibilities, new ways of conceptualising the classroom. This experience changed how I have approached every class since, although I have not repeated this experience in any of them. This happened to be the second time I taught this particular writing methodology course. The first time I had taught it, I controlled the content, the timing, the requirements and the dialogue. By the time I taught this course a third time a year later, I was a different teacher. I neither completely controlled the class nor abdicated control, but I used my inherent control to foster a dialogue . . . I gained the ability and understanding to allow the course to develop in this way only because the earlier process of negotiation had deconstructed my traditional views and new possibilities had risen in their place.

From what those teachers who have initiated negotiation with their students say, it appears, therefore, that the experience is an educative one also for the teacher, whilst inevitably evolving at its own pace and in its own particular way.

Learner response

A clear message from the contributors to this volume is that shifts in teacher attitude may be required for negotiation to be successfully implemented, and that this shift takes place over time. It is equally clear from the teachers' accounts that significant shifts in attitude may be required on the part of learners and that such changes in attitude also require time to develop. The requirement for risk-taking, flexibility and tolerance which negotiation places upon teachers is at least equally matched by similar demands upon the learners, as they are expected to redefine their views of appropriate behaviour in the classroom. In fact, without the background which the professional discussion of applied linguistics affords teachers, the demands upon learners may be even more significant. Learners may have experienced years of classroom work in which they have learned that their role is to behave as if following the path laid down by a teacher rather than sharing in negotiating the route. Such learners may have abdicated their own responsibility for learning and may not be ready to believe the teacher who calls upon it through negotiative work. Newstetter (p. 182), for example, reports that one of greatest difficulties is 'getting them to hear', to understand and make use of the opportunities that negotiation may provide:

> [A]s we neared the due date for the proposals, one student sheepishly asked in class, 'You mean we can decide what we want to do for reports 4 and 5?' The way he asked the question indicated that he was sure he was asking an impossibly idiotic question. Clearly for this student, the idea that he could decide what to write for an assignment was bordering on lunacy.

Undoubtedly, this stems from past experience – from 'years of disenfranchisement' as Newstetter (p. 182) puts it – and beliefs about what 'the teacher's job' is, what the relative responsibilities of teachers and learners are in the classroom and, indeed, how languages are to be learned. As Slembrouck reminds us in Chapter 8, there is often an educational culture which encourages students to focus on achieving the immediate targets and hurdles set by the educational institution and which may appear to be in conflict with any attempts to engage the students in meaningful negotiation about the process of learning in the class. In this case, students may perceive negotiation as simply one more course requirement, and initially try to find the best way (as they see it) to cope successfully with negotiation so that it is not too demanding a change from how they have previously been expected to work. In Chapter 16 Ivanič similarly discusses the gap, typically revealed as the due date for assignments approaches, between the value the students and the tutors variously ascribe to negotiation: some of the students want some tangible evidence of making progress, of learning something, of getting somewhere, while the tutors see learning also in the process of negotiation itself.

A key demand upon learners when they are engaged in negotiated work is a redefinition of how they see the classroom and, with it, the development of abilities for working in groups, analysing, designing and evaluating classroom tasks, and sharing decision-making. Perhaps we need to further explore whether such a shift in perception and the drawing out of such abilities might need to precede a negotiated course (as Ivanič suggests) or whether such changes can be facilitated *during* a negotiated course. It is, however, important to see these changes not as difficulties inherent in negotiation, but as part of the process of achieving the wider educational purposes of negotiated work. Changes in the learners' ability to successfully participate in shared decision-making can be seen as stages in the development of the learners' abilities in the management of learning, alongside other stages in the language-learning process.

Learner voice

As Ivanič points out in Chapter 16, there may be a tension between an aim of engaging students in negotiating the curriculum and the simple fact that they may not always be very good at negotiating. A central feature of a process syllabus is that decision-making is *shared*, that is, that everyone in the classroom group has an equal right to influence the decisions which are made. The danger for any negotiated course, however, is that at these crucial decision-making stages it is the views of the most vocal that predominate, and that those who – for whatever reason – do not voice their opinions do not get heard. For this reason, Ivanič suggests the possibility of some kind of training course for negotiation, or an induction phase, fearful that embarking on a fully negotiated course without preparing the students first may result in a 'sink or swim' situation for students (p. 246):

> One of the roles of the tutor in each sub-group is to support the group members through this experience, to intervene where necessary to ensure that everyone's voice is heard, and to bring

discussion about the negotiation process itself out into the open. This may not, however, be enough. The fact that students do not always seem to benefit fully from the experience of nego- tiation on this course has led us to consider introducing an extra component on the course – possibly as a course within the MA programme as a whole on how to work in small group situations, and how to learn from such situations. This is an issue to be explored further in the future.

Useful though such an induction phase might be it is, however, unlikely over a short period of time to prompt significant changes in students' preferred strategies in learning (such as silence and observation), in character traits (such as shyness), in temporary conditions (such as tiredness) or in deeply held beliefs about the roles of teachers, learners and the classroom. Such pre-existing factors do represent genuine challenges to shared decision-making, which require continued efforts to find ways to draw out students' views. As the range of experiences reported in this book demonstrates, however, and as we summarise below (see p. 293, 'Tools for process syllabuses') there is much that can be done in this respect in the design of questionnaires, elicitation devices, one-to-one consultations and, crucially, evaluation procedures. These factors also suggest that, in many cases, a gradualist approach to the introduction of negotiated ways of working may be appropriate, something which we explore further below (see p. 281 'Guidelines for practice').

Cultural considerations

A number of writers remark on issues deriving from the cultural background and assumptions of their students when faced with the requirements of classroom negotiation. Sokolik (p. 191) for example, found that cultural factors:

> can present resistance to this method in certain students. These students may feel uncomfortable with taking on the role of evaluator. As one student informed me, 'That's your job'. Also, some students may feel it inappropriate to give themselves high marks, or to write positive comments about their own work.

While it is highly likely that cultural factors have a role to play in determining the potential of classroom negotiation, it is possible, however, to overstate the culture-specific nature of student reaction. Just as it may be inappropriate to assert that shared decision-making is feasible in *any* educational context, it may also be inappropriate to assume from the outset that it is not feasible in certain cultural settings. This is a matter for teachers who are most familiar with a particular context, and more experiments in a range of cultural contexts of the kind described in this book need to be undertaken rather than there being a reliance on speculation or opinion. As the accounts provided in this volume suggest, both the potential for successful implementation and the existence of student or teacher resistance to negotiated work is widely evident across a range of cultural settings. There appears to be little evidence that negotiation is 'more appropriate' in some cultures or 'unsuitable' for other cultures. Rather, the requirement to take into account the specific backgrounds of teachers and learners is common to all teaching–learning settings, and the development of negotiated work in the classroom must always depart from that point.

In this respect, Norris and Spencer (p. 201) provide a revealing perspective on the nature of cultural difference and, indeed, whether we look for difference or similarity and take that as the point of departure.

> In general, Indonesian philosophy is based on creating a sense of unity from diversity, harmony, co-operation, self-reliance and national esteem. . . . We, the course organisers, had been trained and educated in the British primary-school philosophy of the 1970s: that of small group activities, learner choice of activity, freedom of movement throughout the class, individual help and class project work which was displayed, published or recorded in some way. Although the Indonesian teachers and ourselves thus came from different ideological and pedagogic backgrounds, underlying both sets of value systems were strong similarities. These were the importance of creating self-esteem and self-reliance, co-operation, freedom of choice and mutual respect of the individual.

Once this 'common ground', as they term it, had been identified and the significance of learning from each other in the classroom group had been established through a 'skills-swap' activity, Norris and Spencer found a reference point from which negotiated work could then success- fully depart. Much, then, would seem to depend on *how* negotiated work is approached, rather than on a general factor of appropriacy or otherwise to specific cultural contexts.

Guidelines for practice

Up to this point we have suggested a number of contextual factors which may affect the extent to which negotiation is possible or likely to succeed. Factors such as the existence of external curriculum plans, constraints on time, class size and diversity of student abilities, the prior experiences of teachers and learners and the wider cultural context background may all have a bearing on the potential of shared decision-making. While it is clear that these factors need to be borne in mind when introducing negotiation, the experiences described in this volume also show that a key aspect is a desire to identify what is possible. It appears that teachers' initial willingness to share classroom decisions and their persistence in trying different ways of engaging student involvement in decision-making may be the decisive factor in any teaching context. Sometimes we may be more held back by our own imagination or assumptions than by any other constraints. The aim of this section is, therefore, to draw from the accounts provided in this book and set out some practical guidelines for implementing negotiation and to provide a framework to guide teachers' experimentation.

Some initial considerations

Meaningful negotiation implies the genuine sharing of decisions, but this decision-making needs to be based on *informed* choices, that is, to be about something with which teachers and learners are familiar. Informed choice requires all participants in negotiation to have previous experience of the course aspects to be negotiated (such as types of tasks or content which are relevant to their purposes in learning) and the opportunity to evaluate this prior experience.

A second significant consideration is something to which we have already referred: the participants' capacity to effectively engage in classroom negotiation and their knowledge of what this may entail. In most situations, classroom negotiation, although drawing on experiences of negotiation in our day-to-day lives, may be unfamiliar to students, as the accounts in this collection have shown.

Given these considerations, it may be fruitful initially to think of either a selective focus for negotiation, where only a particular aspect of the curriculum is negotiated – such as assessment or allocation of time – or a gradualist approach, where negotiation gradually encompasses deeper levels of curriculum decisions – such as moving from the negotiation of how a task will be done to the negotiation of which tasks in future will be selected. Working towards the implementation of a process syllabus in this way is not incompatible with the purposes and spirit of negotiated work, but a practical means by which experience in classroom negotiation may be gained for both the teacher and the students.

The teachers' accounts in this book provide detailed experience of successes and difficulties in negotiated work. Most accounts, in fact, document either a selective or gradualist approach to negotiated work and can, therefore, provide many lessons for us in implementing negotiation in other contexts. Much can be gained by reviewing the experiences of each contributor and examining how he or she approached negotiation. In order to do this it is, however, necessary first to retrace some of the ideas that we discussed in Chapter 1.

A framework for process syllabuses

At this point, it is useful to return to the framework for process syllabuses in order to identify the range of curriculum decisions which may be open to negotiation in any particular context and to identify examples in each of the teacher accounts provided in this volume.

In practical terms, in order for any educational undertaking to become possible, decisions need to be made in relation to a number of key areas. These are:

- the purposes of language learning (why?);
- the contents or subject matter which learners will work upon (what?);
- ways of working in the classroom (how?);
- means of evaluation of the efficiency and quality of work and its outcomes (how well?).

Specific instances of negotiated classroom work can therefore be conceived of as addressing some or all of these decision areas. The Negotiation Cycle in Figure 18.1 (discussed in Chapter 1) shows how each area may be the starting point for a cyclical sequence which can inform future decision-making. At Step 1, teacher and students focus on a decision area and jointly make decisions. These, may for example, be decisions about tasks they will carry out, topics they will focus on or when and how they will be assessed. At Step 2 decisions are acted upon and these become the practical experience of the students. At Step 3 the outcomes of these actions are evaluated. This final step is thus of central importance as it is at this point that decisions previously taken and implemented can be reviewed as a means of shaping future action through *informed* choice; in this way the cycle is initiated once again.

Evaluation at Step 3 may relate to two aspects: *what* (learning achievements, weaknesses and strengths) and *how* (the process followed, types of tasks, modes of behaviour and so on). Thus, the negotiation cycle may relate to evaluation of both attained language abilities and the classroom experience itself. Table 18.1 summarises some example areas which each kind of evaluation may involve. Logically, of course, each kind of evaluation can be subject to evaluation

Conclusions

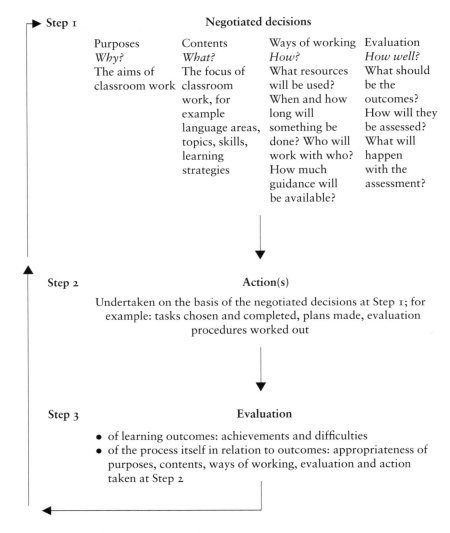

Step 1   **Negotiated decisions**

Purposes	Contents	Ways of working	Evaluation
Why?	*What?*	*How?*	*How well?*
The aims of classroom work	The focus of classroom work, for example language areas, topics, skills, learning strategies	What resources will be used? When and how long will something be done? Who will work with who? How much guidance will be available?	What should be the outcomes? How will they be assessed? What will happen with the assessment?

Step 2   **Action(s)**

Undertaken on the basis of the negotiated decisions at Step 1; for example: tasks chosen and completed, plans made, evaluation procedures worked out

Step 3   **Evaluation**

- of learning outcomes: achievements and difficulties
- of the process itself in relation to outcomes: appropriateness of purposes, contents, ways of working, evaluation and action taken at Step 2

Figure 18.1   The negotiation cycle

from the alternative perspective; evaluation of *what* the students have learned, for example, may be subject to discussion over *how* this evaluation was carried out.

In reality, such explicit evaluation is unlikely to take place after every decision is implemented; this would be cumbersome and most likely extremely tedious. Rather, evaluation may take place at specific

Table 18.1   *Example areas for the evaluation step in the negotiation cycle*

Focus of evaluation	Example areas
What: • What has been achieved? • What has not been achieved? • What has been difficult? • What should be the next point of focus?	knowledge of language forms (such as grammar, spelling, pronunciation, intonation) and language use (such as language functions, appropriacy, dis course structures, genre); vocabulary; abilities in speaking, reading, writing and listening; communication strategies; study and and reference skills; cultural awareness
How: • How was the process carried out? • Was it appropriate/ effective/useful? • How might it be improved?	who does what when; task types used; classroom participation; effectiveness of group work; modes of evaluating learning; timetabling; how feedback is given; how and what guidance is given; allocation of time; homework; sequence of tasks; rights and responsibilities of classroom participants; the decision-making process itself

moments; for example, at the mid-point in a course, after a large scale activity or the end of a 'block' of work. Evaluation may also not be a separate step but in practice be built directly into the decision-making in Step 1, various alternatives being rejected or selected based on previous experience.

Any decisions that are taken manifest themselves in the actions taken in the classroom. These may range from the immediate, moment-by-moment decisions made while learners are engaged in a task (for example, whether they are to work in groups or alone), to the more long-term planning of a language course (for example, what will be the focus of each lesson), and through to the planning of the wider educational curriculum (for example, links between foreign-language teaching–learning and other subject areas). To capture these different levels, the curriculum pyramid in Figure 18.2 shows an increasing breadth of decisions (see also Chapter 1).

At the top of the pyramid we have 'a task' relating to how and on what students are working at any particular moment in the class. Below that, the levels of 'a sequence of tasks', 'a series of lessons', and 'a course' cover increasing frames of time over which more decisions and planning is relevant. A specific subject/language curriculum relates to a wider level of planning in which aims, content, working procedures and evaluation which the course is to address are set out. The 'deepest' level

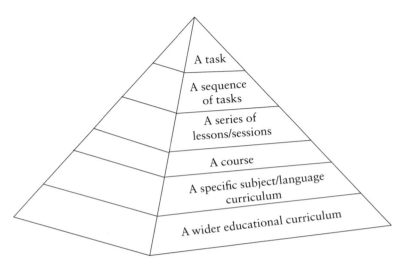

Figure 18.2   The curriculum pyramid: levels of focus for the negotiation cycle

of the pyramid, the wider educational curriculum, refers to the links that the course is to have to other educational subject areas and aims.

Together, the negotiation cycle and the curriculum pyramid allow us to conceptualise a process syllabus as negotiation at specific levels of curriculum planning. Figure 18.3 (see Chapter 1 for further detail) illustrates this, with the negotiation cycle potentially being applied to a particular decision area (purposes, contents, ways of working or evaluation) at each of the different levels in the pyramid.

If we see a process syllabus as the application of a negotiation cycle at particular levels of a curriculum pyramid, this makes possible a working perspective on which negotiation can potentially be introduced in practice. Any teaching situation will inevitably imply constraints, and these can be located in the pyramid. In situations where externally determined syllabus plans exist, for example, this may imply that the deeper levels of the pyramid – a specific language curriculum and a wider educational curriculum – are simply not available for classroom negotiation. In other cases, particular teaching–learning materials may have already been specified, and perhaps also the pace by which teachers are to cover the materials with their classes. Clearly, situations such as these narrow the possibilities for negotiation, but Figure 18.3 helpfully indicates that much may still be available for classroom decision-making by applying the negotiation cycle at the higher levels of the pyramid.

The diagram also shows how a process syllabus itself is not incom-

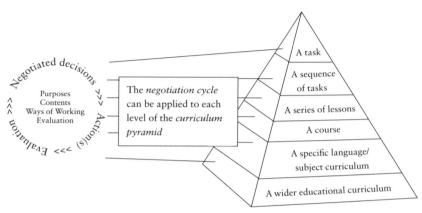

Figure 18.3   A process syllabus

patible with either externally determined decisions or external evaluation. Neither is it incompatible with decisions or proposals made by the teacher: the teacher is a leading participant in the negotiation. The implementation of a process syllabus is never, in other words, an 'all or nothing' situation. In any teaching situation, pre-determined decisions can always form a crucial point of reference for future negotiation and guide the areas around which shared decision-making at higher levels of the curriculum pyramid can take place (as Serrano-Sampedro argues).

The negotiation cycle and the curriculum pyramid together also indicate how a gradualist or selective focus for negotiation may be introduced, particularly where factors such as those we outlined earlier (an external curriculum, time constraints, class size, etc.) apparently limit the potential for negotiated work. Making negotiation available at the higher levels of the pyramid (for example at the level of how students are to work on a chosen task) can offer initial experience for both teachers and students in managing shared decision-making, without jeopardising the structure of the course as a whole. It would then be possible, as circumstances permit, to move to progressively deeper levels of the pyramid as experience is gained; *informed* decisions can then be made. Table 18.2 summarises some example areas of decision-making that may be available for negotiation at each level.

Process syllabuses in practice: teacher accounts

This brief review of a framework for process syllabuses and how a gradualist and selective focus might operate now allows us to locate

Table 18.2   *Examples of decision areas at each level of the curriculum pyramid*

Levels in the 'curriculum pyramid'	Decision areas for the negotiation cycle
1 A task	Who is to work with whom? In pairs, groups or alone? For how long? What is to judged as successful? How shall the task be corrected/monitored? Who shall correct/monitor it? What guidance/support will be available?
2 A sequence of tasks	What tasks will be done? In what order? Which tasks (if any) will be omitted? Should tasks be adapted in any way?
3 A series of lessons/ sessions	In what order will tasks, activities and topics be covered? Should certain tasks/activities/topics be omitted? Do any materials need to be adapted or supplemented?
4 A course	What additional tasks/contents/abilities will the course address? What instances of revision should be included? Which is the most appropriate set of materials for the specified purposes of the course?
5 A specific subject/ language curriculum	What content areas should the course focus on? What areas of language knowledge? What specific content should be included? What topics? What abilities in reading, writing, listening or speaking should be developed?
6 A wider educational curriculum	What wider educational aims (such as the development of autonomy, critical thinking, and so on) should be addressed? What links should be made between other curriculum areas (such as science, nature, geography, and so on)?

each of the accounts presented in this book in terms of how they each variously illustrate negotiation at different levels in the curriculum pyramid and with respect to different decision areas. Table 18.3 provides an overview of each account.

As the table shows, the chapters provide accounts of negotiated work at a variety of different levels in the curriculum pyramid. Two chapters (Chapters 4 and 15) provide accounts at the level of *a series of lessons or sessions*, within a course where wider decisions concerning contents and ways of working have been previously determined. By implication, each of these accounts also covers negotiation at the levels of *a task* and *a sequence of tasks*. Three chapters (Chapters 3, 11 and 12) provide

Table 18.3   *Overview of negotiation in the teachers' accounts*

Chapter	Authors	Context	Level	Decision area
Part 1	**Accounts of practice in primary and secondary schools**			
2	*Anne MacKay, Kaye Oates, Yvonne Haig*	Primary school, ESL in Australia	Specific language curriculum	Purposes Evaluation
3	*Kari Smith*	Secondary school students in Israel	Course	Evaluation
4	*Ramon Ribé*	Secondary school students in Spain	Series of lessons	Contents Ways of working
5	*Marianne Nikolov*	Primary school pupils in Hungary	Specific language curriculum	Contents Ways of working Evaluation
6	*Pnina Linder*	Secondary school students in Israel	Specific language curriculum	Purposes Contents Ways of working Evaluation
7	*Isabel Serrano-Sampedro*	Secondary school students in Spain	Specific language curriculum	Purposes Contents Ways of working Evaluation
Part 2	**Accounts of practice in tertiary education**			
8	*Stefaan Slembrouck*	University in Belgium	Specific language curriculum	Purposes Contents Ways of working
9	*Elaine Martyn*	School of nursing in Pakistan	Specific language curriculum	Purposes Contents
10	*Eddie Edmundson and Steve Fitzpatrick*	Language school in Brazil	Specific language curriculum	Purposes Contents
11	*Wendy Newstetter*	Institute of higher education in USA	Course	Evaluation (of assignments)
12	*Margaret Sokolik*	University writing class in USA	Course	Evaluation (of assignments)
13	*Lucy Norris and Susan Spencer*	Pre-departure course in Indonesia	Specific language curriculum	Contents Ways of working
Part 3	**Accounts of practice in teacher education**			
14	*Suzanne Irujo*	Teacher education at a university in USA	Specific subject curriculum	Contents

Table 18.3 *(cont.)*

15	*Michael McCarthy and Michael Makosch*	Teachers participating in two-week residential seminar in UK	Series of lessons/ sessions	Contents Ways of working
16	*Roz Ivanič*	MA students at a university in UK	Wider educational curriculum	Purposes Contents Ways of working Evaluation
17	*Kate Wolfe-Quintero*	Teaching of writing course at a university in USA	Specific subject curriculum	Contents Ways of working Evaluation

accounts at the level of *a course*, where the specifications of the language curriculum has been previously determined, while a further ten chapters (Chapters 2, 5, 6, 7, 8, 9, 10, 13, 14 and 17) address the specification of the subject curriculum itself. One account (Chapter 16) details work at the deepest level in the curriculum pyramid in which the wider educational aims and nature of a course are negotiated, as well decisions at the higher levels of the pyramid.

While the accounts each focus on a particular level of decision-making, many are also selective with the range of decision areas available. Some accounts refer to one or two decision areas (such as evaluation or selection of contents), while other accounts cover all four of the decisions areas: identification of purposes, contents, ways of working and evaluation.

Most of the accounts appear to document largely successful experiences in classroom negotiation, whilst noting contextual constraints and difficulties as we discussed earlier in this chapter. Each of the accounts can therefore provide us with practical guidance in applying a process syllabus in other teaching contexts. We may also, however, learn much from accounts which document problematic instances of negotiation. Slembrouck's account in Chapter 8, for example, describes a troubled experience of introducing negotiation in the context of a university language course in Belgium. Erratic student attendance, decision-making dominated by one or two vocal students and a sense of distrust as to the 'real' motivation for classroom decision-making all conspired to produce unsatisfactory results for both the teacher and the students such that the course design was abandoned in subsequent years.

What went wrong? Slembrouck himself provides a detailed analysis of the institutional culture which appeared to work against the spirit of negotiated work: a 'cramming' culture, characterised by exams and learned classroom behaviour that effectively silences students and encourages them to take on a passive role in their learning. The result was that students appeared to look for ways to cope with the new challenge to negotiate so that it was not too demanding a change from how they had previously been expected to work. As Slembrouck (p. 149) reports:

> My suspicion is that they did not interpret negotiation as a device for transforming classroom culture and practice, but looked at it more as a way of adjusting classroom activities to what they felt like doing at a particular moment.

He ends with a question which appears to encapsulate a major challenge for procedural negotiation in the classroom (p. 149):

> [O]ne rather urgent question which we need to address is: What is required in a negotiated syllabus to avoid the trap of reinforcing the existing speech/silence regime and, with it, students' preconceived views of classroom behaviour?

Yet, the negative experience which Slembrouck documents does not seem to be evident in most of the other contributions in this book. His account is therefore particularly valuable in alerting us to potential difficulties. There were undoubtedly many different factors at work here, but one of the key problems may have been the scope of negotiation itself. As the summary table shows, the focus of negotiation covered the decision areas of purposes, contents and ways of working but, significantly, did not address the area which Slembrouck describes as a key characteristic of the educational culture: evaluation. In the institutional context in which the course was conducted, the key area of evaluation appeared to be pre-determined and thus non-negotiable. In this respect, a clear account at the start of the course of the requirements of the final examination may have helped to delineate for students the limits of negotiation and how they may have influenced the structure of the course. A result of this may then have been that it more accurately addressed their own purposes in taking the course; these limits could then have been raised for discussion.

An alternative explanation may, however, be that the scope of negotiation went too far and too quickly for those particular students. Consequently, it may be that the negotiation that was introduced was so very different from what the students had previously been used to that the 'leap' they were required to make was too great. In this case a gradual or selective approach to the introduction of negotiation may have produced different results and enabled over time the development of mutual trust, confidence and responsibility upon which negotiated work depends. In this respect, the account by Irujo in Chapter 14 shows how the approach to negotiation must be tuned to the background and expectation of the students.

Forced by circumstances to abandon her plan for a course in teacher education due to its lack of relevance to the enrolled students, Irujo initially found the experience of negotiating course contents a highly successful one. When she tried to repeat the experience a year later, however, with a different intake of students, problems began to emerge (p. 212):

> It soon became apparent, however, that many of my international students were uncomfortable with the results of the negotiation process. Several of them wanted me to tell them what to read and which assignments to do. One wanted a list of readings for all the topics that would have been on the syllabus if we had not negotiated the content. They all resisted having to give themselves grades.

The following year more problems emerged when she provided a list of potential topics for student selection (p. 215):

> This procedure did not work well. Almost everybody wanted to cover everything, they all agreed with my suggestions for assignments and activities, and they wanted to do all of the options that were listed . . . The syllabus that emerged was almost exactly the same as one I would have developed myself, and there were complaints that the negotiation process took too long and was a waste of time.

The lessons that Irujo drew from these years of experimentation have led her to develop an approach which has as its starting point the expectations and previous experiences of the students. In this, she provides a course plan but stresses to the students that this is a proposal, a 'first draft' which can be reworked and refined, much as pieces of written work can be in a process writing approach. The outcome was a much more positive experience for all concerned (p. 218):

> The negotiation process that year was easier than it had ever been. Students understood immediately the concept of the syllabus as a draft that could be changed as we worked with it . . . At the end of the third class, it was obvious to me that we needed more time to discuss the teaching of oral skills, and the students agreed. I asked them to decide what other topic to take

the time from, and a short negotiation produced a decision to eliminate the 'games and activities' topic, incorporating part of that into a second class on teaching oral skills. As the course progressed, the students began to take ownership of the course content.

Irujo's conclusion is that this approach to syllabus negotiation is more suited to the context in which she works and meets the expectations of a range of students, allowing her to fulfil her 'multiple roles of facilitator, expert, and gatekeeper with less tension and fewer contradictions'. Her account is useful in showing how a gradualist approach may work in practice, and how it allows for the possibility of developing negotiated work such that it takes as a point of departure the previous experiences of the students.

Tools for process syllabuses

As we argued earlier, the expression of student views – or 'learner voice' as we have termed it – lies at the heart of a process syllabus, particularly in the decision and evaluation stages. The identification of ways of drawing out these views is thus of prime importance in the development of process syllabuses. Each of the accounts presented in this book is, therefore, particularly helpfully in detailing the various resources used in enabling shared decision-making to occur. Since the very purpose of a process syllabus is to draw out the unique contributions, wants, needs and preferred ways of student learning, it is unrealistic to think that 'off the shelf' resources are likely to be relevant to individual students or groups of students. Nevertheless, each of the accounts gives examples which may be adaptable to other situations. Table 18.4 provides an overview of the uses of these resources and the chapter in this book where further details may be found.

Conclusion

The purpose of this book has *not* been to argue that classroom decision-making based upon negotiation between teachers and students should replace teacher decision-making. Teachers are at the very heart of the process and, as the accounts have shown, a teacher's recognition of the potentials of shared decision-making and a teacher's will to initiate it in the classroom are the two primary conditions for its likely benefit to a student's language learning experience. Nor is procedural negotiation an 'approach' or a particular 'method' which can be claimed to directly

Conclusions

Table 18.4 *Examples of devices used in process syllabuses*

Establishing purposes	
• an initial questionnaire to students	Linder, Irujo
• teacher draft proposals for syllabus items	Slembrouck, Irujo, Wolfe-Quintero
• weekly planning of sessions	Slembrouck, Norris and Spencer
• negotiation with stakeholders	Martyn
• pictures to identify learning preferences and priorities	Edmundson and Fitzpatrick
• eliciting the students' personal syllabus to develop a group syllabus	Ivanič
Decisions concerning contents and ways of working	
• discussion to decide who should do what	Nikolov, Ribé, Ivanič, McCarthy and Makosch
• discussion to establish alternative ways of working through a unit	Linder
• discussion to establish 'rules' for the conduct of a task	Linder
• discussion to establish ways to revise material previously covered	Linder
• a learning plan developed jointly by a teacher and learners	Serrano-Sampedro
• learner-designed activities	Serrano-Sampedro, Norris and Spencer
• syllabus plans presented as a 'first draft'	Irujo
Evaluation of outcomes	
• classroom record sheets, for teacher and student to record achievements; reports to stakeholders	MacKay
• brainstorming what has been learned, identifying a focus for assessment, voting to choose a scale of assessment, agreed assessments between teacher and student	Smith
• a self-assessment questionnaire for negotiated grading	Linder, Ribé
• a self-assessment procedure	Nikolov
• student determined focus of assessment	Newstetter, Ivanič
• establishing criteria for grading and agreeing grades	Sokolik, Ivanič
• retrospective accounts of work covered	Edmundson and Fitzpatrick, Irujo
• journals for student evaluation of process	Ribé, Serrano-Sampedro, Wolfe-Quintero, Norris and Spencer
• learner reflection charts	Edmundson and Fitzpatrick
• one-to-one consultations	Norris and Spencer

enhance the learning of a language. It is difficult enough to prove that any aspect of language pedagogy in the classroom has a direct effect upon a student's learning. The introduction of negotiated decision-making and the gradual development of particular process syllabuses rather serve to complement and enrich the teacher's difficult task of enabling language learning. While incorporating heightened learner responsibility in classroom work, the introduction of process syllabuses leads to the sharing of the task with those whom it most affects.

This is not to ignore the fact that the application of a process syllabus is a challenging and sometimes difficult undertaking for teachers and students. There is no doubt that further practical experimentation is much needed in this area in order to widen our understanding of the nature of classroom negotiation. It is from detailed accounts of negotiated work such as those provided in this book that we can learn more about the complex nature of procedural negotiation, the influence of contextual factors and successful ways of engaging learners in responsible decisions about their work. To contribute to further experimentation, the aim of this chapter has been to offer some practical guidelines for initiating negotiation with students and to support teacher development of process syllabuses that evolve from their own working situations. For teachers and learners new to the practicalities of negotiated work, we have also aimed to show that a selective focus for negotiation and a gradual increase in its scope is a feasible venture, as is more wide-ranging negotiation in appropriate circumstances.

As the chapters in this book have shown, the potential for negotiated classroom work seems considerable. It appears that the implementation of procedural negotiation can be a highly practical alternative to the direct, non-negotiated implementation of a pre-planned syllabus or curriculum – indeed, at times and in certain circumstances, the only viable course of action – which may offer considerable gains in terms of enhanced learning outcomes. The range of types of institutions, class sizes, student ages, levels of proficiency in the foreign language and cultural backgrounds presented in the accounts in this book also suggest that the potential for negotiated decision-making can be realised across a wide range of teaching–learning contexts. As such, process syllabuses and shared classroom decision-making represent one of the most significant practical and theoretical developments in language teaching in recent years.

References

Allwright, D. 1979. Abdication and responsibility in language teaching. *Studies in Second Language Acquisition*, 2(1), 105–121.

Allwright, D. and Bailey, K. M. 1991. *Focus on the Language Classroom*. Cambridge: Cambridge University Press.

Altman, H. B. 1983. Training foreign language teachers for learner-centered instruction: Deep structures, surface structures, and transformations. In J. E. Alatis, H. H. Stern and P. Strevens (eds.), *Georgetown University Round Table on Languages and Linguistics, 1983*. Washington, DC: Georgetown University Press.

Apple, M. 1986. *Teachers and texts: A political economy of class and gender relations in education*. New York: Routledge.

Auerbach, E. R. 1990. *Making meaning making change: Participatory curriculum development for adult ESL literacy*. Washington, DC: Center for Applied Linguistics.

Auerbach, E. R. 1993. Putting the P back in participatory. *TESOL Quarterly*, 27(3), 543–545.

Auerbach, E. R. 1995. The politics of the ESL classroom: Issues of power in pedagogical choices. In J. W. Tollefson (ed.), *Power and inequality in language education*. New York: Cambridge University Press.

Ausubel, D. P. 1963. *The psychology of meaningful verbal learning*. New York: Grune and Stratton.

Bachman, L. F. and Palmer, A. S. 1989. The construct validity of self-ratings of communicative language ability. *Language Testing*, 6, 14–29.

Barnes, D., Britten, J. and Rosen, H. 1969 *Language, the learner and the school*. Harmondsworth: Penguin.

Bernstein, B. 1967. Open schools, open society. *New Society*, 14th September 1967.

Blanche, P. and Merino, B. J. 1989. Self-assessment of foreign language skills: implications for teachers and researchers. *Language Learning*, 39(3), 313–340.

Bloor, M. and Bloor, T. 1988. Syllabus negotiation: The basis of learner autonomy. In A. Brookes and P. Grundy (eds.), *Individualization and autonomy in language learning*, ELT documents 131. London: Modern English Publications and The British Council.

Boerkaerts, M. 1991. Subjective competence appraisals and self-assessment. *Learning and Instruction*, 1(1), 1–17.

Boomer, G., Lester, N., Onore, C. and Cook, J. (eds.) 1992. *Negotiating the curriculum*. London: Falmer Press.

Boud, D., Cohen, R. and Walker, D. (eds.) 1993. *Using experience for learning*. Buckingham: The Society for Research into Higher Education and Open University Press.

Breen, M. P. 1984. Process syllabuses for the language classroom. In C. J. Brumfit (ed.), *General English syllabus design*. Oxford: Pergamon Press and The British Council.

Breen, M. P. 1987. Contemporary paradigms in syllabus design, Parts 1 and 2. *Language Teaching*, 20(1), 81–92; 20(2), 157–174.

Breen, M. P. 1998. Navigating the discourse: On what is learned in the language classroom. In W. A. Renandya and G. M. Jacobs (eds.), *Learners and language learning*. Singapore: SEAMEO Regional Language Centre.

Breen, M. P. and Candlin, C. N. 1980. The essentials of a communicative curriculum for language teaching. *Applied Linguistics*, 1(2), 89–112.

Breen, M. P., Candlin, C. N. and Waters, A. 1979. Communicative materials design: Some basic principles. *RELC Journal*, 10(2), 1–13.

Brown, J. D. and Bailey, K. M. 1984. A categorical instrument for scoring second language writing skills. *Language Learning* 34(4), 21–42.

Brown, J. S., Collins, A. and Duguid, P. 1989. Situated cognition and the culture of learning. *Educational Researcher*, 18(4), 32–42.

Brumfit, C. (ed.) 1984. *General English syllabus design*. Oxford: Pergamon Press.

Budd, R. and Wright, T. 1992. Putting a process syllabus into practice. In D. Nunan (ed.), *Collaborative language learning and teaching*. Cambridge: Cambridge University Press.

Campbell, C. and H. Kryszewska. 1992. *Learner-based teaching*. Oxford: Oxford University Press.

Canale, M. and Swain, M. 1980. Theoretical bases of communicative approaches to second language teaching and testing. *Applied Linguistics*, 1, 1–47.

Candlin, C. N. 1984. Syllabus design as a critical process. In C. J. Brumfit (ed.), *General English syllabus design*. Oxford: Pergamon Press and The British Council.

Candlin, C. N. and Murphy, D. M. (eds.) 1987. *Language learning tasks: Lancaster practical papers in English language education*, Volume 7. Englewood Cliffs, NJ: Prentice Hall.

Candlin, C. N. 1987. Towards task-based language learning. In C. N. Candlin and D. Murphy (eds.), *Language learning tasks*. London: Prentice Hall and Lancaster University.

Carter, G. and Thomas, H. 1990. 'Dear brown eyes': Experiential learning in a project-orientated approach. In R. Rossner and R. Bolitho (eds.), *Currents of change in English language teaching*. Oxford: Oxford University Press.

Carter, K. 1993. The place of story in the study of teaching and teacher education. *Educational Researcher*, 22(1), 5–12.

Carter, R. and McCarthy, M. J. 1995. Grammar and the spoken language. *Applied Linguistics* 16(2), 141–158.

Chaudron, C. 1983. Evaluating writing: Effects of feedback on writing. Paper presented at the *Annual TESOL convention*, Toronto, ERIC document no. ED 227 706.

Chaudron, C. 1988. *Second language classrooms: Research on teaching and learning*. Cambridge: Cambridge University Press.

Chomsky, N. 1968. *Language and mind*. New York: Harcourt, Brace and World.

Clark, J. L. 1987. *Curriculum renewal in school foreign language learning*. Oxford: Oxford University Press.

Clarke, D. F. 1991. The negotiated syllabus: What is it and how is it likely to work? *Applied Linguistics*, 12(1), 13–28.

Coleman, H. 1987. Teaching spectacles and learning festivals. *English Language Teaching Journal*, 41(2), 97–103.

Conner, U. and Kaplan, R. (eds.) 1987. *Writing across languages: Analysis of L2 text*. Reading, MA: Addison-Wesley.

Cummins, J. 1988. *Empowering Minority Students*. Sacramento, CA: California Association for Bilingual Education.

Dam, L. 1995. *Learner autonomy 3: From theory to classroom practice*. Dublin: Authentik.

Dam, L. 1999. Dennis the Menace and autonomy. In B. Mißler, and U. Multhaup (eds.), *The construction of knowledge, learner autonomy and related issues in foreign language learning*. Tübingen: Stauffenburg.

Dam, L. and Gabrielsen, G. 1988. Developing learner autonomy in a school context: A six year experiment beginning in the learners' first year of English. In H. Holec (ed.), *Autonomy and self-directed learning: Present fields of application*. Strasbourg: Council of Europe.

Dewey, J. 1933. *How we think*. Boston, MA: D. C. Heath.

Dewey, J. 1938. *Experiences of education*. New York: Collier Press.

Dickinson, L. 1987. *Self-instruction in language learning*. Cambridge University Press.

Donato, R. and McCormick, D. 1994. A sociocultural perspective on language learning strategies: The role of mediation. *Modern Language Journal*, 78, 453–64.

Doughty, C. and Williams, J. (eds.) 1998. *Focus on form in classroom second language acquisition*. New York: Cambridge University Press.

Dressel, P. 1983. Grades: One more tilt at the windmill. *AAHE Bulletin*, 35.

Edelhoff, C. 1981. Theme-oriented English: Text-varieties, media, skills and projectwork. In C. Candlin (ed.), *The communicative teaching of English: Principles and exercise typology*. London: Longman.

Ediger, M. 1993. Approaches to measurement and evaluation. *Studies in Educational Evaluation*, 19(1), 41–49.

Ehlich, Konrad, Rehbein, J. and ten Thije, J. 1993. *Kennis, taal en handelen:*

Analyses van de kommunikatie in de klas (Knowledge, language and action: Analyses of classroom communication). Assen: Van Gorcum.

Elbow, P. 1993. Ranking, evaluating and liking: Sorting out three forms of judgment. *College English* 55(2), 187–206.

English III: English Skills for Professional Nurses (course outline). 1989. The Aga Khan University School of Nursing, Karachi, Pakistan.

Enright, D. S. and McCloskey, M. L. 1988. *Integrating English*. Reading, MA: Addison Wesley.

Fairclough, N. 1989. *Language and power*. London: Longman.

Forster, P. 1998. A classroom perspective on the negotiation of meaning. *Applied Linguistics*, 19(1), 1–23.

Freeman, D. 1992. Language teacher education, emerging discourse and change in classroom practice. In J. Flowerdew, M. Brock and S. Hsia (eds.), *Perspectives on Second Language Teacher Education*. Hong Kong: City Polytechnic of Hong Kong.

Freire, P. 1970. *Pedagogy of the oppressed*. New York: Continuum.

Freire, P. 1972. *Cultural action for freedom*. Harmondsworth: Penguin.

Freire, P. and Macedo, D. P. 1995. A dialogue: Culture, language and race. *Harvard Educational Review*, 65, 377–402.

Garfinkel, H. 1967. *Studies in ethnomethodology*. Englewood Cliffs, NJ: Prentice Hall.

Giroux, H. 1981. *Ideology, culture and the process of schooling*. London: Falmer Press.

Giroux, H. 1988. *Teachers as intellectuals: Toward a critical pedagogy of learning*. Massachusetts: Bergin and Garvey Publishers.

Hairston, M. 1986. On not being a composition slave. In C. W. Bridges (ed.), *Training the new teacher of college composition*. Urbana, IL: NCTE.

Hatch, E. 1978. Discourse analysis in second language acquisition. In E. Hatch (ed.), *Second language acquisition* . Rowley, MA: Newbury House.

Hatch, E. 1992. *Discourse and language education*. Cambridge University Press.

Heilenman, K. L. 1990. Self-assessment of second language ability: The role of response effects. *Language Testing*, 7(2), 174–201.

Hennings, R. 1972. *Fifty years of freedom: A study of the development of the ideas of A. S. Neill*. London: Allen and Unwin.

Herberg, P. 1991. *Nursing and the health transition*. Grand Seminar, The Aga Khan University Convocation, Karachi, Pakistan. November 1991.

Hoey, M. P. 1983. *On the surface of discourse*. London: Allen and Unwin.

Holliday, A. 1994. *Appropriate methodology and social context*. Cambridge: Cambridge University Press.

Holt, J. 1964. *How children fail*. Harmondsworth: Penguin.

Hutchinson, T. and Waters, A. 1987. *English for specific purposes: A learning-centred approach*. Cambridge: Cambridge University Press.

Hymes, D. 1971. Competence and performance in linguistic theory. In R. Huxley and E. Ingram (eds.), *Language acquisition models and methods*. New York: Academic Press.

Illich, I. 1971. *Deschooling society*. Harmondsworth: Penguin.

References

Janssen-van Dieten, A. M. 1989. The development of a test of Dutch as a second language: The validity of self-assessment by inexperienced subjects. *Language Testing*, 6, 30–46.

Johnson, R. K. 1989a. A decision-making framework for the coherent language curriculum. In R. K. Johnson (ed.), *The second language curriculum* (pp. 1–23). Cambridge: Cambridge University Press.

Johnson, R. K. (ed.) 1989b. *The second language curriculum*. Cambridge: Cambridge University Press.

Kagan, S. 1986. *Cooperative learning and sociocultural factors in schooling*. California State Department of Education. Los Angeles, CA: Evaluation, Dissemination and Assessment Center.

Kelly, G. 1955. *The psychology of personal constructs*. 2 volumes. New York: Norton.

Knowles, M. 1975. *Self-directed learning*. New York: Association Press.

Kohl, H. 1968. *36 Children*. London: Victor Gollanz.

Kozol, J. 1967. *Death at an early age*. Harmondsworth: Penguin.

Kramsch, K. 1993. *Context and culture in language teaching*. Oxford: Oxford University Press.

Krashen, S. D. 1981. *Second language acquisition and second language learning*. Oxford: Pergamon.

Krashen, S. D. 1985. *The input hypothesis*. Oxford: Oxford University Press.

Kreidler, C. 1987. ESL teacher education. *ERIC Digest*. Washington, DC: ERIC Clearinghouse on Languages and Linguistics.

Kroll, L. R. and La Boskey, V. K. 1996. Constructivism in a teacher education program. *Action in Teacher Education*, 18 (2), 63–72.

Kutz, E., Groden, S. Q. and Zamel, V. 1993. *The discovery of competence: Teaching and learning with diverse student writers*. Portsmouth: Boynton/Cook Heinemann.

Lantolf, J. 1994. Sociocultural theory and second language learning: An introduction to the special issue. *Modern Language Journal*, 78, 418–420.

Lantolf, J. and Appel, G. (eds.) 1994. *Vygotskyan approaches to second language research*. Norwood, NJ: Ablex.

Legutke, M. and Thomas, H. 1991. *Process and experience in the language classroom*. London: Longman.

Leont'ev, A. N. 1981. *Problems of the development of the mind*. Moscow: Progress Publishers.

Lester, N. 1992. Cooperative learning is not negotiating the curriculum. In G. Boomer, N. Lester, C. Onore and J. Cook (eds.), *Negotiating the curriculum*. London: Falmer Press.

Littlejohn, A. P. 1983. Increasing learner involvement in course management. *TESOL Quarterly*, 17(4), 595–608.

Long, D. G. 1990. *Learner managed learning: The key to lifelong learning and development*. London: Kogan Page.

Long, M. H. 1981. Input, interaction and second language acquisition. In H. Winitz (ed.), *Native language and foreign language acquisition*. New York: New York Academy of Sciences.

Long, M. H. 1989. Task, group and task-group interactions. Paper presented at the *RELC regional seminar: Language teaching methodology for the nineties*. Singapore.

Long, M. and Crookes, G. 1992. Three approaches to task-based syllabus design. *TESOL Quarterly*, 26(1), 27–55.

Long, M. H. and Porter, P. A. 1985. Group work, interlanguage talk and second language acquisition. *TESOL Quarterly*, 19(2), 207–228.

McCarthy, M. J. 1998. *Spoken language and applied linguistics*. Cambridge: Cambridge University Press.

McCarthy, M. J. and Carter, R. A. 1994. *Language as discourse: Perspectives for language teaching*. London: Longman.

Martyn, E. and Husain, P. 1993. A task-based negotiated syllabus for nurses. In T. Boswood, R. Hoffman and P. Tung (eds.), *Perspectives on English for professional communication*. Hong Kong: City Polytechnic of Hong Kong.

Markee, N. 1996. *Managing curriculum innovation*. Cambridge: Cambridge University Press.

Maslow, A. 1970. *Motivation and personality*. New York: Harper and Row.

Medgyes, P. 1993. The national L2 curriculum in Hungary. *Annual Review of Applied Linguistics*, 13, 24–36.

Milk, R. D. 1990. Preparing ESL and bilingual teachers for changing roles: Immersion for teachers of LEP children. *TESOL Quarterly*, 24, 407–426.

Moskovitz, G. 1978. *Caring and sharing in the foreign language class*. Rowley, MA: Newbury House.

Neill, A. S. 1937. *That dreadful school*. London: Jenkins.

Neill, A. S. 1962. *Summerhill: A radical approach to education*. London: Gollancz.

Nikolov, M. 1994. Some aspects of child SLA in the classroom. Unpublished PhD Dissertation, Janus Pannonius University, Pécs, Hungary.

Novak, J. D. and Gowin, B. D. 1984. *Learning how to learn*. Cambridge: Cambridge University Press.

Nunan, D. 1988a. *Syllabus design*. Oxford: Oxford University Press.

Nunan, D. 1988b. *The learner-centred curriculum*. Cambridge: Cambridge University Press.

Nunan, D. 1989a. *Designing tasks for the communicative classroom*. Cambridge: Cambridge University Press.

Nunan, D. 1989b. Toward a collaborative approach to curriculum development: A case study. *TESOL Quarterly*, 23(1), 9–25.

Nunan, D. 1990. Using learner data in curriculum development. *English for Specific Purposes*, 9, 17–32.

Nunan, D. 1995. Closing the gap between learning and instruction. *TESOL Quarterly*, 20(1), 133–158.

Onore, C. and Lubetsky, B. 1992. Why we learn is what and how we learn. In G. Boomer, N. Lester, C. Onore and J. Cook (eds.), *Negotiating the curriculum*. London: Falmer Press.

Oscarsson, M. 1989. Self-assessment of language proficiency: Rationale and applications. *Language Testing*, 6, 1–13.

References

Papert, S. 1980. *Mindstorms: Children, computers and powerful ideas*. New York: Basic Books

Paretas, G. 1991. *Singing in the rain: Spellbound by a musical* (Cinema original a l'Aula-1). Barcelona: Generalitat de Catalunya, Departament d'Ensenyament.

Parkinson, L. and O'Sullivan, K. 1990. Negotiating the learner-centred curriculum. In G. Brindley (ed.), *The second language curriculum in action*. Sydney: NCELTR, Macquarie University.

Peck, A. and Westgate, D. (eds.) 1994. *Language teaching in the mirror: Reflections on practice*. London: Centre for Information on Language Teaching and Research.

Perkins, D. N. 1992. Technology meets constructivism: Do they make a marriage? In T. M. Duffy and D. H. Jonassen (eds.), *Constructivism and the technology of instruction*. Hillsdale, NJ: Lawrence Erlbaum.

Pica, T. 1994. Research on negotiation: What does it reveal about second language learning, conditions, processes, outcomes? *Language Learning*, 44, 493–527.

Pica, T. and Doughty, C. 1985. Input and interaction in the communicative language classroom: A comparison of teacher-fronted and group activities. In S. Gass and C. Madden (eds.), *Input in second language acquisition*. Rowley, MA: Newbury House.

Pica, T., Holliday, L., Lewis, N. and L. Morgenthaler. 1989. Comprehensible output as an outcome of linguistic demands on the learner. *Studies in Second Language Acquisition*, 11, 63–90.

Pica, T., Kanagy, R. and Falodun, J. 1993. Choosing and using communication tasks for second language instruction and research. In G. Crookes and S. M. Gass (eds.), *Tasks and language learning: Integrating theory and practice*. Clevedon: Multilingual Matters.

Plowden, Lady B. 1967. *Children and their primary schools*. London: Her Majesty's Stationery Office.

Poplin, M. S. 1993. Making our whole-language bilingual classrooms also liberatory. In J. V. Tinajero and A. F. Ada (eds.), *The Power of two languages: Literacy and biliteracy for Spanish-speaking students*. New York and Columbus, OH: Macmillan/McGraw-Hill School Publishing.

Porter, P. A. 1986. How learners talk to each other: Input and interaction in task-centred discussions. In R. R. Day (ed.), *Talking to learn: Conversation in second language acquisition*. Rowley, MA: Newbury House.

Porter, P. A., Goldstein, L. M., Leatherman J. and Conrad, S. 1990. An ongoing dialogue: Learning logs for teacher preparation. In J. C. Richards and D. Nunan (eds.), *Second language teacher education*. Cambridge University Press.

Postman, N. and Weingartner, C. 1969. *Teaching as a subversive activity*. Harmondsworth: Penguin.

Prabhu, N. S. 1987. *Second language pedagogy*. Oxford: Oxford University Press.

Pratt, M. 1989. Linguistic utopias. In A. Durant, N. Fabb, D. Attridge and C. MacCabe (eds.). *The linguistics of writing: Arguments between language and literature*. Manchester: Manchester University Press.

Ribé, R. 1994. *L'ensenyament de la llengua anglesa al cicle escolar secondari (12–18 anys)*. Bellaterra: Publicacions de la Universitat Autónoma de Barcelona.

Ribé, R. and Vidal, N. 1993. *Project work step by step*. Oxford: Heinemann.

Ribé, R., Celaya, M. L., Ravera, M., Rodríguez, F., Tragant, E. and Vidal, N. 1997. *Tramas creativas y aprendizaje de lenguas*. Barcelona: Publicacions de la Universitat Autónoma de Barcelona.

Richards, J. C. and Lockhart, C. 1994. *Reflective teaching in second language classrooms*. Cambridge: Cambridge University Press.

Richards, J. C. 1990. *The language teaching matrix*. New York: Cambridge University Press.

Rogers, C. 1969. *Freedom to learn*. Colombus, OH: Merrill.

Rowe, H. 1988. Metacognitive skills: Promises and problems. *Australian Journal of Reading*, 11(4), 227–237.

Russell, B. 1926. *On education*. London: Unwin.

Russell, D. R. 1993. Vygotsky, Dewey and externalism: Beyond the student/discipline dichotomy. *Journal of Advanced Composition*, 13(1), 173–197.

Serrano-Sampedro, M. I. 1992. *Materiales didácticos. Lengua extranjera: Inglés*. Bachillerato, Madrid: Ministerio de Educación y Ciencia.

Serrano-Sampedro, M. I. 1993. *Materiales didácticos. Lengua extranjera II: Inglés*. Bachillerato, Madrid: Ministerio de Educación y Ciencia.

Simmons, D. and Wheeler, S. 1995. *The process syllabus in action*. Sydney: National Centre for English Language Teaching and Research.

Sinclair, J. McH. and Coulthard, R. M. 1975. *Towards an analysis of discourse*. Oxford: Oxford University Press.

Skehan, P. 1996 A framework for the implementation of task-based instruction. *Applied Linguistics*, 17(1), 38–62.

Smith, K. 1991. Correlation between teacher evaluation and students' self-evaluation in EFL. Paper presented at the *EARLI conference*, Turku.

Smith, K. 1993. The assessment habits of the Israeli English teacher. Paper presented at the *EARLI conference*, Aix-en-Provence.

Stanley, C. 1998. A framework for teacher reflectivity. *TESOL Quarterly*, 32, 584–591.

Stenhouse, L. 1975. *An introduction to curriculum research and development*. London: Heinemann.

Stern, H. H. 1992. *Issues and options in language teaching*. Oxford: Oxford University Press.

Stern, H. H. and Strevens, P. 1983. Georgetown University Round Table on Languages and Linguistics 1983 in retrospect. In J. E. Alatis, H. H. Stern and P. Strevens (eds.), *Georgetown University Round Table on Languages and Linguistics*. Washington, DC: Georgetown University Press.

Stevick, E. 1976. *Memory, meaning and method*. Rowley, MA: Newbury House.

Stevick, E. 1990. *Humanism in language teaching*. Oxford: Oxford University Press.

Todd, S. 1995. Learning the process: A qualitative study of a negotiated course. Unpublished manuscript, University of Hawaii.

References

Tollefson, J. W. (ed.) 1995. *Power and equality in language education*. New York: Cambridge University Press.

Tompkins, C. and McGraw, M. J. 1988. The negotiated learning contract. In D. Boud (ed.), *Developing student autonomy in learning*. London: Kogan Page.

Tudor, I. 1996. *Learner-centredness as language education*. Cambridge: Cambridge University Press.

Underhill, A. 1989. Process in humanistic education. *English Language Teaching Journal*, 43(4), 250–260.

Vale, D., Scarino, A. and McKay, P. 1991. *Pocket ALL: A users' guide to the teaching of languages and ESL*. Canberra: Curriculum Corporation.

van Lier, L. 1988. *The classroom and the language learner*. London: Longman.

Varonis, E. M. and Gass, S. 1983. Native/non-native conversations: A model for the negotiation of meaning. *Applied Linguistics*, 6, 72–90.

Vidal, N. 1989. *The 39 Steps by Alfred Hitchcock: An excuse for project work* (Cinema original a l'Aula-1). Barcelona: Generalitat de Catalunya, Departament d'Ensenyament.

Vidal, N. and Ferrando, E. 1987. The reality of a dream: An example of project work. *A l'ensenyament de les lengües estrangeres*, Volume 3. Barcelona: Generalitat de Catalunya, Departament d'Ensenyament.

Vygotsky, L. 1962. *Thought and language*. Cambridge, MA: Harvard University Press.

Vygotsky, L. 1978. Mind in society. In M. Cole, V. John-Steiner, S. Scribner, and E. Souberman, *The development of higher order psychological processes*. Cambridge, MA: Harvard University Press.

Wallace, M. 1991. *Training for language teachers: A reflective approach*. Cambridge: Cambridge University Press.

Waters, M. and A. Waters. 1992. Study skills and study competence: Getting the priorities right. *ELT Journal*, 46(3), 264–278.

Wells, G. and Chang-Wells, G. L. 1992. *Constructing knowledge together: Classrooms as centers of inquiry and literacy*. Portsmouth, NH: Heinemann.

Widdowson, H. G. 1978. *Teaching language as communication*. Oxford: Oxford University Press.

Willett, J. and Jeannot, M. 1993. Resistance to taking a critical stance. *TESOL Quarterly*, 27, 477–495.

Woodward, H. 1993. *Negotiated evaluation*. Newton, NSW: Primary English Teachers' Association.

Wright, T. 1990. Understanding classroom role relationships. In J. C. Richards and D. Nunan, (eds.), *Second language teacher education*. Cambridge: Cambridge University Press.

Young, M. D. F. (ed.) 1971. *Knowledge and control: New directions for the sociology of education*. London: Collier-Macmillan.

Zamel, V. 1987. Recent research on writing pedagogy. *TESOL Quarterly*, 21(4), 687–716.

Index

age 42, 83
Allwright, D. 95, 226
Altman, H.B. 219
analysis cards 75
Appel, G. 23
Apple, M. 15
assessment 3, 53, 76, 85, 282
  by peers 119, 188–9
  collaborative 241
  continuous 159
  formal 40, 62, 84, 101, 111, 134, 140,
    148, 158–159, 291
  negotiated procedures 41, 55–62, 85,
    90–91, 99, 102, 135, 207, 242, 252,
    262–263, 291
  of individual progress 56
  of self 57, 58, 90, 119, 120, 197, 225,
    249, 274
  procedures, 39, 42, 57, 58, 59, 60,
    90–91, 110, 141, 221, 237,
    240–241, 283
  scales 55, 56
attendance levels 144–147
Auerbach, E.R. 14, 248, 268, 269
Ausubel, D.P. 108
Australian Language Levels projects (ALL)
  45, 47
autonomous learning 1, 63, 66, 80, 159,
  220, 221
Bachman, L.F. 57
Bailey, K.M. 185, 226
Bangalore project 109
Barnes, D. 14
behaviourism 12, 13, 15
Bernstein, B. 14
Blanche, P. 57

Bloor, M. 150, 152, 153, 160, 161
Bloor, T, 150, 152, 153, 160, 161
Boerkaerts, M. 58
Boomer, G. 14, 25
Breen, M.P. 5, 18, 24, 25, 79, 85, 96, 109,
  163, 165, 248
Britten, J. 14
Brown, J.D. 185
Brown, J.S. 177
Boud, D. 245
Brumfit, C. 18
Budd, R. 250
Campbell, C. 163
Carter, G. 80
Carter, K. 245
Carter, R.A. 223, 224, 225
Canale, M. 17, 108
Candlin, C.N. 18, 79, 109
can-do cards 75
Chang-Wells, G.L. 219
Chaudron, C. 14, 25, 185
Chomsky, N. 15, 16, 17
Clark, J.L. 150, 153, 160
Clarke, D.F. 150, 160, 161, 229, 249
classical liberalism 11, 12, 15
class presentation 70–75, 77–82
class size 14, 109, 124–126, 221, 235,
  273, 275–276, 282, 287
classroom
  culture 20
  curriculum 27
  decisions 5
  discourse 25
  record sheets 47, 48 (fig.2.2)
Coleman, H. 199
collaborative learning 1, 206, 219, 241

communicative competence 17, 19, 26
communicative language teaching (CLT)
    1, 17, 18, 19, 26, 235, 240, 241
Conner, U. 185
constructivist models of education 177,
    220
cooperative learning 63, 64–82, 94, 159,
    166, 218
Coulthard, M.R. 226
Council of Europe 17
Counselling Learning 109
course assignments 135
Crookes, G. 18, 79, 225
cultural awareness 45
cultural syllabus 23
Curran, J. 94
curricula
    external 110, 113, 114, 273, 282, 285,
        286, 287, 290, 295
    implementation 234
    learner-centred 219
    national 94–107
    negotiated 108–132, 156, 183,
        246–247, 279, 283
    planning 234, 286
curriculum pyramid 29, 35, 36, 37, 38,
    285–290
Dam, L 109
decision-making 28, 29, 30, 32, 33, 37,
    38, 42, 54, 55, 57, 164, 166, 178,
    227, 283, 285, 287, 290, 293
    reflection on 168
    shared 1, 2, 3, 24, 153, 206, 208, 218,
        242, 272, 276, 277, 279, 280, 282,
        287, 293, 295
    student 94, 140, 178, 184
Dewey, J. 11, 12, 13, 14, 15
dialogue journals 212, 250, 252–269
diary keeping 63–82, 119–124, 131, 195,
    200, 207, 250, 252, 267
Dickinson, L. 57
discourse analysis 225, 227, 231, 232
discourse-based descriptions of language
    learning 223–224, 227, 232
diversity of student abilities 40, 177–178,
    206–207, 220, 275–276, 282
Donato, R, 17
Doughty, C. 26, 108
Dudley-Evans, T. 163

Edelhoff, C. 80
Ediger, M. 57
Edmundson, E. 135, 272
educational cultures 19, 20–21, 23, 27,
    40–42, 44, 53, 62, 83–84, 134, 135,
    138–139, 146–149, 150–151, 154,
    176–178, 201, 212, 223, 272, 278,
    280–281
Ehlich, K. 148
Elbow, P. 185, 189
English for academic/other purposes
    (EAP/EOP) 163, 164, 171
Enright, D.S. 80
essay writing
    negotiated 185–194
ethnographic interviewing 179
evaluation 4, 31, 33, 36, 45–47, 183,
    198, 200, 219, 224, 234, 286, 290,
    293
    by peers 113, 121, 125
    by teachers 113, 121
    cards 75–78
    continuous 44–54, 228
    of difficulty of tasks 166
    joint 37, 112, 199
    of learning 52, 110, 123–124, 202
    of learning outcomes 42, 76–79, 225,
        284, 285
    negotiated 40, 44–54, 150, 154–155,
        185–194
    procedures 91, 117, 119–121, 280
    questionnaires 76, 103, 105, 106, 107,
        119, 120, 124
    recording of 45–46
    self 45, 48, 49, 52, 96, 103, 106,
        107, 121, 125, 126, 187, 189–190,
        193–194
    systems 53, 103, 166, 283
exams
    negotiated 102, 103
experience
    reflection on 245–246
Fairclough, N. 15
Farrando, E. 80
feedback 39, 40, 61, 71–73, 83, 84, 85,
    92, 114, 121, 125, 132, 164, 182,
    183–184, 198, 200, 203, 227, 241,
    249, 256, 268, 276
Fitzpatrick, S. 135, 272

Forster, P. 225, 226
Freeman, D. 219
Freire, P. 13, 135, 177, 248, 250, 261, 268
Gabrielsen, G. 109
Garfinkel, H. 7
Gass, S. 108
genre analysis 225
Giroux, H. 15
Gowin, B.D. 108
grades 60, 183, 185, 186, 189–191, 210, 275, 292
  negotiated 102, 106, 120–1, 135, 212, 242, 262–3
  of self 76, 211
grammar exercises 90
grammatical syllabuses 2
Graylands Intensive Language Centre 44–54
group work 63–82, 121, 252
  problem solving 227
group presentation 74
Haig, Y. 40
Hairston, M. 191
Hatch, E. 7, 16
Heilenman, K.L. 57
Hennings, R. 14
Herberg, P. 151
higher education 58
Hoey, M.P. 226, 231
Holliday, A. 250
Holt, J. 13
homework 56, 61, 88, 92, 102, 106, 107
Husain, P. 152, 154, 155
Hutchinson, T. 163
Hymes, D. 17, 108
Illich, I. 13
immigrant students 44
individual task evaluation 66
Indonesia-Australia Language Foundation (IALF) 195–203
institutional culture 13, 14, 15, 27, 53, 133, 138–139, 291
International Certificate Conference 223–232
International English Language Testing System examination (IELTS) 163
Irujo, S. 206, 207, 272, 277, 292
Ivanič, R. 207, 208, 272, 279

Janssen-van Dieten, A.M. 57
Jeannot, M. 253
Johnson, R.K. 163, 185
Kagan S. 185
Kaplan, R. 185
Kelly, G. 12, 24
kibbutzim 94–107
Knowles, M. 57
Kohl, H. 13
Kozol, J. 13
Kramsch, C. 23
Krashen, K. 7, 16
Kreidler, C. 219
Kroll, L.R. 218
Kryszewska, H. 163
Kutz, E. 248
La Boskey, V.K 218
LAP (Learning needs Analysis through Pictures) 135, 163–175
language awareness 45
Lantolf, J. 17, 23
learner autonomy 13, 19, 20, 21–22, 24, 42, 45, 54, 57, 64, 95, 110, 123, 124, 125, 140, 159, 166, 177, 184, 206, 209, 219–221, 243, 295
learner-centred teaching 1, 18, 24, 206, 209, 219–220, 248, 249, 253
learning chart 169
learner contract 171
learner diversity 109
learning difficulties 169, 173
learner independence 95
learner needs 18, 171
learning outcomes 52, 53, 164, 274
learner participation 109
learning plan 127–128
learning preferences 163, 168
learning procedures 56, 61, 94, 99
  value judgements on 61
learning resources 45
learning strategies 199, 203
Legutke, M. 80
Leont'ev A.N. 17
Lester, N 21
lexical syllabuses 2
lifelong learning 95, 220
Linder, P. 42, 273, 274
Littlejohn, A. 250
Lockhart, C. 219

Long, D.G. 161
Long M.H. 7, 16, 18, 79, 108, 225
Lubetsky, B. 23
Macedo, D.P. 248, 250, 261
MacKay, A. 40, 272, 275
Makosch, M. 207, 208, 273
Martyn, E. 134, 152, 154, 155, 272
Maslow, A. 12, 13, 24
McCarthy, M.J. 207, 208, 223, 224, 225, 273
McCloskey, M.L. 80
McCormick, D. 17
McGraw, M.J. 153
memorising 70
Merino, B.J. 57
method 31 fig.1.1, 32 fig.1.2, 18, 34, 108, 116, 141–142, 225, 228, 232, 240, 244, 252, 274, 286, 290, 291
Milk, R.D 218
mixed ability classes 41, 95, 98
migrant children 41
Moskovitz, G. 13
negotiated assignments 178–184, 206, 242
negotiated creativity 63–82
negotiated participation 85–87
negotiated procedures 87–88, 90, 99, 102, 136, 153, 206, 207, 209, 242, 261
  as requirement 135
  continuous 221, 226
  gradual introduction of 134
  implementation of 150, 154–155, 156, 157, 281, 282–295
  in mother tongue 90
  in planning of course 150, 154–155, 156
  spontaneous 221
negotiated work 64, 176–184, 247, 295
  arguments against 140
  constraints operating on 122–124, 160–161, 273–274, 281–282, 286, 287, 290, 291, 295
  difficulties with 61–62, 92–93, 121–124, 143 149, 212, 230, 246–247, 281, 290, 291
negotiation
  participatory dialogue 248–271
  time-consuming process 28, 30, 61, 122, 143, 274–275

gradualist approaches to 280, 282, 283, 287, 291, 293
inter-group 70–75, 78, 80
interactive 6, 7, 8, fig.1.1, 10, 11, 16, 18, 19, 24, 25, 29
non-negotiable elements 216, 218, 221, 237, 240, 243, 247, 252, 291
  of format 248
  of learning strategies 203
  of method 240, 252
  of negotiation 259
  of ongoing learning needs 163–175
personal 6, 8, fig.1.1, 10, 11, 18, 19, 24, 25, 29
procedural 6, 7, 8, 9, fig.1.1, 10, 11, 18, 19, 25, 27, 29, 30, 272
process 58, 63–82
  of purposes 135
  of revision 100
  of role-boundaries 201, 209, 211
  of subject matter/course content 42, 88–90, 102, 110–113, 116, 135, 136, 138–149, 206, 207, 209, 234, 235–240, 242, 248, 249–250, 252, 261, 267, 283, 291–293
  of tasks 42, 6771, 110–116
  selective approach to 283, 287, 291
  teacher-learning 94
  three-way 44, 46, 134
negotiation cycle 29, 31, 34, 37, 38, 283, 284, 285, 286, 287
Neill, A.S. 14
Newstetter, W. 135, 272, 278
Nikolov, M. 41, 42, 92, 272
norming sample papers 188–189
Norris, L. 136, 281
Novak, J.D. 108
Nunan, D. 18, 56, 79, 153, 156, 163, 219, 249
Oates, K. 40
objectives 42, 44–54, 57, 58, 61, 67, 76, 79, 80, 94, 96, 200, 202, 219, 286, 290, 291
  personal 109, 119, 203
  course 110, 111, 113, 114, 163, 164, 168, 169, 210, 234, 235, 249, 250, 274, 278, 285
  formulation of 42, 67, 161, 165
  shared 134

Onore, C. 23
Oscarsson, M. 57
O'Sullivan, K. 153, 250
Palmer, A.S. 57
Papert, S. 177
parents 41, 44–46, 49–51, 53, 54
Paretas, G. 80
Parkinson, L. 153, 250
participatory dialogue 248–271
participatory frameworks 97–99
participatory pedagogy 14, 248, 249, 250, 263, 264
Peck, A. 219
pedagogic decisions 41
peer co-operation 100, 185
peer correction 74, 99, 124
peer feedback 157, 158
peer tutoring 87, 212, 216, 218, 276
Perkins, D.N. 177
personal agendas 235, 243, 245
Pica, T. 79, 108
planning 202, 210, 229, 292
   of content 70, 234, 276
   documents 47
   future 52–53
   learner designed plan 129
   learning plan 127–128, 178
   long-term 53, 285
   short-term 53, 285
   strategies 65, 105, 106
Plowden Committee 14
Poplin, M.S. 220
Porter, P.A. 108, 218
portfolio work 56
Postman, N. 13
Pratt, M.L. 147
preparation 101
primary school practice 2, 39–45
problem posing 177, 248
problem-solution discourse 228, 231
problem solving 228, 230, 275
procedural cards 69–71
process
   as opposed to product 243–244
   in relation to content 244, 251
productive learning 243
project work 41, 56, 80, 157, 226–232, 281
   creative 63–82

negotiation 67–82, 108, 226
   framework for 66
questionnaires 96, 97, 213–215, 216, 280
reflection chart 170
reflective approaches to teaching 227
reflective teaching 219
report cards 45–52, 54, 55
reporting 59, 70–73
   oral group reporting 71–73
reports 180, 181, 183–184
retrospective accounts 237, 242
revision 100, 116, 202–203
   procedures 70, 185, 187–191
Ribé, R . 41, 63, 64, 79, 80, 273
Richards, J.C. 219
Rogers, C. 12, 13
role boundaries 4, 198, 201, 231
role negotiation 28, 209, 224–225, 231, 248–250, 251, 252–269, 280
Rowe, H. 57
Russell, B. 11, 12, 13, 14, 15
Russell, D. 249
school reform 13
secondary school practice 2, 39, 41, 55–62, 63–82, 94–107, 108–132
second language acquisition (SLA) 1, 7, 15, 16, 18, 25
self-access materials 63, 69, 71, 171, 235
self-actualisation 13
self-assessment 41, 91, 209
self-correction 91
self-directed learning 151, 222
self-esteem in students 135, 137, 164, 201, 281
self-evaluation 45, 48, 49, 52, 96, 187, 189–190, 193–194
self-regulation 57
self-study periods 200
Serrano-Sampredo, M.I. 42, 112, 273, 275, 276, 277, 287
Simmons, D. 160, 162
Sinclair, J. McH. 226
Skehan, P. 225
skills-swap activities 197–198, 201, 281
Slembrouck, S. 133, 134, 135, 272, 278, 290–291
Smith, K. 41 56, 57, 273, 274, 275, 277
social interactionist perspective 16

Index

Sokolik, M. 135, 136, 274, 280
Spencer S. 136, 272, 281
Stenhouse, L. 14
Stanley, C. 219
Stern, D. 23
Stern, H.H. 218
Stevick, E. 13, 95
story work 98
Strevens, P. 218
student expectations 134
study buddy groups 195, 198–199
subject curriculum 35, 36
Summerhill school, 14
Swain, M. 17, 108
syllabus
    actual 9
    content syllabus 17, 29, 85
    design 84
    draft 217, 218, 270 (Appendix 17.1)
        292
    functional 2
    negotiated 92, 94–107, 150–162,
        179–184, 206, 210, 211–212, 216,
        219, 229, 236 (fig 16.1), 238 (fig
        16.2), 243, 257, 261, 264, 271
        (Appendix 17.2) 292
    prescribed 9, 94–107, 249, 292, 295
    prospective 245
    retrospective accounts of 237, 245
    story-based 85, 88, 89
    task-based, 161, 196
task work 166
task sequences 66
task-based approach to language learning
    18, 223, 226, 227, 232
tasks
    descriptive 69
    design 95, 240, 241, 279
    narrative 69
    for group work 69
    whole-class 198
teacher development 126
teacher education, 205–271, 278
teacher role 134, 205, 287, 293
teacher's comments 49 (fig.2.3)
teachers' meetings 64

teacher-dependent 178, 206
teacher-led activities 199, 227, 251, 272
teacher-trainer development seminars
    process-based approach to 223–232
teaching spectacle 199
technical-writing class 176–184
tests 56, 59, 61, 84, 91, 92, 119
    group tests 119, 120
    learner-designed 119
Thomas, H. 80
three-way
    dialogue 41, 51, 53
    evaluation 49, 53
    negotiation 150–151, 153–154
time sequences 69
Todd, S. 251, 254, 259, 269
Tollefson, J.W. 15, 21
Tompkins, C. 153
topic-based activities 171, 242
training seminars 64
transmission model of education 177, 209,
    219, 240, 272, 274
Tudor, I. 18, 219
Underhill, A. 28
van Lier, L. 24, 25
Varonis, E.M 108
Vidal, N. 80
voting 59, 73, 86, 88
Vygotsky, L. 16, 17, 24, 249
Wallace, M. 227
Waters, A. 163, 166
Waters, M. 166
Weingartner, C. 13
Wells, G. 219
Westgate, D. 219
Wheeler, S. 160, 162
Widdowson, H.G. 6, 17
Willett, J. 253
Williams, J. 26
Wolfe-Quintero, K. 14, 208, 277
Woodward, H. 40, 45
World Health Organization 156
Wright, T. 218, 250
Young, M.D.F. 14
Zamel, V 185